D1211943

*FIGHTING*
*THE UNDERWORLD*

'Dapper Jackie' French
bookmaker, 1920–21
7 to 10 years

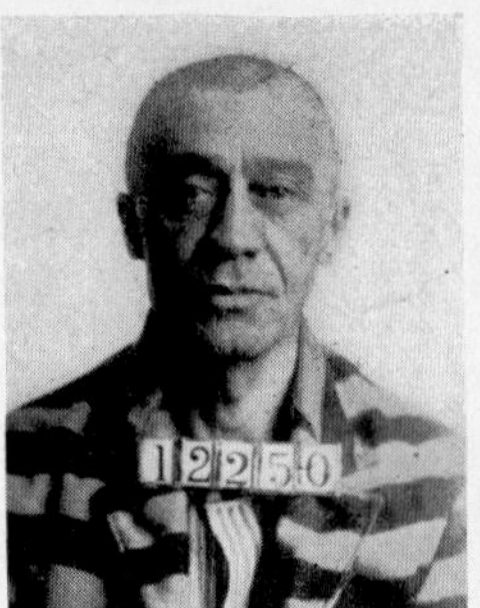

Adolph W. Duff
'Kid Duffy' —
The Manager
7 to 10 years

George 'Tip' Belcher
'The Tailor'—1921–22
7 to 10 years

Lou Blonger, King of the
Bunks — 'The Fixer'
7 to 10 years
(Died in the penitentiary)

Arthur B. Cooper —
'Tex' — Spieler,
1919–20–21–22
7 to 10 years

Leo Kelley — 'Pretty'
Spieler, 1919–22
3 to 10 years

Walter Byland — 'Sox'
Spieler and Steerer
1919–20–21–22
7 to 10 years

BIG SHOTS OF THE BUNCO RING

# Fighting the Underworld

PHILIP S. VAN CISE

WITH ILLUSTRATIONS

*Boston and New York*
HOUGHTON MIFFLIN COMPANY
The Riverside Press Cambridge

The Riverside Press
CAMBRIDGE · MASSACHUSETTS
PRINTED IN THE U.S.A.

# *Dedication*

---

IT SEEMS to be the customary thing to dedicate a book. This one could very properly be dedicated to Kenneth W. Robinson, my associate in the events described herein, who for over eleven years has been my partner and closest friend. It could be dedicated to my wife, Sara Reeves Van Cise, who was of material assistance in my fight against the underworld. It could be dedicated to juror Herman M. Okuly, who by his honesty, integrity, diplomacy and strength of character did more than any other man to insure a verdict of guilty in the case against the confidence-men. It could be dedicated to the thirty-one friends of Denver, whose unhesitating co-operation and financial assistance made it possible successfully to rout protected criminals.

But team work, not separate individuals, won the battle. Therefore, this book is dedicated to all those who in any manner aided in the fight against a protected underworld.

# *Foreword*

The underworld is not a figment of the imagination. It is composed of active, alert and in the main young men and women, determined to make a living in defiance of Law.

In the United States hundreds of confidence-men, usually protected by public officials, and using various kinds of sure-thing rackets, annually steal millions of dollars from over-trustful citizens.

These slick swindlers are finished actors. So expert are they in their lines that they fascinate their victims by the apparent safety of their schemes and the quick profits to be made by the participants. Shunning friends and advisers, the dupes rush headlong into the traps prepared for them, and in a few hours lose the savings of a lifetime.

Organized gangsters are lawless business men, who congregate in cities where money can be made. Wherever they flourish the ugly whisper of bribery is heard, as no such group exists without protection. Given the least encouragement they smash the lid which society attempts to clamp upon them, and in many cases they dominate government.

The character of a town is readily revealed by the situation upon the beat of a policeman — if organized crime is there continuous, either he is stupid, is crooked, or is taking orders from superiors. The great majority of policemen are honest. brave and eager to do their duty, but the grafters in their ranks imperil the lives, reputation and *esprit de corps* of an entire force.

The enforcement of Law depends upon team work between all governmental agencies, upon absolute secrecy of police movements while criminals are being rounded up, and upon the ruthless exposure by the Press of the alliances between public officials and their favored criminals. It depends upon aggressive governors, mayors and prosecuting attorneys, upon able and fearless judges, upon honest, well trained and well equipped police and upon a militant citizenry. Governors and mayors are responsible for the police, who usually follow the policies of their executives. In most of the Commonwealths sheriffs still are included in the forces of the State, but their selection for political reasons, rather than for their knowledge of criminals, handicaps them in a modern era. They should be abolished and be replaced by State police. When all the power of the State can be integrated under one non-political head, criminals and gangs will no longer prosper in America.

It is hoped that this book will disclose protection as it exists in large cities, and will arouse the citizens of this Nation to aid in the constant warfare against organized enemies of the Law.

## *Contents*

# *Illustrations*

*FIGHTING THE UNDERWORLD*

# I

## *The Underworld Organized*

Crime is of two kinds — organized and unorganized. The ordinary murderer, highwayman, thief, or embezzler is an unorganized criminal who operates by himself. When he commits a crime the hand of everyone in society is raised against him. He is easily apprehended, speedily convicted, and lands in the penitentiary with very little difficulty.

The other class of criminals, however, the organized groups, work in gangs running from two or three to almost any number. They may devote their energies to one community, or spread across the country from coast to coast, or become international in their scope. Among these are racketeers of all kinds — kidnapers, bank-robbers, bootleggers, dope-peddlers, and confidence-men.

All of them secure some measure of protection either from the police departments, Federal agents, or elected officials. In some towns only a limited assistance is given; in others the system is almost airtight — so much so that criminals belonging to the organization may ply their trade with impunity, while those outside the pale are arrested and run out of town, or suffer the extreme penalty of the law.

In 1922, Denver was in the ironclad class and had been for many years. The evil genius and dominating power in its underworld was Lou Blonger, a short, heavy-set, affable fellow of French-Canadian descent, who came to this country from Canada in his early boyhood, and settled in the Western mining camps. He first appeared in Denver in 1880 with his brother Sam as a bartender, then became the proprietor of a saloon with all the early-day accessories of a dance-hall and the necessary girl attendants, roulette wheels and all kinds of gambling. As society became more respectable in the West, the girls were first eliminated, then the gambling, until only the saloon was left.

Accustomed from the early days to paying the police for protection and special privileges for his own place, and owing to his native shrewdness and innate knowledge of police conditions, Blonger gradually attained a position of affluence in the community. In the late eighties he became a 'fixer' and the friend of the Chief of Police, and in large measure determined what protected crooks should operate in the town. This power once attained was pushed to the utmost, so that, as time passed, he gradually 'got something on' various aspirants for, or those holding, public office, until his will and money were powerful factors in the political field in the Rocky Mountain metropolis.

At one time, while Blonger was operating a saloon, a private telephone line ran directly from his office to that of the Chief of Police, and upon his orders men were arrested or turned loose. He was the king of the Denver underworld.

In the early nineties Soapy Smith came to town. Soapy was then known throughout the West as a slicker, or con-man, and his method of operation was rather open and aboveboard, simply setting up a wagon with flaring gasoline torches and a large number of packages of soap wrapped up in paper, standing by a little table giving the 'ballyhoo' talk to get a crowd together, and then offering to sell soap with five- or ten-dollar bills in it for one dollar a cake.

He would pick up several bars and apparently wrap a five-

or ten-dollar bill with each, then carelessly throw the cakes on the table with the others, mix them up, and sell them at one dollar apiece, or bet any amount with any of the spectators that they could not pick a package with the cash in it. The money, of course, he would always palm, although once in a while a sucker, as victims are called, would get a cake to stimulate trade. Soapy would harvest from fifty to a hundred dollars a night. Blonger got half as his share for keeping the police away.

In those days the gold-brick artist flourished and every circus carried its quota of pickpockets, shell-game experts, and other grafters. When they came to town, all called at Blonger's office to get permission to operate, and one of his men would be on the job to get his fair share of the cut.

By 1898, so notorious had Blonger become that in that year the *Rocky Mountain News* carried a front-page article about his having been trimmed by an even cleverer rascal. Its headlines read: 'Got caught — Lou Blonger complains that he has been buncoed. Strange news for the police.'

And then it went on to state:

> Lou Blonger has been buncoed. This is about the most startling piece of news the police department has received in a long time. It was not hard work to find it, either, as Blonger 'yelled' louder than the backwoodsman from Indiana who bought the gold brick. It was a long time before Blonger could induce the detectives to take the 'yell' seriously.
>
> Yesterday evening Blonger appeared at the police station much excited and exclaimed that he had been buncoed. All the detectives were taken with a fit of laughter. Their mouths stretched and their sides shook. Tears rolled down their cheeks and it was fifteen minutes before they could compose themselves. They were listening to Blonger's tale of woe.
>
> Blonger has the reputation of being a bunco-man himself and for years had everything his own way on lower Seventeenth Street, where he successfully managed a gang of the shrewdest confidence-men in the country. This was the reason the detectives laughed so heartily when Blonger said he was buncoed.

Two years later Dick Turner, a deputy sheriff from Weld County, came to Denver and stopped at the Albany Hotel. Shortly afterwards, while in the lobby, he was 'picked up' by a con-man who tried to swindle him, but Turner was too shrewd, and got away. He then went to the police, secured a detective and went back for his man. The fellow was still there, looking for another victim, and as he was being arrested Lou Blonger came in.

'What's all this fuss about?' demanded Lou.

'Nothing much, except one of your boys is running a little wild,' responded the detective.

Quickly getting the details, Blonger turned on the man and said: 'You were recommended to me as a first-class bunco artist, and the first thing you do, you damn ——, is to pick up a deputy sheriff. What the hell are you tackling the Law for, anyway? Don't you have sense enough to let Colorado people alone in Denver? I paid your transportation to Denver and put you to work. Now you walk back, and start now.'

And getting a hack, Blonger, the deputy sheriff, and the city dick accompanied the disconsolate crook to the city limits, where, under Lou's caustic tongue, he started the hike east over the railroad ties.

Lou also liked the ladies. In his early days he had married a successful variety actress, who was a high-class woman, but as he grew older they drifted apart. They were never divorced, and he spent some of his time with her. But his real romance arose out of an arrest. Two of the city detectives were not in the good graces of Mike Delaney, Chief of Police in 1904. So, one evening, when they were having dinner with two girls, the patrol wagon backed up to the door, and under Delaney's orders all four were arrested and thrown into jail. The officers made bond and got out at once, but Mike refused to release the women.

One of the men then went to Blonger and told him about the girls, and Lou at once telephoned Delaney and ordered him to let them go. He did, and the next day they called on Blonger to thank him for his help. Immediately he was attracted to the younger one. She was only about nineteen. He gave her a musical education and lavished money on her until her marriage a few years later.

Shortly afterwards, however, she divorced her husband, and from then on was Blonger's mistress. She called for him in the evening, drove him out to his farm, and was constantly subject to his beck and call. Her name in this book is Berna Rames.

In 1921, Blonger built a beautiful bungalow for Berna on Capitol Hill, at 601 Williams Street, right across the alley from fashionable Ascension Episcopal Church. It cost thirty thousand dollars. Nothing was spared in its construction, and only the best material was used.

A large garage was in the high-ceilinged basement, with a covered roof over a walled-in entrance-way. Small windows enabled the occupants of the house to see what visitor was calling before opening the door for his car. And at night prominent politicians, with side curtains drawn to hide the occupants, drove to the garage entrance, there to be identified and admitted for their private business. An adjacent large billiard room, with cozy fireplace and comfortable chairs, was the setting for the conferences.

The town became more and more protected as the police and various officials came under the sway of the underworld, and many kinds of confidence-games began to be evolved. At first there would be only three or four men in each group and they would use a 'salted' mine, or a swindle of any sort to separate the victim from his money. Then came the era of fake horse- and foot-races, and wire-tapping, which allowed much larger gangs to operate.

In them the victim always engaged in a crooked deal, and this narrowed the field of suckers to the inherently shady classes of the community. This weakness made it impossible for gangsters to reach out for honest but careless men who might be willing to go into a good investment if it looked as if they had a sure thing for their money. But for fifteen years these fake-race swindlers flourished all over the country.

In the foot-race the victim would usually have a secret meeting with the man whom he was betting against in which that fellow would agree to throw the race.

In the horse-race he would be led stealthily to the stall where dope was apparently shot into the opposing animal.

In the fake wire-tapping he was taken to a room fixed up as a pool-hall with telegraph instruments ticking merrily, with huge blackboards on which the names of the horses appeared with the betting odds, and the results of the races. A good-sized crowd of boosters would be present making bets and winning and losing money in large amounts. He was then taken to another room which had only a single telegraph instrument, an operator, and a great air of mystery. Here he was told that this was a tap on the main wire of the telegraph company, that the operator was bribed so as to relay the races slowly to the pool-hall, and that they therefore got the information and final outcome of the race in advance of the time when the pool-hall downstairs closed its bets. So he was told that in this way they could go down and make a great cleaning playing any horse.

In these dealings, of course, the victim was trying to win by a dishonest transaction, but was dealing with rogues smarter than himself. When he lost his money and started to fight, they laughed at him and told him that he was a crook himself — that if he wanted to prosecute he could go as far as he wished, but that he couldn't get anywhere, and might land in the penitentiary himself.

While this was an incorrect statement of the law, and a vigorous prosecution would have convicted the gang, the sucker was so guilty and they were so adroit that only a small percentage ever complained to the authorities. When they did, the police departments in turn also called them crooks and refused to help them, so that a prosecution was almost unheard of. The Federal Government finally stepped in with its famous Maybray gang prosecution at Council Bluffs in 1910, in which all the defendants were convicted and this class of criminality effectually stopped. But the Denver chieftain, though involved, escaped.

As soon as prosecution was rumored, powerful political influences were set in motion to prevent any exposure of Blonger's connection with the gang. To insure success, the partner of a United States District Attorney, accompanied by a deputy United States Marshal, went to Council Bluffs. They persuaded the Federal authorities to omit Lou Blonger from the list of those indicted. But to make sure that no possible whisper of that name should occur, all during the trial, which lasted several weeks, the lawyer and the Deputy Marshal were in daily attendance. Their efforts were successful, because not a witness testified about Denver or its squat overlord.

Meanwhile, to Blonger's charmed circle had been added an assistant who relieved Blonger of details and left him free for larger operations. About 1896 this man — a little fellow, only twenty-two years old, agile, wiry and active, about five-feet-five in height, with a heavy head of wavy black hair, named Adolph W. Duff, alias 'Kid Duffy' — appeared in the underworld in Colorado Springs. He was a pickpocket, opium-smoker or hop-head, and gambler. He was befriended by a man named Byron Hames, who lent him enough money to get on his feet. Duff established friendly relations with the police department, ran out the other grafters, and became an underworld leader, ending by chasing his friend Hames out of the place without repaying him anything.

Duff soon became one of the members of the old Webb City gang, later the Maybray, already referred to, and helped to trim suckers in fake foot-races in the Garden of the Gods. He never served time, though he was frequently arrested and had many felony cases filed against him in the District Court. On at least four occasions these cases were dismissed by request of the District Attorney of El Paso County.

Then, in 1902, it was charged that the Colorado Springs Captain of Detectives, gangster Adolph W. Duff, and six others unlawfully hired, persuaded, and induced Pat McNellis, the prosecuting witness against Duff on a con-game charge, to leave the State of Colorado. The case was never tried, but the Chief of Police and Captain of Detectives lost their jobs.

Duff had made two early attempts to extend his operations to the richer Denver field, but failed to contact Blonger, and so was unsuccessful. The Denver police blotter shows arrests of Duff in 1897 and 1903 on the charge of 'bunco'; both times a conviction in police court, with sentences suspended on condition that he leave town! So he returned to the city at the foot of Pike's Peak.

Finally Duff's power in Colorado Springs completely collapsed when in 1904 he was charged with keeping a policy wheel. Later the same year he pleaded guilty to gambling and was sentenced to thirty days in the county jail and fined seven hundred dollars, his first conviction of any kind! All punishment was canceled, however, when his attorneys filed a plea that he had no money and his family was suffering.

His power in Colorado Springs broken, Duff went to Denver and joined Blonger. The latter had now reached the point where he craved respectability, and wanted to work from behind the scenes, where he would never come in actual contact with the victims. Lou had always shunned the spotlight, so much so that except for a few occasions in the early days when the city directory gave his occupation as 'saloon' and 'clubrooms,' he was listed as a business man under the head of 'mining.' So in a short time Duff became the active manager of the Denver gang, and Lou's first lieutenant.

Duff spent his summers in Denver with Blonger. During the fall he operated with con-men in other States. In those places he was usually only one of the players, though occasionally he was a partner of the local fixer. He was arrested in San Francisco and Kansas City, and his picture placed in their galleries, but his pull enabled him to escape trial. In fact he had such good connections in Kansas City that he first had his picture sequestered and then removed from its police records. Then after Duff joined Blonger, his old Denver police record was 'lost' and could not be found; and was not located until 1923.

Duff was married to his own niece, a very handsome woman. She had two small brothers who passed as his boys. When they reached college age, they entered the University of Colorado, where their money was of material assistance in their induction into the exclusive ranks of an Eastern fraternity which catered to the socially élite.

As Blonger's and Duff's activities spread, both acquired wealth and large real estate holdings followed. They opened offices on the third floor of the American National Bank Building, where the name of each appeared on the door, Blonger as in mining, and Duff in the insurance business.

Blonger also blossomed out as a farmer, and bought a cherry orchard at Beehive, five miles west of Denver. Here he grew the finest dark red cherries which could be produced in Colorado. The main purpose of the orchard, however, was not to make money, but to furnish presents of the fruit for his political friends. Each July drays were busy carrying full crates of Blonger's best to judges and other office-holders, policemen, party committees, and favored underworld friends. This annual event was eagerly looked forward to, and became a sure index as to whether or not one was still in the good graces of the boss.

Yet behind the scenes the gang was in full operation. In June, 1916, a number of their men went up the South Platte to Gill's Resort for a few days of fishing and poker. There they got into a fight, as a result of which one Frank Hughes Turner was shot and killed by Christopher Wilson, alias Brown, and the rest of the mob helped him escape. None of the witnesses were put under bond, and a few days later all of them quietly left the State.

During the next four years, Blonger saw that these members of his gang were well scattered and remained outside of Colorado. Wilson then came back in January, 1920, and gave himself up. He was promptly released on a $5000 bond, furnished by his Denver leader. Three months later he pleaded guilty to involuntary manslaughter and was sentenced to one day in jail, which he cheerfully served. Wilson, however, was now a well-known character in Denver, so Lou never allowed him to return. But his hide was saved!

After Blonger and Duff got together, they and other confidence-game artists developed the 'pay-off' game, a big money deal which numbers its victims by the tens of thousands, which drags in millionaires, play-boys, ministers, bankers, business men, lawyers, and others, and which furnishes steady employment — except when interrupted by short visits in the penitentiary — to over five hundred of the cleverest crooks in America. They fight for big stakes, from $5000 up, and they rely on crooked bankers, politicians, and police for protection. For the pay-off game organizes the underworld vertically. Built on deception, manned by rogues, and covered up by respectable veneer, it is a national problem. In 1934 the United States District Court in New York City tried a $1,500,000 case involving transactions in Reno, Nevada, and daily for twenty-five years the press has carried stories of the depredations of these pay-off mobs.

And so the gang throve, getting more and more bold and powerful. Entrenched locally, they had their allies in similar gangs all over the country. The Wolves of Seventeenth Street roved Denver, arrogant, powerful, and wealthy. They feared neither law nor man, as all apparently had their price.

# II

## *Running for Office*

In the primary campaign of 1920, Philip S. Van Cise became a candidate for the Republican nomination for District Attorney of the City and County of Denver. He had been practicing law for eleven years, had been an officer in the Colorado National Guard for five years, six months of which were spent on strike duty in the coal-fields, and had been a lieutenant-colonel of infantry during the War. As such he saw service in France with the First and Eighty-First Divisions, and was on the General Staff of the American Expeditionary Forces. As assistant chief of staff, and G–2 of the Eighty-First Division, he was in charge of enemy intelligence.

In his campaign he was opposed by two principal candidates, one backed by the City Hall machine, the other by the Republican United States Senator. Largely because the politicians were split into two camps he was successful in his race and received the nomination, but at the same time incurred the enmity of the City Hall gang, the politicians, and the underworld. So bitterly was his selection disliked that caricatures of him were posted around Republican County Headquarters and a branch office of his Democratic rival was opened across the hall, and on election day automobiles, ballots, and workers for his opponent went out under the direction of the Republican

County Headquarters. He was anathema to the established ways of politicians and their underworld allies.

A few days after the primary, Leon Dean, a former inspector of police and at that time the proprietor of the largest private detective agency in the city, called at his office.

'Congratulations on your nomination,' he said. 'Now I've come over to help you, and I have a friend who controls at least fifteen hundred votes and he wants to meet you. I think I can line him up solid, and he can do more to elect you than any man in Denver.'

'Thanks, Dean,' rather curtly responded the lawyer. 'I'll be glad to meet him one of these days'; and turned to speak to someone else.

The detective did not state who his party was. Dozens of politicians had been making extravagant claims as to the votes they owned, and the candidate was beginning to be bored with that line of talk. Besides, he did not like Dean, and made no further effort to get in touch with him.

But Dean was persistent and wanted to establish a contact. So he went to see Samuel J. Sackett, an influential attorney who had strongly backed the Colonel's candidacy.

'Sam,' he said, 'you've been boosting Van Cise for District Attorney. If you teach him some manners, and a little politics, he might be elected.'

'What's the trouble with Phil?' said Sam.

'Why, he hasn't any political sense at all,' he replied. 'I went over to help the fellow and he got high-hat at once, as if he didn't care for my support at all. And I have a friend I want him to meet who can get him a pile of ballots. You tell him to 'phone me and I'll fix him up, and we'll elect him yet.'

So Sam said, 'That's awfully nice of you, Leon, and I'll get after him.'

When the detective left, Sam telephoned: 'Say, Phil, did Leon Dean come around to see you?'

'Yes, he had some cock-and-bull story about a guy with a

pocket full of votes, and that's just building himself up for a stand-in. I'm not interested.'

'Now look here, soldier. You're asking for votes, not giving orders. Votes are votes, and his kind count just the same as anybody else's.'

'I know, Sam, but I'm going to get my votes on the Hill, and you tell Dean and his friends I don't want their support.'

'Don't be crazy. It may be on the level. You go to his office, see his man, make friends with him, and get his support if you can. You don't have to make promises to get votes. Just be sociable.'

'Oh, all right, Sam. But I'm not keen about it.'

As a result, Van Cise called Dean and made an appointment to be at his office at nine-thirty the next morning. And Dean still retained the name of the man with the votes.

When the candidate arrived, there was Lou Blonger. The Colonel had met Blonger before when he was a newspaper reporter, and knew his reputation as the head of a gang of some sort operating against tourists and suckers on Seventeenth Street, but had no idea as to its method of operation.

'Here's where I'd better keep a poker face,' said the visitor to himself, while he did all he could to keep from laughing at the play which he saw was just ahead.

Blonger had a softly modulated voice and pleasing manner, and started in at once to make his guest feel at home. He was then seventy-one, and schooled in the art of guile over a long life spent at the game. After some preliminaries, he said:

'Colonel, I am a veteran of the Civil War. I wear the same G.A.R. button that your father did. I have marched in Memorial Day parades with him before his death, and he was a grand old man. Now his son's following in his footsteps and has been in the War. Do you know, we old soldiers feel mighty proud of you young fellows.'

The old man was asking no questions, so the candidate let him talk.

'What's the matter with these politicians, anyway? Aren't you the only candidate on either ticket who saw service in France?'

'Yes.'

'Why, the veterans should be on both tickets, and all the jobs given to them. We G.A.R.'s had them for almost fifty years. And here you are the only one. It's a damn shame. Got any practice?' he asked.

'Not much. You see I gave up my business when I went to training camp in May of 1917, then I have been campaigning the past three months, and clients want someone who is on the job.'

'How about money?'

'Oh, I've still got a little. Enough to see me through, I guess.'

'Say, do you know how much it costs to get elected District Attorney in this town? Have you any rich friends who are putting up for you?'

'No, I don't know anything about it. I've paid my own way so far, but it shouldn't cost more than two thousand dollars.'

'Two thousand dollars! It'll cost twenty-five if it costs a cent. It's the most expensive campaign to run for in Denver outside of the Mayor.

'Now look here. I'm serious about this. I guess I am a sentimental old fool, but I've recently made quite a clean-up in some mines. I like your style, and I want to help you, and because you are the only soldier on any ticket, I'll put up that twenty-five thousand. You can either have it now, or call on me as you need it, and you don't owe me a cent. I'll make some of the boys down at the Hall chip in to help me out. What do you say?'

That poker face was having an awful time staying put, but it did. The candidate studied Blonger a long time, as if pondering over the matter, then replied:

'I can't tell you how much I appreciate that offer, Mr.

LOU BLONGER, THE FIXER

ADOLPH W. DUFF, 'KID DUFFY,' THE MANAGER

Blonger. This is the first time I ever ran for office, and I don't know much about the game. I don't need your money now. I want to get through without any outside help. But I may need it, and if it costs as you say it does, I will certainly call upon you. I don't know just how to thank you.'

The old rascal beamed, and stalled along for a while on the weather. Then he got down to business again, and stated that most of his old friends had died off, that their sons were now well along in years, and in turn their grandsons had reached young manhood, and were out in business for themselves.

'Why,' he said, 'you know how it is. Some of these boys sometimes sell people oil stock or mining stock, or something like that — perfectly legitimate transactions, but the purchaser gets scared and runs to the District Attorney's office and makes a complaint. Now, the District Attorney does not have time to investigate, so he swears out a warrant and throws the man in jail.

'The boys then come to me and want me to make bond for them, and I have to go to the trouble and expense of taking care of something that turns out to be nothing, because the District Attorney always dismisses their cases. Now, Phil, what I would like to have you do is to agree with me that whenever I have to go on a man's bond, you will fix it at a thousand dollars. Then I can just have a regular arrangement with a bondsman and not have to bother at all.'

Here was the pin-down for the candidate. How should he answer?

'Blonger,' he said, 'I have had no experience as District Attorney, and practically no criminal practice, and so I don't know anything about bonds; but my hunch would be that the safe rule to follow is to fix the bond at double the amount which the defendant is said to have stolen. Then there would be no question about his appearance at the trial.'

Blonger seemed to lose interest in the soldier candidate then and there, and as the conversation lagged, the lawyer got up and left. As he went away he wondered how much of a boob Blonger thought he was. His con-men could swindle a victim out of $25,000, and if by some chance they were arrested and the bond was fixed at $1000, the overhead cost of business would not be very great; $25,000 from the victim, $1000 forfeited on the bond, a certain amount lost for 'gravy,' and the balance pocketed by the gang.

On election night at the Republican Headquarters, the candidate and his wife were watching the returns. The early ballots from the downtown districts were strongly Democratic, and he was running far behind his ticket. Blonger, Hal Crane, the chief deputy sheriff, and the Republican County Chairman, were closeted in the latter's office and were jubilant.

About eleven o'clock the returns from the residence districts began rolling in, and they showed that a new District Attorney had been elected. At midnight, visibly disturbed, and cursing loudly, Blonger and Crane left.

The end of December, 1920, and a few days before taking office as District Attorney, the newly elected official telephoned Blonger and asked him to come to his office. He did not know that a man of Lou's age could move so rapidly, because it seemed as if he had hardly hung up the telephone before the old man arrived, probably hoping that the long-expected touch had come.

Although the District Attorney-to-be knew that Blonger was no longer a gambler, and had little, if any, interest in any gambling-establishments, he decided to make him believe that he thought he was mixed up with that line.

The fixer looked at his host, and the latter looked at Blonger, and there was utter silence for several minutes.

Finally the younger man spoke. 'Lou, what is your honest opinion of that conversation we had in Dean's office last September?'

Again the visitor sat still, trying to make up his mind as to what was behind the question, and finally said: 'That was the damnedest fool stunt I ever pulled in my life.'

The lawyer answered: 'You're right; we might as well understand each other right now.

'Blonger, you are running the Quincy Club [this was a protected gambling-den two blocks from Blonger's office] and other crooked gambling-joints, and I am going to close them and shut you up on these gambling activities.'

To put it mildly, Blonger was astounded, and vigorously denied the charge.

'Why,' he said, 'I haven't anything to do with the Quincy Club. I haven't run a gambling-place or saloon for years. I am in mining and investments. There isn't a thing wrong with my business. If you don't believe it, ask any bank in Denver as to my credit standing and you will find my unsecured note is worth a hundred thousand dollars at any of them.'

'Well, Lou,' was the reply, 'I just wanted to give you notice to quit while the quitting is good. I intend to smash these protected gambling-houses in Denver, and then I am going to get the real owners and send you to jail along with the rest of them.'

'But, Colonel, I haven't a G—— d—— thing to do with them. If you think I have, go ahead and raid them. You don't care if I go down to Hot Springs, Arkansas, for the races, do you? You do what you want to with the gambling-joints while I am gone.'

The prosecutor-to-be said, 'Go where you please, but don't run any gambling-dens around this town while I am District Attorney.'

And Blonger left, a somewhat mystified man.

# III

## *Crime Viewed by a Police Chief*

Shortly before this last talk with Blonger, the newly elected prosecutor went down to the City Hall to see the Chief of Police, Hamilton Armstrong. He was a square shooter, if ever there was one, and an able and fearless officer, but had to take his orders from 'upstairs.' Armstrong was a queer duck. He called everybody younger than himself 'son,' and could hardly say a sentence without cussing.

'Son,' he said, 'how well do you know this town?'

'Not as you do, Chief,' was the answer.

'I want to have a talk with you about it,' said Ham, 'but I don't want to waste time on you until you know some of the ropes. I better have somebody take you around.' So he called in Captain August Hanebuth, whom he said was absolutely reliable.

'Gus,' said Armstrong, 'this is the new District Attorney. Take him out and show him the town.'

'What do you mean, Chief,' said the Captain, 'how much shall we see?'

'Everything,' was the answer.

So under the escort of Captain Hanebuth, the Colonel visited the gambling-joints of Denver, both white and colored, marched up to the doors, knocked, was inspected through the peepholes, waited a reasonable time until the apparatus was put away and the players occupied in other pursuits, then walked in. All he found, of course, was a bunch of slightly embarrassed men who were introduced to the new District Attorney, and who were anything but pleased at his visit, even though nothing could be seen.

Hanebuth gave him rather full details of the operations of each place, and the history of the proprietors and hangers-on. He also explained the lookout system, either by peepholes or by a man loafing around outside the door.

'Watch for the buzzer on the wall near him,' he said. 'When the lookout sees something suspicious, he rings the bell. Then you never find anything when you get in. You can't convict of gambling on suspicion. We raid them once in a while, drag everybody down in the wagon, and of course they all get loose in police court because we haven't any evidence.'

Then they went through the row. Some sixty houses were operating, in addition to the girls in the small downtown hotels. Then the small hotels and rooming houses were queried and their registers examined. Candy punch-boards were going full blast in the drug stores and in the little shops near the schools, and dice games were being played in the cigar stores.

'How about bootlegging, do you have much?' the Captain was asked.

'Have much! The town's full of it. You can't enforce that law. Every soft-drink parlor, pool-hall, whorehouse, hotel, or resort of any kind can get it for you in five minutes.'

Chinatown wound up the tour. From a population of several thousand in the eighties the Celestial Republic's citizens had dwindled to a bare two hundred. Fan-tan and lotteries were going full blast, and Hop Alley was the center of their activities. But all that appeared on the outside were a few Chinamen slinking along the alley, or standing quietly by entrances. The interiors of the buildings had large wooden bars to block the doors, and the rooms, when entered, though filled with tobacco smoke, were bare of players. The exits were not visible.

Several nights were spent with the Captain, who did his best to initiate his protégé into the Denver underworld.

After these trips the new prosecutor wondered about the situation. There were strict laws against gambling, the old row had been shut up, prostitutes were supposed to be run out of the section formerly occupied by them, yet Denver in 1920 was practically a wide-open town. Gambling-houses and bootleg joints were running with the full knowledge of the police and prostitutes were occupying somewhat the old section of the city, though slightly less brazen in their activities. Why was it?

The answer came a few nights later when he went back to the Chief. The latter asked him if he had seen the town. The Colonel told him generally what Hanebuth had shown him.

'So you saw the line, did you? Who do you think runs it?'

'I don't know,' the lawyer answered.

'Well, I do,' said the Chief. 'Abe Silver, the constable, collects from all of them. That's his graft. You'll have to watch your juries in his justice court too, or all your misdemeanor cases will blow up. He's the Court.

'Then in the West Side District Court you've got Hal Crane. He's the chief deputy sheriff, is one of the gang, and will throw you whenever he gets a chance. Never tell him anything and keep watch of him. He and the Mayor are old-time pals and were in the United States Marshal's office for years. He kids the Mayor and gets him to do whatever he wants. Crane runs the niggers; their gamblers and women all see him.

'The candy boards get the kids' money, and that starts them gambling. The dice games don't amount to much. The candy and cigar men get by on the claim that this petty gambling helps business.

'So Gus told you about the bootleggers. This prohibition business ruins every police force. When officers can get money just for not seeing things, it takes an unusual man not to get blind once in a while. You can get booze anywhere. And the Mayors have hung on to all the bonded stuff. They keep that under lock and key in a huge room in the basement of the auditorium, and issue it for political parties. It insures a good crowd and goes over big. At present prices that stock is worth 'way over a hundred thousand dollars.

'Some of the big fellows cut in on the large-sized gambling-houses. But, son,' he continued, 'you haven't seen or heard of half of it. You did not run into Blonger and Duff, did you? What the hell do you think they are doing around this town?'

'I don't know anything about Duff, but I know Blonger has some sort of a con-men's gang on Seventeenth Street.'

'Hell! they own the town,' said the Chief. 'What Blonger says goes. I tried to run Duff out of here and had him in jail. Then Hal Crane went "upstairs" and I got orders to release Duff and to leave him and Blonger alone. The first thing you find out, son, in being a policeman, is to obey orders and I take mine, and so Blonger and Duff do as they want to in this town, and we don't touch their men either.'

'What would happen if you went on the rampage, cut loose, raided all these places, and put the Mayor and his bunch on the spot?' said the visitor.

'Say, you are green,' answered the policeman. 'What would happen? Just two things — my raids would all be tipped off, and I'd arrest a lot of people but have no evidence. And Denver would have a new Chief of Police, and the Mayor wouldn't be on the spot. I can get the big criminals, the murderers, stick-ups, and protect the average citizens. But the politicians have to get theirs, and when I'm told what's theirs, that's that.

'We have a lot of square men on the force and a lot of crooks, and the two biggest ones of the bunch are over there in the detective department, and they are in on the cut with Blonger on every deal he makes.'

And then the Chief proceeded to regale the District Attorney with stories of the two detectives, both of whom were powers in their department.

'Son,' he said, 'they are smart. Look out for them. They are Blonger's men, and he has a lot of others in this burg. All through the political jobs you will find his gang; but, son, if you are on the level, I will get you the dope and you do the work, and we will smash the whole damn bunch of them.'

Two months later Hamilton Armstrong was dead and his assistance was never obtained. But the foundation was laid through the information supplied by him.

# IV

## *Protection*

ABOUT the time that he visited Armstrong, the District Attorney-elect began to check into the pending criminal cases. Almost at once he found the trail of Blonger, in a confidence-game charge against Robert Ballard, accused of obtaining $25,000 from one E. Nitsche, a florist of Dallas, Texas, in Denver in the fall of 1919.

Nitsche had returned to Colorado about ten days after he had been swindled and had made a complaint to the Denver Police Department. Though that was July and the summer operations of the con-men were then in full blast, the detectives were unable to give him any information whatsoever, and he went home without results.

However, he did not give up hope, but printed a circular which he sent, among others, to the Colorado Springs Police Department, and in the fall of 1920 it picked up Ballard. The latter was working that city and Denver as a 'steerer' or pick-up man under Duff's direction.

Colorado Springs had an excellent force, and its officers were honest. At their head was Chief of Police Hugh D. Harper, and his Captain of Detectives was Irvin B. (Dad) Bruce. They were relentlessly on the trail of the con-men, because Blonger's gang frequently dropped into their town and picked up a sucker and then brought him to Denver to trim him.

As soon as they arrested Ballard, Harper wired Nitsche that he had him under arrest, and the latter went to Denver and filed a case against the con-man in the West Side Criminal Court. The machinery of the law now faced the tactics of the underworld, and the latter went to work.

Though Ballard had no visible occupation, though he had a police record, though he was charged with stealing $25,000, the prosecutor had recommended bond of only $5000, which the judge fixed without investigation. But even a fifth of the loss was deemed too high for the gang. So Tom Ward, Blonger's personal attorney, and a former United States District Attorney, appeared for Ballard, and without objection, had the bail cut to $2500. Blonger then personally put up cash and Liberty bonds with a surety company and the latter went on Ballard's bond. Thus released from jail, with part of the victim's own money as his security, he was free to ply his trade of swindling the public. And free was right, as he had been in Denver, without molestation, all the summer of 1919 and 1920, though his picture was in the police gallery and the authorities had been asked to find him!

After several continuances, secured by the defense on the ground that the defendant was busy, the case had been set for trial for January, shortly after the new prosecutor took office. Nitsche was absent, but Ballard appeared in court on the day appointed, and his attorney insisted on immediate trial or a dismissal of the case. However, Nitsche had wired that he would be delayed a few days, and the case was put over until the following week. When Ballard found that Nitsche was on hand to prosecute him, he jumped his bond and has never since been found in Denver.

Score one for the underworld. Cost to it: only ten per cent out of a $25,000 steal for a forfeited bond, plus attorney fees to the regularly retained attorney for the crowd. Add to that the build-up of its morale, that Blonger's men always 'beat the rap,' and that the new District Attorney had had his first con-man slip out right under his fingers. Why worry about the Law?

Cost to the State: the loss of respect for government by one more victim of a criminal gang. But add to that the fact that Nitsche's tale was the first time the new District Attorney had heard the story of how the con-men operated. His eyes were now opened to the game. Had the underworld really scored, or was it only a touch-back?

In brief the victim's story was as follows:

Nitsche met a man named Crosby, whose true name was Ballard, in Manitou, near Colorado Springs, the latter part of June, 1919. They drove out to the Broadmoor Hotel, a fashionable summer resort south of Colorado Springs, and there Crosby saw a man whom he claimed he had seen with a judge friend of his in Minneapolis.

This man at first denied his identity, but after Crosby told him about the judge, he admitted that his name was Ware, and said that he was under a security bond of $75,000, which he showed them. He also exhibited to them a letter from his firm, an alleged New York syndicate of stock-brokers. He had received some publicity in the paper about the winnings he had made, and the letter said that he would be discharged if he had any more unfavorable notoriety. He further stated that he was constantly being checked by the company's auditor.

They had a little talk about investments on the stock exchange, and Ware agreed to make them a little money, so Crosby gave Ware ten dollars, and Ware went into the Broadmoor Hotel to invest the same in an alleged brokerage office in the hotel, and later returned and handed them twenty dollars. Ware suggested they go to Denver and deal on the main 'exchange,' so they drove there that afternoon, and went to a room in the Kittredge Building, which was equipped with a blackboard, stock quotations, telephone desk, and chairs, and which Ware said was a branch office of the stock exchange. It was presided over by a manager or broker.

Crosby and Nitsche invested small amounts and always

got two for one in return. Ware then suggested that they buy $50,000 worth of Mexican Petroleum; that they would get twenty-five per cent of the profits if they went into the deal with him.

Ware then had Crosby buy the stock, and they sold it at a profit. So Ware and Crosby went in to collect their profits, and the transaction went so far that the broker put the money in Nitsche's hands. Then Crosby asked for their credit slips back, as they had been buying on credit. At that point the manager refused to let them take the money away unless they could show that they could have made good on their credit slips if they had sold at a loss.

The broker then agreed to give Ware a thirty-day option on the winnings, at which time they were to have money equal to the amount of their purchase on deposit in a Denver bank. Nitsche went home to get his money and returned and placed it in the designated institution on July 7. There had been something about wrong initials, which Nitsche did not understand, but because of them he and Crosby were required to take their money in cash to the brokerage office. They turned this over to the broker to count, and he said he would have to wait until he got in touch with the main office and have it send up a check.

While they were waiting, Crosby went in and made some deal whereby the entire winnings and all of their money was lost. Ware at once knocked Crosby down and pulled a gun on him. Ware then told Nitsche that he would repay his loss, but he had to leave that afternoon for Kansas City, where he would get the money, and for Nitsche to go to Oklahoma City and wait for him there. At that point Ware gave Nitsche the money for railroad fare. When Nitsche arrived in Oklahoma City, he received a telegram from Kansas City stating that Ware had to go to Chicago, but for Nitsche to wait for him. Nitsche then concluded that he had been swindled, and went back to Denver and reported to the police.

As a result of Ballard jumping his bond, the prosecutor

checked back on old confidence-game cases in the West Side Court, to see what had become of them. His force was composed of three experienced old men and six young deputies, the latter with little previous trial experience. As all of them were strangers to him as far as working together in a law office was concerned, he began the investigation by himself and decided not to take any of his deputies into his confidence until he became better acquainted with his own staff.

He found that in 1913 two confidence-men named Jackie West and Frank Goodrich, alias 'Diamond' Frank, had been convicted and sentenced to the penitentiary. Their case was appealed to the Supreme Court, where the decision was affirmed in 1915. Goodrich went to the penitentiary and served his term, but West jumped his bail. The securities for the bonds in both District and Supreme Courts were put up by Blonger through the same bonding company.

A later investigation revealed that West's real name was John J. Egleston, of Worcester, Massachusetts, with a criminal record of many convictions and arrests dating back to 1908, while Goodrich was Frank Gerlach, who had drifted into the con-racket from an early career as a bartender in Tacoma, Washington.

February 1, 1921, a Denver paper carried an article from Goshen, Indiana, stating that the Reverend Albert S. Menaugh, a Brethren Church minister, had committed suicide. The article stated that in 1920 he had confessed to a shortage of trust funds of $12,000, claiming that he had been fleeced out of the money by confidence-men in Denver, Colorado.

The District Attorney at once wrote a letter to Menaugh's wife, and was answered by her attorneys, who told a story something on the order of that of Nitsche. After Menaugh returned home, he went into court, stated that he had used trust funds left with him, and asked that he be sent to the penitentiary, and he was placed in jail. His attorneys had then gone to court and said that, inasmuch as those who had placed the money with him did not want to prosecute, he could not be convicted of any crime, and he was released. However, Menaugh, disgraced, broken-hearted, and unable to pay back the funds which had been entrusted to his care, took poison and added one more to the list of men whose lives had been destroyed by con-men in the United States.

On February 14, another letter came, this time addressed to 'State Attorney, Denver,' from C. E. Henson, of Haskell, Oklahoma. He stated that on September 7, 1920, he was swindled out of $14,500 in Denver on a fake stock-market transaction; that he spent nearly all the money he had left trying to locate the men; that he was not able to offer a reward, but wanted to run them down and prosecute them.

And then Henson added this sentence: 'Please let this be confidential, as I do not want my friends at home to know of my misfortune.' He later released the District Attorney from that confidence and testified for him, but his statement was one which was so much relied on by confidence-men that they figured that nine tenths of their victims would keep quiet rather than let their friends or associates know that they had been played for suckers.

Later the District Attorney's office found out about numbers of men who had been swindled in Denver, but who refused to answer any letters whatsoever, or give any inkling of any kind that they had ever lost money in such a transaction. Henson's story was the same old transaction on the stock market.

The next day still another victim wrote about crooks in Denver, this man being Albert Backus, a lawyer of Okmulgee, Oklahoma. He had been defrauded out of $8500 in Denver in 1918, had returned to the city, and had gone to the then District Attorney. There he swore out a complaint and had a warrant issued for the arrest of the three confidence-men implicated in his case.

Backus's letter was quite pointed. He stated:

> In February, 1919, I traced J. P. Kinsman to Sanford, Florida, and had him arrested and held for ten days awaiting extradition

papers from Denver. I failed to get the extradition papers, and he was released. Later he was arrested in New York City, and extradition papers were requested from Denver, but the District Attorney, Mr. Fox at that time, flatly refused to issue them.

I offered a $1000 reward for arrest and conviction, and spent a good deal of money in tracing them, but I have lain off until a change in the District Attorney's office should occur at Denver, hoping that some day the State of Colorado would have officers who would have an interest in the prosecution of those who rob tourists at Denver. I have not renewed my reward and am spending no more money in tracing the crooks, but if you are interested in the prosecution of these men, I will appear as a witness at my own expense at any time you may bring any or either of them back to Denver for prosecution.

I would like to either have you make an effort to get these men back to Denver for prosecution or dismiss the case, so that I can proceed against them in a civil action for the recovery of my money. As I understand it, I cannot hold the criminal action over them while I am attempting to recover my money, which as yet I have not attempted to do. I much prefer to have them prosecuted.

I think I have done my part in trying to apprehend these crooks, and now it is up to the State of Colorado to either let them go unmolested or to prosecute them. The offer of a reward is useless as detectives will not work without their regular per diem and expenses. I cannot pay for any more detective work, and the time of the posted reward has expired. It seems to me that the State of Colorado should go to some expense in the interest of justice and protection of society, in view of the fact that I received no co-operation from the District Attorney at Denver when I had one of my men arrested and held twice for extradition.

In his letter Backus enclosed a circular, which gave the names and pictures of J. P. Kinsman, Thomas Beech, and William E. Mead, alias the 'Christ Kid,' as the men who had defrauded him. These pictures were to be the beginning of the gallery of confidence-game men which was to be assembled by the District Attorney. Both Mead and Beech were dangerous felons.

In 1896 Elmer Mead was sentenced to the penitentiary at

San Quentin, California, for three years for robbing a passenger on a Santa Fe train. He escaped from an officer while en route to the penitentiary, but was later recaptured, and served that term. After that he stole fifteen hundred dollars' worth of valuable furs from the Daniels and Fisher's store in Denver in 1913, but evaded arrest for it. However, he was from time to time apprehended in many other cities on miscellaneous charges, mostly with con-men, but escaped successful prosecution.

The Thomas Beech record commenced in 1895 when he was sentenced to six years in the Columbus, Ohio, penitentiary for forgery. In 1900 he had served three years in the Jackson, Michigan, penitentiary for picking pockets. In 1904 he had been sentenced to five years in the Stillwater, Minnesota, penitentiary for shoplifting, and then became a con-man and as such had acquired a long list of other arrests, but with no additional convictions. To be a con-man seemed like an insurance policy against arrest.

As evidence began to accumulate, it was found that both Mead and Beech had been members of the gang and worked in Denver in 1918, 1919, and 1920. Here were two men, professional criminals, one wanted at that time for a depredation on a local store, and both wanted for a Denver swindle of $8500, yet roaming the streets of the city, untouched by the police. Why was this so? Is Society helpless, that it cannot seize and hold the gangsters and thus protect itself against their constant attacks?

The action of the St. Louis police partly answers the questions. It was 'Hell on con-men,' and those gentry entered the portals of that city at their peril. Albert Backus's circular was in the rogues' gallery of nearly every large city in the country, and St. Louis and Denver each had it. Thomas Beech, though in Denver every summer for three years, could not be found by its police.

But December 21, 1921, he stepped off a train at the Union

Station in St. Louis, and was grabbed by its detectives as he walked through the gates. Mugged, finger-printed, and identified, he was quickly tied to the Backus circular.

St. Louis at once wired the Chief of Police at Denver:

> WE HAVE THOMAS BEECH, CHARGED WITH CON-GAME IN DENVER ON COMPLAINT OF ALBERT BACKUS. DO YOU STILL WANT HIM?

By return wire came the message from Denver:

> CANNOT LOCATE COMPLAINING WITNESS. TURN HIM LOOSE.

Which St. Louis did, ordering him out of town. And the next day the Denver department tried to save its face by wiring:

> HAVE LOCATED BACKUS CIRCULAR. HOLD BEECH FOR WARRANT.

But Beech, of course, was gone. He didn't seem to like St. Louis.

# V

## *Gamblers*

SHORTLY after the new District Attorney took office, he asked all the owners of gambling-establishments to meet him one evening at the West Side Court. About sixty attended, wondering what it was all about. They quickly discovered.

'Boys,' he said, 'I have no quarrel with you personally. Nor do I intend to prosecute you for what you have done up to this time. That's water under the bridge. But Colorado has very strict laws against gambling and the District Attorney has the job of enforcing them.

'You men have been operating under protection. Some of you have been running straight and some crooked. But in either event your protection isn't going to help you, and the game is over. Will you close up by yourselves, or do you want me to shut you up?'

There was silence for a long time, each waiting for the other to speak. Then Andrew H. Sorenson, of the Quincy Club, got to his feet. He was a large, surly, heavy-set Swede. 'You're the bunk,' he said. 'You're not the whole police department, and you can't shut me up and you know it. The Quincy Club is incorporated, has a private membership list, and is going to run as it pleases, just like the Denver Club where the swell business men go. So far as I am concerned, you can go to hell.' And with that statement he walked out, accompanied by his partner, James A. McAdams. Frank K. Miller, of the Dry Climate Club, made the same statement about his organization, but stayed in the meeting.

The views of the others, however, were well expressed by one of their number, who was a stranger to the official. 'Well, Colonel, if you tell us nothing doing, I for one don't seek any trouble, and I'm moving on.' And as a result most of them closed up, but watched the Quincy Club to see when, if ever, Sorenson's bluff would be called.

Important murder and other felony cases consumed the first months of 1921, but by summer, when court vacation came, the office was thoroughly organized and the gambling situation demanded attention. Meanwhile, some other establishments, emboldened by the lack of action by the prosecutor, had also opened up. But the Quincy Club was to be the first point of attack and the raid had to be a complete knock-out, not a mere tap on the wrist.

In preparation for the assault the District Attorney had made periodical visits to the place, but had always gone openly to the door and knocked for admission, and consequently had never seen any evidence of gambling. These trips, however, had familiarized him with the construction of the joint. It was built to insure its patrons the entire destruction of evidence before the Law could break in.

Externally the 'Quincy' was a typical gambling-den on the second floor of a building of the same name. There was a creaky elevator which could be used, but the fraternity and the victims preferred a long flight of stairs which led up from the street. It bore the disguise of an incorporated club, and admission supposedly was by card only, but any sucker or sport could get one, and the police entered at will. But when a reform wave was on, or newspaper reporters or officials who were not 'right' desired to enter this or other places of chance, they could not get in until all evidence of gambling was removed.

The rooms themselves, U-shaped, ran on either side and

across the end of a wide hall. The bottom of the U was the room used by the lookout, and the peephole commanded the approach of all coming down the hall from the stairs or elevator, and nothing obstructed the view, which was made better by unusually large lights furnished by an accommodating landlord.

But the interior was where the real protection lay. The windows were covered with sheet-iron painted to represent the window-panes and sash. Huge hooks and bolts fastened them tight to their frames. The glass panels on all the doors adjacent to the hall were painted black on the inside, and two inches of newspapers were laid against them. These in turn were covered by plates of one-eighth-inch sheet-iron. Then over this armor were built wooden boxes, half a foot deep, filled with sawdust. The place was axe-proof and sound-proof.

Craps was the principal game, played on billiard tables with a small 'lay-out' or sheet of oilcloth, with numbers painted on it. Roulette wheels were no longer used, as they could not be concealed, and were subject to destruction on sight.

Thus the enemy were revealed entrenched in their fortress. The problem was how to take it. The District Attorney had no officers of his own. The assistance of the police was needed, but which ones could be trusted?

Edmond C. Young was one of the outstanding members of the force. He towered well over six feet in height, weighed about two hundred and twenty-five pounds, and had the largest foot of any 'copper' in the city. This had been used with advantage by him in kicking in doors when pursuing criminals. He had been put on the vice squad and given a little leeway, and the District Attorney told him his problem. So together they laid out their plans.

Ed persuaded a friend of his, who was a member of the Club, to go in and engage the lookout in conversation. Then Young sneaked down the hall, and hid in the corner next the wall. He then had another club member knock on the door, and Mc-

Adams, one of the owners, himself acting as lookout, opened it wide. Young at once crashed into the place, followed by the District Attorney and his men, who were close at hand.

Sheet-iron and lookout all had failed. Gambling was going full blast at all the tables, money and paraphernalia were seized and the actual evidence obtained. Then the inmates were lined up, searched, identified, and turned over to the police for the city magistrate's court.

Sorenson was on hand, too, but this time was quiet.

'How about it, Sorenson?' asked the District Attorney. 'Do I go to hell, or do you plead guilty? I always call a bluff, and this is yours. Now I'm going to tear this joint to pieces so you will never recognize it.'

The partners were ordered held separately from the other prisoners for a state case. Then axes and hammers were called into play, the sheet-iron was ripped off doors and windows, buzzers torn out, and peepholes destroyed. Vans were called and the entire contents of the place moved out, only bare floors being left. The 'Quincy' was cleaned.

The owner of the building was notified that a reopening would lock up the place for a year, and Sorenson and McAdams were given the option of having everything destroyed by court order, or of acquiescing in giving the furniture to fire stations and to charity. They chose the latter, and as a result, from this and similar raids, almost every fire house in Denver received a billiard table, chairs, tables, and cards enough to last them for years.

Shortly after the attack on the Quincy Club, the District Attorney and his deputies raided Julius Epstein's bookmaking and gambling-joint, arrested him and two of his men, and secured his books, showing that he had made a net profit from crap-shooting alone of $47,650 for the first six months of 1921. Unfortunately, the books did not reveal the details of protection, which were apparently included in a large item listed simply as 'expenses.'

The district court was in vacation. The justice courts were both dominated by Abe Silver, the constable, who controlled the prostitutes. The county court appeared to be the only chance for that quick trial and speedy conviction which is so essential in criminal procedure.

The prosecutor went to the County Judge, told him his situation, and asked if he would call a special jury to hear these cases. He agreed to do so, and set aside a week for the work.

The cases were set for trial, a special jury called, and the District Attorney personally went to court to present the evidence. Sorenson and McAdams of the Quincy Club had their cases set for Tuesday. That of the Epstein crowd was to follow.

The lawyer for the Quincy Club stated that, if the case was put over until afternoon, his clients would plead guilty. Epstein's attorney announced that his men would probably do likewise, so the jury was discharged and Epstein's case put over until Wednesday.

That afternoon Sorenson and McAdams pleaded guilty to keeping a place for gambling and were sentenced to forty-five days in the county jail, which they started serving at once. The next morning Epstein and his men pleaded guilty, and then things began to happen. The documentary evidence against them was all out on the table ready to be presented in evidence. When the judge took the bench it was apparent that he was badly out of sorts. The District Attorney stated he would like to put on his testimony as a guide for sentence. The Court said the District Attorney was taking up altogether too much of his time (he had promised a week for a special jury, and the cases had gone off on pleas of guilty), refused to hear any evidence whatsoever, and continued the case for thirty days.

When the thirty days were up, two outside judges were on hand to assist the local judge in handling his docket. A court attaché, who was a friend of the District Attorney, told him that he was going to be double-crossed by the outside judge to whom the case was assigned, and that he had better watch out.

He at once asked the local county judge to have the other outside judge try it. But he stated that it had been set, and he couldn't change his docket, so the case went as posted.

The new judge sentenced Lewis D. Pardue, Epstein's clerk, to three months in the county jail — where he was sent forthwith and served his sentence. H. H. Weiler, the lookout, was fined fifty dollars and costs, and paid up.

Then the Judge turned to Epstein, the proprietor, and a Jew, and said, 'The judgment of the Court is that you be fined three hundred dollars, and costs, and be confined in the common jail of the City and County of Denver, at hard labor, for the full period of six months, provided, however, that the jail sentence be suspended on condition that you attend church each Sunday for six months!'

Epstein paid his fine, his bond was vacated, and he left the courtroom!

The next day when the offending judge was threatened with mandamus proceedings for making an illegal sentence, he backed down completely, revoked the church provision, and ordered him sent to jail. But in the meantime Epstein had left the State for parts unknown, unextraditable because his conviction was only a misdemeanor.

Such are the devious ways of justice with the underworld.

Candy men with their punch-boards and cigar men with their dice were far easier to handle. Both were called into separate meetings about the same time that the gamblers were assembled. Each put up the old plea that their particular kind of petty gambling was good for business and should be overlooked. But when that was turned down, the confectionery dealers promptly agreed to quit, and did. Some of the tobacco men stalled, and claimed that they had large stocks of certain kinds of cigars on hand which could be disposed of only by dice games, that they had laid these in on the assurance of a prior prosecutor that they would be allowed to operate and that they should be permitted to dispose of them before quitting. The man who made this objection was asked the locations of the stores he operated and the brands of cigars included in his statement, and the dealers were asked to reconvene a week later.

Investigators were sent at once to purchase full boxes of the cigars in question, but were told at several of the stores that they didn't have that quantity in stock! The garrulous gentleman was then called in, confronted with the facts and backed down. This got around and the dice games stopped without a second meeting.

A second link was being added to the chain of evidence on why we have criminals. Some business men seemed perfectly willing to have the Law stretched if it would fill their own pocketbook.

# VI

## *Federal Activities*

Chief Armstrong had told the new District Attorney to trust no one in investigating the Blonger gang; that his friends and lieutenants were everywhere. The city administration was hostile, had backed another candidate in the primaries, and had done everything that it could to defeat him in the final election. He had little personal acquaintance with the police, and Armstrong was dead, so that all he could do was to feel his way carefully, watching every step that he made, and trying to make sure that those to whom he talked were not Blonger's men.

He was very well acquainted with Rowland Goddard, the head of the Federal Secret Service, and so went to see him. Goddard gave the District Attorney a lot of information corroborating Armstrong's statement. He told him he could trust Roy Samson, Division Superintendent of the United States Bureau of Investigation, and Harry Williamson, District Supervisor of the Federal Narcotic Department, and all the Post Office Inspectors. So the prosecutor called upon them and established friendly connections, which became invaluable as matters progressed.

Williamson proved the best immediate lead. He became interested as soon as he was told about confidence-men. He went into a back room and came out with a small box such as carpenters use for a chest for their best tools.

'Here is just what you want,' he said. 'W. S. Patterson, of this office, nabbed a con-man named Charles F. Dixon when we were looking for dope last year and got a boxful of con-men's paraphernalia. You can take it and look it over, but keep it for us because the judge will probably make us give it back if Dixon's attorney demands it at the time of the trial. However, there is a lot of duplicate stuff in there and I don't care if you keep some samples.'

This was the District Attorney's first introduction to the layout of the con-man, and his education started in earnest. The most imposing-looking document of the lot was a bond for $100,000 of the Metropolitan Bonding and Security Company of Newark, New Jersey, bonding Dixon, and with the rogue's picture printed on the bottom, something done by very few con-men because the bond might get lost and the identification be easier.

The bond disclosed a peculiar failing of criminals. Dixon's full name was Charles Frankie Dixon. The bond was for Carlisle F. Davenport. Criminals lack imagination and fear they will forget their assumed names, and therefore the usual alias contains the same initials as the real name of the criminal. Dixon had two bonds in his tool box, and the District Attorney kept one.

Among other things there were tin signs for 'Notary Public,' 'Manager,' 'Clerk,' etc.; stationery of all sorts with the names of various business men and fraternal organizations, including the Thirty-Second Degree Masons; blank telegraph sheets and envelopes; red and gold seals; newspaper clippings about the tremendous winnings made by a young man on the race-track; a letter of warning from a brokerage house; and buy and sell tickets on 'International Exchange.' Just how they were used, or what they meant, neither Williamson nor the prosecutor could tell. Here is one of them:

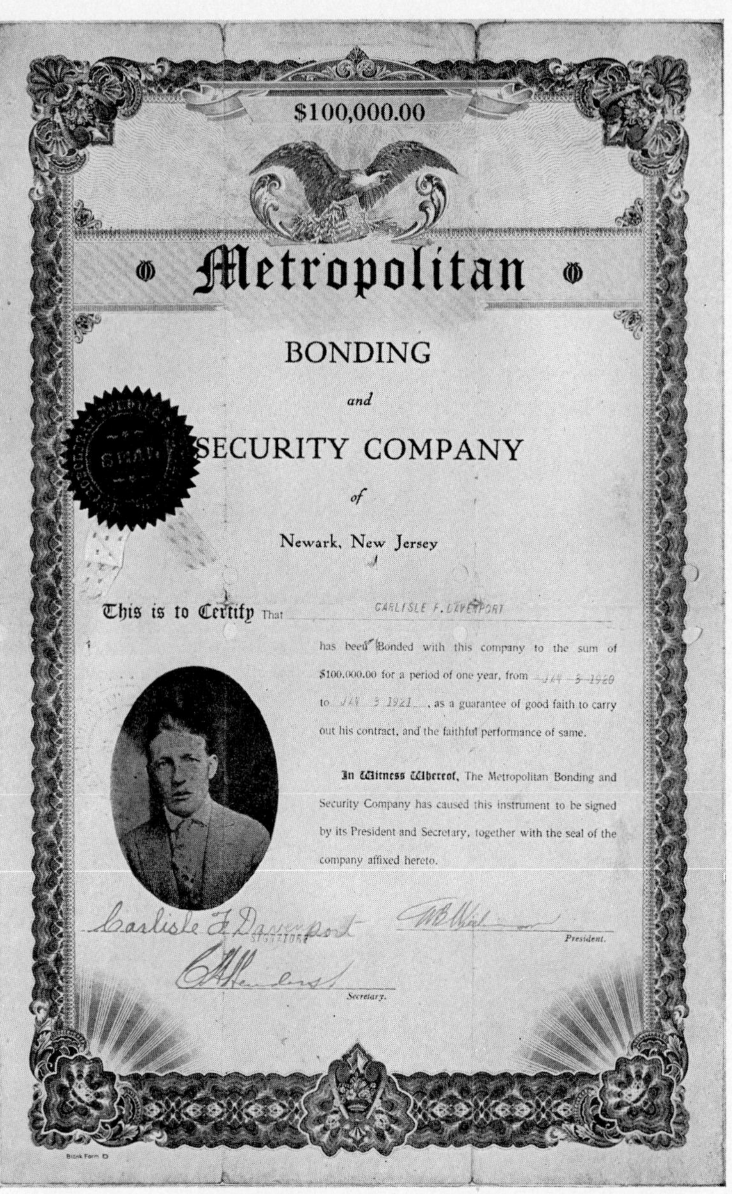

$100,000.00

Metropolitan

BONDING

and

SECURITY COMPANY

of

Newark, New Jersey

This is to Certify That CARLISLE F. DAVENPORT

has been Bonded with this company to the sum of $100,000.00 for a period of one year, from JAN 3 1920 to JAN 3 1921, as a guarantee of good faith to carry out his contract, and the faithful performance of same.

In Witness Whereof, The Metropolitan Bonding and Security Company has caused this instrument to be signed by its President and Secretary, together with the seal of the company affixed hereto.

Carlisle F. Davenport
SIGNATURE

President.

Secretary.

Blank Form D

A TYPICAL CON-MAN'S BOND

Taken from Charles Frankie Dixon, alias Carlisle F. Davenport

CABLE: BROWALL

W. S. SHEPPARD, PRESIDENT
A. R. VAN COURT, VICE PRESIDENT

J. A. BRAINARD, SECRETARY
D. W. SHERWOOD, TREASURER

CAPITAL $350,000,000

**Sherwood, Sheppard & Company**

**BROKERS**

OFFICE 42 WALL STREET
PHONE HAYS 245

NEW YORK CITY, *June* 3, 1921

Carlisle F. Davenport,
Rome Hotel,
Omaha,
Neb.

DEAR SIR;

It is with regret that upon the recommendation of the Board of Directors I call your attention to the recent press notices you have been unfortunate enough to receive.

While we know that these incidents will occur notwithstanding the utmost care and while we feel real regret in the dismissal of the unfortunate victim, still the fact remains that it is results we pay for and expect rather than causes and excuses.

Obviously, the moment your operations attract sufficient comment and attention to cause the various heads of the brokerage houses against whom we operate to suspect your connections with us, YOUR USEFULNESS TO US ENDS.

I am instructed to inform you that this will be your last notice and warning,

Very Truly Yours,
J. A. BRAINARD
*Secy.*

Williamson stated that one of their leads took them to the Iron Building, on Arapahoe Street. Across the street was a sporting-goods concern which carried in its window a large supply of fishing tackle, gloves, and other paraphernalia.

Agent Patterson had covered the building for a week or so. He found that Duff went to the room daily, and that fifteen to eighteen men went in and out of the place each day. Blonger was there two or three times, but did not stay very long. The door opened on the clock at nine A.M. and closed at four P.M.

A typewriter stood on a desk in front of the window and a man was always seated behind it looking out. He never seemed to be doing anything with the machine unless the door opened, at which time he got busy and pounded the keys vigorously. Patterson noticed also that whenever a con-man stopped in front of the sporting-goods house across the street, one of the con-men in the room ran down the stairs and went down the street, but why he did not know.

The Federals were watching the room from a studio across the hall. The colored janitor, evidently tipped for that purpose, informed the occupants of the room that they were under surveillance, and Duff was very much excited, and ran down to police headquarters to find out about it.

A detective investigated, and found out that 'it was only Federals looking for dope.' Finding no narcotics on any but Dixon, the Federals arrested him. Blonger went on his bond.

Under our system of law enforcement, the Federals work their field and look for their particular crime, and usually say nothing to the State authorities about State crimes which they daily see. The State authorities do the same, and give no information to the Federals, and crooks operate under the eyes of authorities, both purposely blind if they are fixed, or if their particular field is not being trespassed upon by the criminal.

However, in this case Williamson went to the City Hall and had a conversation with the Captain of Detectives, John Bacon, about the matter.

'Captain,' said Williamson, 'we have been checking on some hop-heads, and arrested a fellow named Charles F. Dixon, and have indicted him in the U.S. District Court. We found in his possession an entire con-man's lay-out, and we also found that Room 1 in the Iron Building is the headquarters for the con-men who are operating in Denver. I wanted to tell you so that you could close it up. Here is their lay-out.' And Williamson started to open Dixon's box.

'Hmmm,' said Bacon, 'you know, that is a funny thing. We haven't a single way in this department of counteracting those fellows. They never trim any Denver men, and consequently you can't get any interest in doing anything against them. Our appropriation is all taken up in other ways, and we haven't any money we can spend on paying any attention to them. No, I don't care to waste time looking at that stuff. I am too busy on other matters.'

So Williamson, disgusted, took Dixon's paraphernalia and left.

The Post Office Inspectors also had some data about the Denver con-men. They showed the District Attorney a report about two of them named Frank Irving and William L. Lewis.

Irving was known in the underworld as the 'Rocky Mountain Goat,' but in reality he was Charles W. Rockwood, from Iowa and Eldorado, Kansas. Lewis had a bad record. His real name was Edward O. Ellis, of Birmingham, Alabama, and he had there been convicted of murder. Later, however, he participated for several years in con-games in Atlanta under the notorious Floyd Woodward, alias Tommie Harrison, the fixer of that city. When Solicitor-General John A. Boykin made his successful drive in November, 1920, both of them skipped out and have been fugitives from Georgia since that time.

Irving and Lewis had used the mails in an attempt to defraud Gust Bergstrom, a wealthy farmer of Hudson, South Dakota, of $10,000 in September, 1919. The scheme of introduction to the second man was a little different from that worked on Nitsche, Menaugh, or Backus. Bergstrom had been accosted by a stranger, and they went around town together. While walking in one of the city parks they had found a large pocketbook, which contained considerable money, a surety bond for $100,000, and other papers showing the financial responsibility of the owner. A few minutes later a man appeared and asked if they had found a pocketbook, identified its contents, introduced himself, and in gratitude for their services very shortly afterwards took them into a stock exchange.

Bergstrom made quite a winning, but it was necessary for him to have $10,000 on deposit in a Denver bank in order to get the money. Consequently, he went to the Metropolitan Bank and signed a note for $10,000, which was sent to his home bank.

However, the banker in South Dakota differed from the Denver banker. He was suspicious of the transaction, and so wrote Chief of Police Armstrong that Bergstrom was trying to get $10,000 on some deal in Denver, and that he thought something was wrong.

Armstrong called in a detective and personally instructed him to cover Bergstrom and any man who went with him to the Metropolitan bank, and that he would hold the detective personally responsible for the arrest.

When Bergstrom showed up at the bank with Lewis and Irving, the latter two were arrested and taken down to the Chief. Bergstrom, however, was so well sold on the proposition that he was indignant, and refused for some time to tell the Chief of Police anything about it.

A Federal case was filed against the men, the bond of each fixed at $10,000, and Blonger again put up the security with the surety company. The report of the Post Office Inspectors stated, 'Irving and Lewis are doubtless members of the gang of confidence men who have operated at Colorado Springs and Denver during this summer, and many thousands of dollars have been obtained from victims.'

When the case came up for trial, Tom Ward, Blonger's attorney, was on hand as usual. He had already arranged with the United States District Attorney to recommend fines. So he promptly entered pleas of guilty for both, each was fined $1000 and costs, which Ward paid at once, and they walked out of the courtroom.

Emboldened by escaping prison, each continued active in confidence-game circles. Irving is today the 'boss' and 'fixer' of the con-men who operate against tourists in Quebec, Canada, where the much-reputed 'British justice' holds full sway.

Ellis went to Phoenix, Arizona, and likewise became the 'boss' and 'fixer' in that town, to which for over ten years his steerers brought their victims from Southern California. The Federals finally caught him again, however, and now he is serving a five-year sentence at Atlanta.

# VII

## *Kanavuts the Greek*

THE latter part of August, 1921, there was a small article in the *Rocky Mountain News*, stating that a man named George Kanavuts, a moving-picture proprietor from Sapulpa, Oklahoma, had reported to the police that he had been trimmed by con-men, but that none of the crooks had been located.

Picking up the telephone the District Attorney called the detective department.

'Captain Bacon,' he said, 'what's this story in the papers about some Greek from Oklahoma being trimmed out of $25,000? That's a lot of money.'

'I don't know much about it,' answered the Captain. 'Those things happen in every town, some con-men slip in, pick up a sucker, trim him, and get out again without anyone knowing who they are. We have never been able to catch any of them.'

'Well, what are you doing about it?' was the reply.

'Oh, I've detailed my best men, Pete Land and George Lusk, on the job, and they have looked around with him, but he's so dumb they can't get any help out of him. I don't think he ever had that much money, anyway. We haven't told him yet, because we have to jolly him along a little, but we're going to drop it because we can't land them, anyway.'

'Can you get hold of him?' asked the prosecutor.

'Sure,' said Bacon, 'he's outside right now.'

'Send him over, then, I want to talk to him,' was the order.

A few minutes later in came Land, Lusk, and Kanavuts. Land was a huge, fat, lumbering, bald-headed fellow, with a lot of real ability, but one who always was where the getting was good. He and Bacon were the two men whom Chief Armstrong had said were the main lieutenants of Blonger in the detective department. Lusk was also a large man, although he was more powerfully built than Land. He possessed only average ability, but always managed to get in with the big boys.

Kanavuts was introduced to the prosecutor, and the latter began to question his visitors about the case. But all during the conversation the detectives were watching the District Attorney, who was just as carefully studying them. Kanavuts had no idea of the tension in the room.

'Tell me,' said the Colonel, 'what there is to this article in the paper about Kanavuts being swindled out of $25,000 here in Denver. When did it occur, who were the men, and what have you done to catch them?'

'All I know about it,' said Land, 'is that Mr. Kanavuts came to the Captain's office with some story about losing twenty-five grand to three men, and we were detailed on the case with orders to try and get them. So we asked him his story, and it's the same old racket about the stock market. We tried to locate the place, but though he has taken us all around town he can't find the building where it occurred. And he can't describe the men. He says one had a green shade over his eyes, that some tall fellow picked him up, a short fellow joined them, and that he lost everything to the third man at some broker's. But that doesn't help us any. We are willing to do all we can, but we've got to start somewhere.'

Turning to Kanavuts, the District Attorney said, 'How about it, can you locate that building?'

'No, I don't find,' answered the Greek. 'But I know them fellow if I see them.'

'Have these detectives been helping you?' he asked.

'Well, I no know. They ask me questions, we walk, but we no find.'

The prosecutor got Kanavuts's Denver and Sapulpa address, and his business, and then said:

'There's nothing this office can do to help you. These are the two wisest dicks on the force, and if anybody can locate your men they can.'

The detectives smiled, but the irony of the remarks went over their heads.

'Well, much obliged for coming over,' said the Colonel, getting to his feet. 'Kanavuts, you might as well go on home and not waste any more money looking for your crooks. If the police catch them, we will let you know and you can then come up for the trial.'

So out they went, Kanavuts nonplussed over the brevity of the interview and the detectives delighted. So pleased were they that they dropped the Greek before he got back to his hotel, simply telling him that they would keep looking for his men.

And at the police station the word went out that the District Attorney didn't know a con-case when he saw it.

But at the prosecutor's office action was on foot. 'Send me Sanborn,' said the Colonel, and in came Fred Sanborn, a conscientious, conservative, thoroughly reliable deputy.

'Fred, I want you to go down to the Saint Elmo Hotel and wait for George Kanavuts. When he comes in, make sure no city dicks are with him, and as soon as you get him give me a ring and bring him straight back to the office. Keep this quiet.'

And Fred, a former officer in the Eighty-Ninth Division, said, 'Yes, Sir,' and went out. Within the hour he returned with his man.

Meanwhile, the District Attorney had been closeted with Kenneth W. Robinson, his chief trial deputy. Robinson was then only twenty-five. At the outbreak of the War he was too young for a commission, so had enlisted as a private and had been promoted to a sergeant in a regular army regiment. After the War he had returned to school and finished his law course. When appointed a deputy, he had never tried a lawsuit. And he took the position over the strenuous objection of his father, an able member of the bar, who did not like the practice in the criminal courts as a training school for his son. Only on condition that the young lawyer be kept out of the justice courts and be given trial experience in felony cases did Robinson senior withdraw his protest.

'Justice court is no place to learn law,' the father said. 'The procedure is sloppy, the environment usually crooked, and no man can become a real lawyer in such a place.'

So Kenneth, a novice at the bar, had been plunged forthwith into the trial of major cases. And from the start he had made good. A tall, good-looking brunet, charming in personal manner, a real student, he possessed an excellent memory and early acquired an uncanny faculty of holding a witness to the subject and compelling him to answer the question asked. In six months he was looked upon by judges as the equal of any practitioner in the criminal courts, and was shortly to become one of the outstanding trial lawyers of Colorado. He had only two hobbies, the law and fishing. Law books were taken home by him to read for the recreation that others found in novels. He was later made first assistant in the office, and was untiring in his work.

'Kenneth,' said his chief, 'I am going to let you in on an absolute secret, the most confidential matter in the office. I have a fight on that may take a year to break, and I want no word of my actions revealed to anyone until the proper time. I want you to hear a story.' So behind locked doors he was given a hurried summary of Blonger's activities and was then brought into the center of it when Kanavuts was again ushered into the room.

Kanavuts had the same old story of being picked up by a stranger, introduced to the man who had the tip on the stock market, being taken to the exchange, making a big winning, and then going home for his money. He had been neatly trimmed out of his $25,000, knew it, and was boiling for revenge. Though he spoke broken English, he was intelligent, and if one went slowly with him he could be easily followed. He showed that he could be trusted.

'What do you think of those detectives?' queried the prosecutor.

'They no good,' he answered; 'all they do is say, "You are crook, go on home," and no try to do much.'

'Well, Kanavuts, they won't do anything, and we can't do much more now, but give us some time and we think we will get your men. We will keep in touch with you, and don't give up hope. Will you keep away from the police department and never tell them anything and only work with us?'

'Sure will,' he said; and went his way.

Kanavuts's story keenly interested Robinson, who interrupted it repeatedly to get the full details of a situation which was entirely new to him. And after the Greek left, the Colonel spent the rest of the afternoon detailing to his deputy all the data which he had gathered on the con-men up to that time. He told Robinson that the situation had become too big for one man to handle, and from that time on the two were inseparable in the fight.

And so the District Attorney and his chief deputy set out to cope with Blonger, the fixer, and Duff, the manager, and the con-men's gang. It was to be army training and legal lore against the cunning and trickery of the underworld. Which would win?

# VIII

## *Anonymous Letters*

THE raids on the Quincy Club and Julius Epstein were the first direct attack on organized crime by the new District Attorney. And when McAdams and Sorenson were placed behind the bars on a case so airtight that they had to plead guilty, the underworld knew that protection might keep out the police, but it did not exclude the prosecutor.

Tearing up and moving out an entire gambling-establishment was a novelty to the knights of the cloth. They were used to the old method of a camouflaged raid, where the patrol wagons rushed up to the door, and the proprietors and all inmates were hauled away to the station, but who seldom went to jail, as bonds were promptly made. Then the cases would be dismissed or small fines assessed in police court, and the joint would do business the next day as usual.

But at the Quincy and Epstein's nothing but the bare walls remained. There was no paraphernalia for operations, and the places were never reopened.

Down through criminal circles went the word that these dens were closed up. And old animosities, long slumbering but bitter, came to the surface, and tips of all kinds, by telephone, from strangers on the street, and finally by letter, came to the District Attorney. They turned out to be the opening wedge in the attack on the con-men.

The most interesting and detailed stories of all were a series of five letters, one from Colorado and four from Kansas, written in longhand, except the last one which was printed in ink. All spelled the District Attorney's first name 'Philp,' and were obviously from the same person. Stripped of many of the details, and with assumed names substituted for some of the real ones given by the writer, and with his peculiar spelling and lack of punctuation, they follow:

Aug. 11

I am going to let you know about a situation * Sam Abrams * runs an open saloon * he has full Protection even from your office and you dont know it * his supposed wife * use to work on the Streets * under name of Jennie Brown now he has her stay home to Make Gin and Whisky and she does all the labeling and corking He supplies all his Customers in his Place in a little office * You caught him once in his cigar Store * he has Protection from Geo Peters Seargent Police he pays him $75 a month * and Oliver Smith from your office gets 50 a month to telephone him when his name is mentioned in the office *

Now take my tip Dont tell Smith when you go to Sam Abrams place * Smith has done Business with all those fellows before he went to your office * Abe Silver is now doing Business with all Bootleggers Big ones he collects 125 a month out of that he is supposed to Pay Horace and Strike from Police Headquarters *

all they arrest is a few suckers that dont Pay and dont know the ropes and Put it in the Paper, and the Public thinks they are enforcing the law take my Tip anything important never let Smith know it

A. Friend

Aug. 13

I will give you full Particulars of the Vice Trust in Denver — will of later date tell you who I am Abe Silver and Hal Crane handles everything in the Protection line They get 25 P/c off of * all Gambling * the house at 19th & Larimer * Quincy Club * 16th Market in Cigar Store * Glenarm Place

Silver handles Police Judge always and Crane and Abe the Police on Beat on account of * being friends of Mayor * also they get 25 a week from every house on Larence and Araphoe and

I will give you full Particulars of the Vice Trust in Denver. I know you real well and you know me But will of later date tell you who I am

Now the Bunko Man from all over U.S. has Made 2 Million dollars in Denver the last 2 Years Louie Blonger Protects them Little Duffy runs the Place they have had 40 Men working in Colo. Springs and Manitou they Bring them in and Trim them in Denver.

A LETTER FROM 'A FRIEND'

Larimer for Protection all those little Roomg. house and the Pimps have all to Pay Abe $15 a week *

they all have Abe's phone in trouble he send Petie Beers a Taxi Man and Sam Fields down to Bond them and he squares case in the Morning with Judge *

Now the Bunko Man from all over U.S. has Made 2 Million Dollars in Denver the last 2 years Louie Blonger Protects them Little Duffy runs the store I mean the false stock exchange they have had 40 Men working in Colo. Springs and Manitou they Bring them in and Trim them in Denver * Bacon gets 10 Per cent Land 5 P/c and the Steerer 50 P/c and Louie Blonger gets 35 P/c Duffy and Blonger Splits the 35

out of the Steerers 50 P/c comes 2½ to the Bank to cash the Suckers Draft they have to have a Bank They had the Hibernia Bank to cash all Drafts Bacon and Crane only Protects Blonger * when the Kick comes Bacon gets it only so he doesnt allow a Newspaper Reporter to hear it they get rid of Sucker in a day

Keep this letter Confidential dont let no one know you get a letter as all Reporters are friends of Abe and Crane and Bacon all Police Captains take Money from Gambling House and Prostitution house Abe Handles them all But they can't do Nothing with Reed or Barry They are all in one Clique

if the Chief of Police gets heavy they all send Land to him * The Chief is ascared of Crane and Silver because he know they are strong with the Mayor So he lets them go they dont interfere with one another Now you can stop all of it and Denver is the Worst Town in U.S. en worst then Frisco was when they Put Mayor and all of them in Jail *

Hire * Burns Agency they will Empersenate them self as Prostitutes and gamblers and they will get Evidence on the whole Combination and * Police force they can reprenst as Bunko Man and grab Duffy Blonger Bacon Land and Abe and Crane in a Month You would know things People of Denver would cause a riot * if you give them 6 months and a year they will Start telling on one another *

Mayor is a sucker and he believes No One like Abe and Crane * Next Month you Might see me in Denver and I will connect with You But get Busy on these Particulars Pay no attention to Police Dept. as they all work against you they tip you off every Move you Make —

A Friend

In the last letter the writer went into details, giving the names of the gamblers who owned the various places. Raids later conducted by the District Attorney, based on these letters, verified the locations and ownership, and resulted in the conviction of nearly all the proprietors.

Aug. 15

you see Man from Oklahoma got it for 25,000 thats only one of 500 that was gotten in the last 2 years * Duffy just Bought a Piece of Property on Broadway and 13th for 150,000 * You see the way they work they railroad Sucker out of town to a couple of towns and [when] he is safely away from Denver he drops it its very seldom they report If a Kick comes in from a Man that lost Bacon turns it over to Land his duty is to walk the sucker all Day and tell him to go home and he will send for him thats the last of it Not one in twenty comes back No other Detectives hears about a Bunco case * only Land handles for Bacon

Same Friend

The property in question proved to be the Capitol Apartment, a valuable three-story building which belonged to Duff.

Aug. 23

I wrote you twice before about * the Con Man that was working for Lou Blonger under Protection of Police Deprt Hal Crane Abe Silver Bacon * and Land have all got rich in 3 years * off of Lou Blonger of course ½ went to the steerers * any time one of there men got grabbed accidently by some Man they beat [in] some other town like happen last summer in Colo. Spgs they always get Tom Ward Crane gets him to go to Judge to get Bond lowerd and they get Bonding Co. Ralph Smith to Put Bond up for Blonger and he forfiets it thats what the Gang calls Protection every detective gets Paid every week so much if one of there Man gets picked up accidently the police releases them at once * Blonger gets This Phone through Hal Crane everything O.K. go back to work because every man that just beat a Man must Stay home till he gets a Phone that sucker left town from Land

A. E. Williams
5 West 12th St.
Kansas City Mo.

This letter confirmed the earlier lead that Blonger obtained all his bonds through the National Surety Company headed by Ralph Smith and at the proper time the latter furnished very valuable information. Smith's connections with Blonger were perfectly legitimate, as Blonger always put up full collateral, which he forfeited to the surety company if the bond was jumped.

The next letter was printed by hand.

Oct. 9

I have been working as a Bunco steerer for Lou Blonger and Duffy for 3 years * and I got doubled crossed this summer I will tell you who got this 25,000 from George Kan Buts of Salolpa it was Jack Flartery and Duffy Blonger right hand man * Police took Duffys picture out of rogues gallery for Blonger but it is in Colo. Springs gallery Flarity picture is in Kansas Penitenry he served a year Flarty and Duffy got 12500 and Blonger give plenty to the police *

The police know there is only two places in United States we all work That is Florida in Winter and Denver in the summer They are the only paces that has got protection We cant work without as the police would come down with sucker and pick us out any time * Florida police and Denver police tip us off when any state want us so we leave We also got protection in Cuba Frak McWherry handles Cuba police and Lou Blonger handles Denver police Crane Bacon and Land They have been on Blongers pay roll for twenty years before they were big *

Youse people only hear of one case in twenty as police dont let reporter hear about it unless reporter happens to be rigt there when sucker comes in *

We use to play the race game Make the sucker belief we are tapping the wire but that has had to much publicity since the war We use the stocks racket We drop a pocket book in front of sucker A card is in the pocket book belonging to owner offering a reward That is my partner We then show him where he cant lose We take in a office in charge of milloianre supposed witch is Duffy and he has bundles o money in front of him And tell sucker he will buy stock at two dollars and steerer shows sucker where he can buy same stock for a dollar so sucker buys at dollar When he goes to sell the millionar broker is out of buisness Steerer gets sucker out of town promising to give him his back

In order to get every Bunco man every sucker must go in person to Miami and Daytonia Florida or Havana They will meet there swindler But they must not go near police in those places * Havana and Denver because that what police get payed for when there is a rap for one of us Bacon notifys Blonger and he has hide out for couple of days until coast is clear

Flarity is in New York on track playing horses There is fourty five of us work in Denver in Summer for Blonger and in winter we go to Florida We are under protection of Pepper in Florida Like Blonger in Denver *

Dont let them know how you got the Information But go to work on the quiet because if police get wind of it you will never get no body They will tell Blonger He will wire every body to duck * They use to get protection in Los Angeles but dist atty put police in jail so we coulnt work without protection so we quit Will give you more news next week

But next week never came, so far as any letters were concerned.

Duff's picture was obtained from Colorado Springs and Flarety's from the Kansas penitentiary. But the latter was not recognized by Kanavuts and was never identified as a con-man of the Denver gang.

Duff's picture was almost twenty-five years old. It showed that he was then a neat dresser, and had wavy hair and heavy eyebrows. But did those characteristics still exist?

A registered letter was sent to Williams at the address given on the fourth letter, but was returned with the notation 'vacant lot.' Despite every effort to locate him, the 'friend' apparently lost interest in Denver and could not be found.

# IX

## *Planning the Campaign*

THE time had now arrived for action. The underworld was active, and the only place in which organized crime had been disturbed was in the closing of the gambling-joints. What the criminal enemies of society were doing was generally known by the prosecutor. The problem was how to prove it in court. So a plan of campaign had to be made.

The problem was threefold: first, to ascertain what local influences, outside of the underworld and its political allies, might be dangerous; next, what officials might be counted on for active assistance; lastly, what persons might donate funds so that investigators could be employed to secure the evidence.

While the press, almost without exception, stands vigorously for the enforcement of the Law, and against criminals of all kinds, their very activity in this respect presents one of the greatest American problems in apprehending malefactors. All the news about criminals who are evading arrest, regardless of whether it hinders the officials or not, is usually printed. The result is that all a pursued outlaw needs to do, to avoid capture, is to purchase a copy of any newspaper published near the seat of the crime, and turn to the front page. There, blazoned in huge type for the benefit of the entire underworld, the criminal usually finds a complete statement of what the police are doing, whom they suspect, where they have been, and what they intend to do next.

When harried officials refuse to give out any information about their operations, the press seeks to obtain it regardless of its effect. And it usually secures its facts from officers who curry favor with the papers, either for a monetary consideration or for favorable publicity for themselves. These men whisper tips to their reporter friends, or telephone the secrets to the editors.

The resulting situation is that the officials distrust the press and get rough with the reporters, and the papers retaliate by getting the news, anyway, and each side blames the other.

Would conciliation, and frankness on both sides, help? In his experience as District Attorney, the prosecutor had found that it did. He had formerly been a Denver newspaper reporter, and was somewhat familiar with newspaper practices. Denver at that time had one morning and three afternoon papers, the Denver *Post* being the largest and most powerful, and the other papers were bound to follow its lead.

Consequently, early in his term the District Attorney had, on several different occasions, gone to the papers with requests that they give no publicity to certain cases. A bank defalcation was one of these. Carl Smith, vice-president of the Central Savings and North Denver Banks, had embezzled quite a large sum of money at a time when the bank situation in Denver was critical and when news of Smith's peculations might have occasioned a serious run on the two institutions. The bank official had been arrested by the District Attorney, a confession obtained, and an agreement secured from him to plead guilty. None of these facts were known by the newspapers.

Then the Colonel went to see Fred G. Bonfils, one of the proprietors of the *Post*, and gave Bonfils all the facts about Carl Smith and the banks. The prosecutor stated that he hoped there would be no publicity about the case until the situation quieted down, and that, if Bonfils would agree to keep the matter out of the *Post*, the District Attorney would try to have the other papers assent to the proposition.

Bonfils demurred at first, stating that his business was publishing the news and not suppressing it, but finally, when appealed to that it was in the public interest to protect the depositors of the banks, and that oftentimes it would aid in law enforcement if he refrained from publishing the activities of officials against criminals, he acquiesced.

The other editors were then approached, and, although all three of them were afraid that the *Post* would run the story, they finally agreed to drop the case. Following that episode the papers had co-operated when given the facts, and had been of material assistance in several cases.

But Harry H. Tammen, the business partner of Bonfils, was a close personal friend of Lou Blonger. Hence if the *Post* knew about the investigation there was no chance of concealing it from Blonger. So the press had to be regarded as dangerous, and all reporters, so far as the confidence-game matters were concerned, had to be considered as public enemies.

The second feature was then considered. What local agencies might actively help?

'Robinson,' asked the District Attorney, 'what's the chief reason the trial deputies lose cases?'

'Lack of evidence,' he replied. 'The police arrest the men, but fail to arrest the evidence. That's because they are not properly trained and overlook important facts.'

'Then,' said the Colonel, 'that's exactly where we must commence. We are lawyers, and if we can't recognize evidence when we see it, we'd better quit. So in this fight let's mass our facts, seize every one of them, and arrest no man until the proof is on hand for conviction.

'And right here let us remember that where the police fall down is that they rush in and arrest as soon as they get an idea, instead of spotting mob criminals and giving them a little rope with which to hang themselves.'

'That's the way to handle it,' responded the younger man, 'because if these gangsters go free, the victims can well say there is no protection in the law.'

'In France,' said the Colonel, 'we always tried to find out all we could about the enemy. We used observation posts, balloons, airplanes, listening-posts, spies, raids, and everything else. And we particularly watched the avenues of communication, and cut them when we could.

'Here we can watch Blonger's mail, telegrams, telephones, and maybe get his janitor. Now I'm on my way to see what I can do.'

So to the post office he went as the most important place to start. The United States mails afford one of the most valuable places to obtain a clue to apprehend criminals. This is the 'cover' on the mail. It is against the law to open letters while in the custody of the Government, but not after delivery. But the inspectors will delay the mail sent to persons suspected of crimes until all data appearing on the envelope are copied, even to the extent of tracing it where written by hand.

And with copies of all envelopes to Blonger and Duff, many con-men who belonged to the gang could be located, and in turn covers put on them, so that the writing members of the bunco ring could be located and identified.

The Chief Postal Inspector promised the utmost co-operation, and he and his aids forthwith started their long task. Their first move was to call in the mailman on Blonger's building and instruct him to keep a list of designated letters handled by him, so as to be able to testify to their delivery.

Then J. F. Reade, the superintendent of the Western Union, was seen.

'Mr. Reade,' said the prosecutor, after explaining the situation and committing him to secrecy, 'I want your help. I want copies of all telegrams received or sent by Blonger or Duff for the last year and from now on.'

'I can't do it quite that way,' answered the superintendent.

'Our communications are confidential. But we want to help you. Here's how we can handle it. We will search our files for all back telegrams — we usually keep them for only a year — and get them out. And we will set aside all new wires. And whenever you get a court order we will produce them for you.'

'That's easy,' answered the District Attorney. 'We nearly always have a grand jury, and I will get out a subpoena *duces tecum* every so often for you to produce them there, then I will put them in my pocket and everything will be lovely.'

The same plan was arranged with the Postal Telegraph Company and with the president of the telephone company, Ben S. Read. The latter stated that anything his company could legally do to aid in the enforcement of the law was at all times subject to call by the District Attorney. And that promise came in handy in very short order. Read agreed to prepare all data on long-distance calls, their records, of course, only showing the parties, times, and cities.

How could the janitor be approached? Sanborn got a list of tenants in the American National Bank Building where Blonger had his office, and the task was simple. Philip Zang, a prominent business man and the former manager of the structure, had a room on the top floor, not far from Blonger's office, and he was a friend of the District Attorney.

Zang had a passkey to the offices, which he lent to the prosecutor, and then introduced Sanborn to the janitor. The latter then went to the Colonel's office and agreed to deliver daily the contents of Blonger's waste-basket.

This left the remaining question of who would donate funds and where could honest detectives be secured? Where could men be found, who, anonymously and without hope of reward, would furnish funds for the protection of the general public? And who could be trusted to furnish the right kind of investigators?

The District Attorney made up a list of about fifty men who

had reputations for philanthropy. He took these names to his friends among the lawyers and bankers, asked them what kind of public service would interest those parties, and particularly whether they could be trusted to keep a confidence. In a short time he found it necessary to get from three to five opinions on each man, because, while very often two or three would vouch for his secretiveness, the next one would tell an incident which would require the striking off of the name.

Finally thirty names were left, and now the District Attorney had to forsake the rôle of prosecutor for that of salesman, and sell his proposition to hard-headed business men. With Dixon's 'box of tricks' for his sample case, the anonymous letters to 'Philp,' and the letters from victims, he had the basis for a wonderful talk. And the response was amazing. Not one on the list turned him down, and the contributions totaled almost $15,000, ranging from $100 to the $1500 contributed by Mrs. Verner Z. Reed, the sole woman in the group. Charles Loughridge, a retired business man, agreed to collect the subscriptions as needed, and acted as liaison man to keep the donors advised of the progress of the work.

An interesting sidelight on human nature occurred almost a year later. J. K. Mullen, one of the wealthiest and finest citizens of Denver, heard about the fund, rushed into the District Attorney's office, asked to see him personally, and said: 'Colonel, is there anything wrong with me? Haven't I lived a long and upright life in this city? Haven't I contributed to every worthy enterprise in the history of Denver? Why didn't you come to me and ask me for funds? Why was I left out? Do you need anything more to pay your expenses?'

The District Attorney answered: 'Yes, Mr. Mullen, your reputation is of the highest in Denver. The only reason we did not come to you is that we did not know you as well as some of the others.'

'Do you need any more?' Mullen asked. 'How much is necessary to pay your bills?' And on being told the balance,

Mullen sat down forthwith and wrote a check for the entire amount.

Now for the detectives. They had to be men of experience who could get facts and report them accurately without color, men whose notes would stand the acid test of searching cross-examination in court. They had to be entirely different from the ordinary private detective, many of whom are discharged police officers of shady reputations, and a very large percentage of whom are dishonest, untrustworthy, lazy grafters, whose work is worse than useless. They had to be absolute strangers to Denver, yet able to make connections and acquaintances in short order.

The United States officers knew the Denver ropes and had nation-wide connections. Their aid was sought. Roy Samson, of the Department of Justice, recommended Fred M. Tate, a former United States Secret Service Agent, who had offices in Kansas City and St. Louis.

Tate came to Denver early and agreed to undertake the work. His job was to furnish detectives for Denver and any part of the country, and to work himself when called upon.

The funds were provided; what kind of men would they produce?

'Tate,' said the District Attorney, 'this is a new field to all of us, so we must go slowly and work into the situation gradually. Send me just one man now, the best you can find. We want him to get right in with the underworld, live with the grafters, bootleggers, pimps, and the rest of them. Let him find out which cops and higher-ups are crooked, and have him make his approach to Blonger and Duff from beneath, rather than through respectable circles. Take your time in getting him.'

The office telephone switchboard was all right for general use, but not for confidential calls. So a private line, with a secret number, was installed on the prosecutor's desk.

The plan of campaign was now complete. A detective for the underworld, others on Blonger's trail as needed, the mail, telegraph, telephone, and janitor all working for the Law.

The conspirators were pretty thoroughly covered and underworld news was about to roll in. What would it be?

# X

## *The Gang Starts South*

By November the Denver tourist season was over, the pickings were poor, and the con-men quit their activities for the summer and moved on to their new fields.

The Blonger gang worked Denver in the summer, Kansas City in the fall, and Florida, Cuba, or Mexico in the winter. In each place a different man held what could be termed the franchise with the police. Blonger never operated outside of Colorado, but when Duff moved, the Colorado season was at an end.

The District Attorney had been trying for some time to get a recent picture of this roving con-man. An early 'mug' had been in the Denver rogues' gallery, but had been removed. A poor and old picture of him had been secured from Colorado Springs, but in every other place where Duff had been arrested, when the District Attorney tried to get his picture, it was reported to be missing from the files.

Duff went to Kansas City before the District Attorney knew it, but a telegram from him to Blonger on November 16, gave this information:

> FORWARD MY MAIL TO BALTIMORE HOTEL NO SALES MADE UP TO DATE WILL WRITE YOU TODAY.

This was followed by a letter which Blonger kindly threw in the waste-basket.

K C 11/16/21

Dear Lew

Wired you today to send my mail to Baltimore Hotel here but since I have wired you thought it over and think you had better write me also forward my mail and write me to the Majestic Hotel as it belongs to Jack Haskell and he is a friend of mine and should anything come up would hold my mail for me. We are stopping at the Baltimore but of course might move from there.

Jack is leaving here for Florida today so I will take store and see if we can get out of the nut at least, some few boys here but it seems they cannot make any sales the one they had for twenty fell through and our friend Cooper had one tied but he also lost him, they just played in bad luck is all I can say as I know from what all tell me that all have been trying very hard.

Will take a chance and keep things running for three or four weeks unless something comes up that does not look good to me, if so will of course close at once so do not worry as I will not take any chances....

Hope you take good care of yourself and get things in shape to take your trip to Hot Springs as I am sure it will do you a lot of good as your last years trip did. I will write you often and if you want to get in touch with me you can write and I will leave my room number with Jack Haskell and he will call me on Phone at once if any wire comes for me to his hotel.

A. W. Duff

Majestic Hotel, Kansas City Mo.

Most of this letter was Greek to the District Attorney. He did not know who 'Jack' was, or 'Cooper,' or what was meant by 'nut,' or 'tied,' or 'sales.' He knew that 'twenty' meant twenty thousand. From the anonymous writer he knew 'store' meant fake stock exchange. He knew that Duff was at the Baltimore Hotel and got his mail at the Majestic, and found that Jack Haskell was a former Western League umpire who was running that hotel.

None of the District Attorney's force was skilled in dealing with criminals. None of them knew underworld parlance. None of them had any contact with any city policemen who were free to help against Blonger. All the prosecutor could do was to blunder along for a time until the investigators could get the inside data. His first mistake came almost at once.

On November 19, 1921, which date should be carefully noted, the Denver District Attorney very foolishly sat down and wrote this letter to the District Attorney at Kansas City:

District Attorney,
Kansas City, Mo. *Personal and Confidential*

DEAR SIR:

An all-around confidence-man and crook named Adolph W. Duff, alias 'Kid' Duffy, is stopping at the Baltimore Hotel in Kansas City. He has a few of his gang working with him, and they are trying to frame some of your citizens or visitors for good-sized wads. Jack Haskell, who runs the Majestic Hotel, is a personal friend of his, and it is possible he may be hanging around there. He expects to be in Kansas City for about a month before going south for the winter.

I do not want any inkling to go to anybody that I have given you this information, as it is the most confidential thing in my office. This gang operates in Colorado, and occasionally in Excelsior Springs, Mo., in the spring, summer and early fall, and then stops off in Kansas City on its migration south, and spends the winter in Cuba and Florida. It has cleaned up in the neighborhood of a quarter of a million dollars during the summer, and it is strongly protected politically. I am hoping to get to the bottom of it, and convict many members of the gang, including the higher-ups, but it will take me at least six months to get my data in shape. The rogues' gallery of Denver formerly had a picture of this man, together with his record, but it has recently been removed, and I have no way of identifying him with the suckers. I am very anxious to get a picture and the finger-prints of this party, and if you can get him seized on your own initiative, and take him to the Police Department, as a suspect for a Kansas City job, and there have him 'mugged' and finger-printed, you would find he would make no protest whatever, but would beat it out of town the instant he was released and you would be free of his gang, and the Kansas City people would be protected; and I would have the all-important data for my office.

This man Duff is about 50 years of age, 5 ft. 6 in. in height, 150 lbs., sallow complexion, wavy brown hair, dark blue eyes, gold filling in some of his teeth.

If you have to give out any reason for investigating him, you can state you have a complaint from Oklahoma, as many of his victims have been Oklahoma men. This man is undoubtedly using an alias at the Baltimore Hotel, but will get all his mail and telegrams at the Majestic. The 'mob' is stopping at the Baltimore.

The letter shows how little the District Attorney's office really knew about the summer clean-up in Denver, which, instead of being a quarter of a million dollars, ran from one million to two or three millions.

This letter was dictated to May Golin, a rare girl who knew how to keep her mouth absolutely shut. By this time she had been handling a lot of data on con-men, coming to the office early or working late so that no one in the building, aside from Kenneth Robinson or the District Attorney, could have any possible chance to see these letters. She was number three in the secret.

The letter was placed on the prosecutor's desk and he decided not to mail it until he could make some investigation of the District Attorney in Kansas City. Not until early in December did he get a report from former Governor Herbert Hadley of Missouri, who was then Professor of Law at the University of Colorado at Boulder, that while the prosecuting attorney of Kansas City was none too energetic, he was honest and could be trusted. Unfortunately, no heed was given to the admonition of the Colonel's father several years previously, 'Better walk a thousand miles than write a letter.'

The letter was mailed on the 9th of December, without rewriting, and under its original date-line of November 19. The District Attorney thought that he had done a fine job; that Duff would be arrested, his picture taken, some of his gang discovered, and perhaps some identifications would be made.

Then came a telegram on December 13, 1921, from Duff to Blonger, reading as follows:

LEAVING TONIGHT WILL WRITE FROM ST. LOUIS EXPLAINING MY DELAY IN WRITING DO NOT TALK TO ANYONE UNTIL YOU HEAR FROM ME.

And the next day came a letter to Blonger as follows:

FRIEND LOU

I am dropping you these few lines while waiting for my train have just wired you.

Be sure and be very careful what you say. Also try and remember who you have told I was stopping at the Baltimore — and that I was getting my mail at the Majestic — as our friend Van Cise has all the dope — if you have not told these parties I mention — then he got the dope in some other way.

Will write you more from St. Louis as I will be there a couple of days before going on to Miami — and will explain just what has happened here. Information came direct from Van Cise.

Be sure and do not mention this to any one for if it should get out it will cause lots of trouble here.

A. W. DUFF

On December 15 came another interesting epistle from Duff, now in St. Louis, to Blonger, telling all about the Colonel's letter of November 19, and stating:

Wired you on leaving K C also had Joe drop a few lines as I thought it best on account of a letter that was wrote by Van Cise to the District Attorney at K C, telling him that there was a con man with a lot of boys in K C who were there trying to sell some goods that they had made a lot of money out in Denver and as he wished to get the higher-ups he wished the District Attorney of Kansas City to have them pick me up and get my mug also finger prints. He asked him to please keep the letter confidential as it would take him about six months to work up his case and to save me I cannot see where he got the dope. Letter was mailed from Denver on December 9 but the date on the letter was November 19. I cannot understand why in hell those fellows down here took so long to get it to me. It seems to me that I either wrote you and told you that I was stopping at the Baltimore but that you had better write me at the Majestic. If I did not I put it in a letter to Redmond so if I did he might have told someone and that might be how Van Cise got that dope. Lew be sure and whatever you say do not let this letter get out for it will get my friend in trouble in K.C.

We will leave here tonight for Miami, so write me down there care of General Delivery. Also wish you would call Redmond and tell him to address me down there and not to give my address to anyone. You had better burn this letter after reading.

Your friend

A. W. Duff

This was a nice situation. The District Attorney had been working on the Blonger matters for about a year, and now by writing a letter he had given his entire hand to the enemy. They knew he was after them; they knew that he knew they were protected politically, and that he was going to try to convict them, including the higher-ups; that it would take at least six months to do so, and that the District Attorney had been looking for Duff's picture and found it missing from the Denver gallery.

Not long afterwards Tate found what happened to the letter. The Kansas City Prosecuting Attorney gave it to the Chief of Police; the latter gave it to the Captain of Detectives, who called in Detectives Severn and Odden, who took it up and gave it to Duff. No answer was received from the Kansas City Prosecuting Attorney, but drastic action was necessary to try to cover up a bad situation.

Luckily the District Attorney had made an application to the Mayor for $10,000 increase in his budget for an investigation fund, ostensibly for enforcement of the Prohibition Law. The Mayor was a bitter political enemy of the District Attorney, and not only turned down his request for $10,000, but attempted to cut off $6000 from his District Attorney's normal budget, and this matter was still pending. So a letter was composed in the hope that it would follow the same route and cover the situation.

December 19, 1921

*PERSONAL*
District Attorney,
Kansas City, Mo.,

DEAR SIR:

On the 19th day of November I wrote you in regard to a 'con' man named Adolph W. Duff, and asked you to see about arresting him, so we could get identifications. I have never received any kind of an answer to that letter, and therefore suppose that you have been unable to locate him, or do anything in the matter. At the date I wrote you I was quite confident of getting the sum of $10,000 from the Mayor and City Council for an investigation of this matter. I have had complaints of two or three 'con' games this summer, and a host of rumors that made me believe this man Duff is at the head of the organization, and I had hoped to get the money from the City Council to make an investigation. However, the Mayor did not see fit to put this sum of $10,000 in his budget, and the City Council cut almost $6000 off the running expenses of my office. Consequently, I am so badly handicapped for funds that I have been obliged to stop all further investigation of this matter until the end of next year, when I will make another attempt to get money from the Mayor and City Council.

That letter, or a copy, likewise reached Duff, because shortly afterwards he wrote Blonger from Florida, giving the latter the substance of the letter, and stating that their friends in the Hall had shut off the District Attorney's funds.

# XI

## *Analyzing the Enemy*

Roy Samson, the Department of Justice agent who had recommended Tate, brought in a report that W. H. Wurzbach, of Pueblo, had met a stranger in Denver in August, 1921, and then had gone with him to Excelsior Springs, Missouri, where he had been swindled out of $6800. Wurzbach had also complained to the Denver police department, and had been turned over to two detectives, who accomplished nothing.

Their chief advice to him was: 'Don't tell anybody about this, particularly the papers. If you just keep quiet, we will locate your men in two or three months, but if you talk to anyone, you will never get them.'

Samson gave the swindlers' descriptions to the District Attorney. He hoped the latter had some pictures or data which might be helpful in running down the men. However, at that time the prosecutor had only a very meager gallery of con-men, which was of no value to Samson.

The Wurzbach case showed that the con-men, even with their gilt-edge protection, were afraid to trim Colorado residents in Denver, but did not hesitate to pick them up in that city and then take them into another State to get the money. His story also differed from the others in that the game played on him was what was known in underworld circles as the 'play-to-the-wall,' the sucker dealing almost entirely with the first two men. The swindlers in such cases operate without much police protection, and do not have a stock exchange or pool-hall, or any office equipment. While they use con-men's literature, it is apt to be pretty poor-grade stuff. In many cases they do not even use the third man, and when they do, he appears only for a moment, so that it is rarely possible later to identify him.

The operators of the play-to-the-wall convince the victim that the stock exchange is a private club, and the second man goes in and out of the sucker's room, apparently being in contact with the exchange in the interim.

Early in November, Hugh J. Alexander, president of the First National, the largest bank in the Rocky Mountain region, telephoned.

'Phil,' he said, 'I wish you would drop in and see me. I have a matter in which I think you would be interested.'

The District Attorney went to see Alexander. And the latter handed him a twenty-five-page letter in longhand from Herbert J. Gray, of Exeter, Devon, England, giving the details of how he had lost $25,000 in August. Gray gave an unusually correct picture of the transaction, but the story by now was so old that it was no longer interesting. However, Alexander's statement was:

'Gray came to us originally,' he said, 'to see about opening an account. He cabled his bankers, Lloyd's of London, to remit £6000 to our bank, but they refused to do so on a wire order, and told him he would have to go to London in person to get the money, or to draw a draft through regular channels.

'So he went back to London and got a letter of credit for his deposit. You will notice in his letter that one of the con-men met him in New York and escorted him back to Denver. He gave Gray the excuse that he had to be in New York in order to get his draft.

'When Gray returned, he presented his letter of credit to our bank and opened an account. A few days later he wanted to draw it all out in cash. The teller sent him to me. I told him that $25,000 was too large a sum to get in money; that we would give it to him in any other form, but it was dangerous to carry that much currency. I asked him what he wanted it for, and at once his best English manner asserted itself.

'"My good sir," he said, "my letter of credit is valid. I have asked for $25,000, and am not in the habit of answering anyone's questions as to what I want to do with my money. I demand I be paid at once."

'"But," I said, "why do you want it in cash?"

'"It is none of your business why I want it in cash. It is none of your affair if burglars steal it from me. I demand my money at once."

'I told him,' Alexander said, '"if you are that big a fool, we will give it to you. But I want to warn you that crooks will get it, and we don't think you will have it long."

'So at his request we gave him the $25,000 in $100 bills, and from his letter it was gone in half an hour.'

Gray was very fair in what he wrote: 'You very kindly warned me to be very careful as to the manner I was investing this, as there are so many men around who are preying upon strangers. This advice I very much appreciated and only wish I had been able to confide in you, but the very nature of the deal prevented this, and I regret to say that I was victimized to the whole extent of my capital.'

His letter went on to say that the men he was dealing with had cautioned him very carefully not to tell his bankers or his brokers, or anyone else what he was going to do with the money, but to go to England, sell his securities, and cable them the boat on which he was returning.

The con-men, in one of the fake telegrams sent him after they took his money, wired him funds for his passage home, and he first found he had been swindled when they failed to appear in England to restore his money.

'Phil, what can you do about it?' said Alexander.

The District Attorney told him the history of his activities to date and asked for and at once obtained his complete co-operation.

'Mr. Alexander,' said the District Attorney, 'suppose you search your draft register and see what large items have been paid in cash during the last few years, and we may get some more victims.'

The bank president did this at once and in a few days reported that J. L. Tilton and Aaron Cobbs, of Ottowa, Iowa, cashed a $10,800 draft at his bank in September, 1920, and that William E. Griffith, of Walnut, Iowa, secured $20,000 in July of that same year.

'How big is this going to be?' asked Alexander. 'Blonger's gang certainly made a killing around here.'

The same month a letter came in from W. A. Carnes, an Iowa farmer, about his loss of $15,000 in September, 1921. After losing his money, his con-men paid his transportation to Chicago. At that point one of them sent him two telegrams, one from El Paso and the other from Kansas City, both of which he had retained. The letter contained these telegrams.

EL PASO TEX
1921 OCT 6 PM 1 24

W A CARNES

CARE PLANTERS HOTEL CHICAGO ILL

MONEY ARRANGEMENTS OK HAVE BEEN CALLED TO KANSAS CITY BY FIRM FOR INVESTIGATION DONT KNOW NATURE OF SAME YOU BE SURE AND WAIT THERE FOR FURTHER INSTRUCTIONS AM SURE EVERYTHING WILL BE OK I WIRED WEBB

LOWERY

KANSAS CITY MO
1921 OCT 8 AM 5 39

MR W A CARNES
CARE PLANTERS HOTEL CHICAGO ILL
HAVE BEEN SUSPENDED LEAVING FOR NEW YORK TO HAVE MATTERS STRAIGHTENED OUT YOU GO HOME WILL WIRE YOU WHERE TO MEET ME JUST AS SOON AS I GET BACK TO WORK HAVE YOUR BUSINESS ARRANGED SO YOU CAN MEET ME WHEN WIRE YOU I WIRED WEBB
LOWERY

After getting the last message, Carnes had gone home in disgust.

James F. McGrath, of Sayre, Oklahoma, wrote and stated he had lost $5000. He said one of his men wore a number 11 shoe; that he found this out when they were in their room and he put on the other fellow's by mistake. This made identification of one of his swindlers an easy task, and he readily picked the picture of Ed White, alias Ed Filger, from the photographs of tall, skinny men forwarded to him.

It was now time to analyze the situation to date, and the tabulation showed the following:

| | Swindles | |
|---|---|---|
| | 1918 | |
| August | Albert Backus | $8,500 |
| | 1919 | |
| June | E. Nitsche | 25,000 |
| | 1920 | |
| July | William E. Griffith | 20,000 |
| September | C. E. Henson | 14,500 |
| | Tilton and Cobbs | 10,800 |
| | 1921 | |
| August | W. H. Wurzbach | 6,800 |
| August | Rev. E. Menaugh | 12,000 |
| August | James F. McGrath | 5,000 |
| August | George Kanavuts | 25,000 |
| September | Herbert J. Gray of England | 25,000 |
| October | W. A. Carnes | 15,000 |
| | Attempted Swindles | |
| September 5, 1918 | Gust Bergstrom | 10,000 |

One hundred and sixty-seven thousand, six hundred dollars actually stolen from nine victims, one of them a suicide as a result, and ten thousand dollars attempted to be stolen from another! One man had hired his own detectives, identified his men, arrested one of them, and been refused extradition by the then District Attorney. Two others had sought the aid of the Denver police and received no help. Each year for the last four years showed confidence-men operating in Denver, and the 1921 swindles, under the new District Attorney, made an imposing record.

The anonymous letter-writer had told about the protection, and the evidence was rolling in to prove his statements.

# XII

## *The First Waves of the Offensive*

The latter part of December, 1921, Rowland Goddard, of the United States Secret Service, told the District Attorney that it would pay him to see the Colorado Springs Police Department and to talk with the Chief and the Captain of Detectives; that they could give him a lot of information about the Colorado activities of con-men. Accordingly, the Colonel and Robinson went down a few days before Christmas and had a long visit with them.

Chief Harper said: 'Denver should have got Blonger a long time back, but he's plenty strong up there. We ran Duff out of here years ago, and he doesn't bother us any more. But their men come in by the droves every summer and try to catch suckers here among the tourists. Then they take them to Denver and trim them there. As a consequence we never have any cases against them in Colorado Springs. All we can do is to protect our people against them. When we find any con-men here we arrest them, "mug" and "print" them, bring them in for the "show-up" in front of the full force, and then run them out of town. Occasionally we catch a con-man like Ballard, who is wanted elsewhere, and then we hold him until extradited.'

Harper then turned his visitors over to Captain Bruce, who took them into the detective department. 'We haven't many pictures of these gentry,' he said, 'but I can show you some who have been operating around here the last few years.' So he produced the photographs of about one hundred con-men and went into detail on many. He promised copies of the entire group and sent them up in a few days.

'The man for you to see,' said Bruce, 'is District Attorney Thomas Lee Woolwine, of Los Angeles. That man has made a real record. And he knows the entire inside of the activities of con-men, and about their operations all over the world.'

As Woolwine's work offered a wonderful opportunity to find out his method of attack, and as he was an expert in that game, it was decided that first-hand information should be obtained from him. So on January 1 Robinson left for Los Angeles to see its famous prosecutor. The latter turned over his entire office facilities, assigned his deputy, H. C. Kirkman, to full time on the work, and was of invaluable assistance in giving the first accurate information as to the manner in which a gang of confidence-men operated.

Woolwine was a Southerner. 'Mr. Robinson,' he drawled, 'you're up against quite a party, and you won't get as far as you want to. I doubt if you convict any police officers, because the con-men don't take witnesses when they pay public officials. And you may not get Blonger. But if you take your time you can put them out of business.

'We had some luck here. These gentry had trimmed a man named J. Frank Norfleet down in Texas. He has since become quite a famous character and you must write to him, because he can probably help. Well, he came here on the trail of some of his men, arrested one named Joe Furey, and left him with some deputy sheriffs.

'While Norfleet was over in my office getting his extradition papers fixed up, Furey bribed his way out from the deputy sheriffs. We opened their safety-deposit box and found the $20,000 bribe and we sent them over the road, then convicted some of our local bunks or con-men, and though we didn't get a case on any cops, we made it so hot that the Chief of Police and the entire bunco squad had to resign. Most of that bunch were con-men themselves.

'Then this may surprise you. We also convicted Otis V. Barry, a local banker, as an accomplice of the gang. When you get into this, you'll find that in nearly all cases a bank teller is part of the crowd. The sucker must cash his draft and get real money, because the con-men can't handle anything else.

'An honest teller won't pay out cash on a large draft without a protest and the approval of a higher bank officer who will want to know the facts before letting a customer run the chance of being robbed. And that won't do. So they bribe the teller to hand over the cash without a question. And they pay him five per cent of the draft for his services in pushing out the cash in whatever denomination the victim asks for. But Barry's conviction has opened the eyes of the bankers.

'Con-men are always protected. The larger the gang in your town, the more officials are on their pay-roll and the harder it is to get them. Make sure your own men aren't with them.'

Robinson spent many days in Woolwine's office, and brought back with him a suitcase filled with pictures of well-known con-men, besides case records and voluminous data of all kinds.

Then with all Woolwine's material before them, Robinson and the Colonel queried: How far do criminal activities extend? The police, the sheriff's office, politicians, and now bankers; and all for a price!

Just prior to Robinson's departure, the first detective, Arch Cooper, reported for duty. He was a tall fellow of about six feet in height, with blond hair, florid complexion, and large nose and features. He had been on the police force in Kansas City, and Tate said he was an experienced investigator. He turned out to be a good mixer, was rather lazy, spent money freely, and was always watching out more for Cooper than anything else. But he knew how to get in with criminals, and was fitted for the work to which he was assigned. The

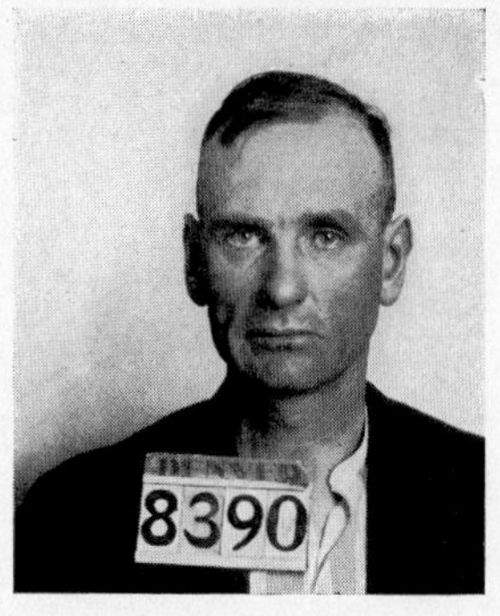


William E. Mead
'The Christ Kid'

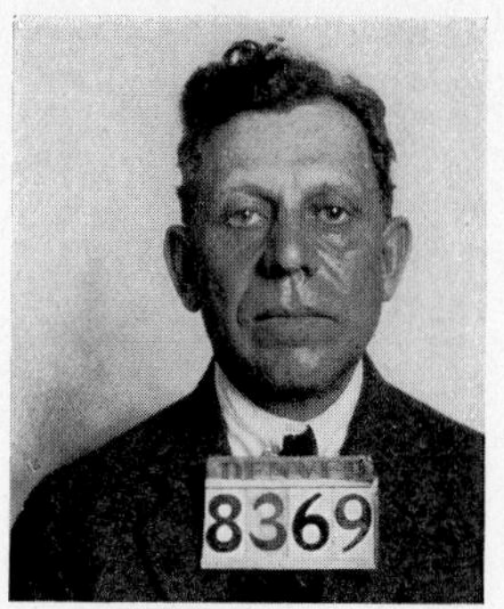


Thomas Beech

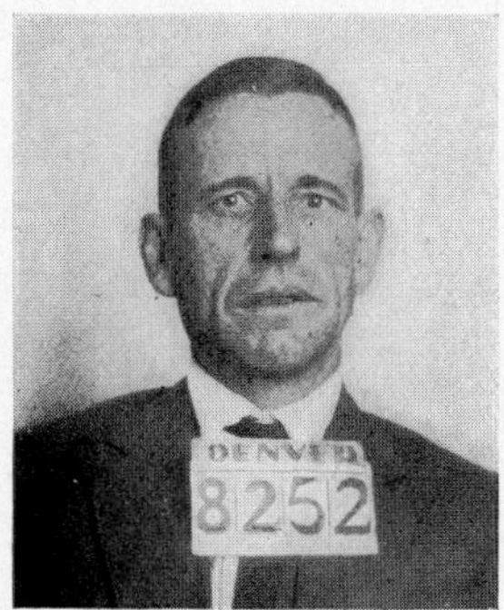


Walter Byland

Leon Felix

Arthur B. Cooper, Spieler

FOUR STEERERS AND A SPIELER

plan called for him to work the underworld, get acquainted with the gang, and if possible to join it, so as to get the inside facts on the conspiracy.

His reports give an excellent picture of the underworld of bootleggers, prostitutes, pimps, police court, and of the petty graft as it exists in most large cities. He was on the job until the end of August, 1922.

To prevent discovery, should any of the detectives' reports become lost, it was decided that numbers, rather than names, should be used to identify the men under suspicion. Accordingly, Duff and Blonger, many of the con-men, and certain police officers were assigned specific numerals. The prosecutor took the alias of 'M. Reeves,' and all reports were addressed in that name. This was because his mother-in-law's name was Maria Reeves, and she lived at his home, and no suspicion would attach to letters so received.

However, instead of the numbers, the real names themselves, except where aliases are used, have been substituted in the extracts from the reports used in this book.

Arch Cooper's early statements gave the following:

> I met a fellow from St. Joe who is a whisky hauler, his name is Fitzgerald and he was in one of Petie Beers' cars. I rode around with him and we went to Beers' place, the A & B taxi stand, Champa 2, where I met P. Beers and Dago Mike and Abe Silver and a gang of pimps.

> Gene Rossi asked if I was any relation to the Cooper that worked out of the Big Store, and said Cooper was in Houston, Texas, and will be back here in the spring and Gene will introduce me to him. I am told to join this mob it is necessary to see Red Hogan.

> I have been around with this bunch every day since I met them and I believe we can get Crane and Silver this way, and am sure this Silver is a tough bird, as he calls one of the judges 'his judge.' Am spending some time around Dawes' Smoke House getting acquainted as this is supposed to be the hang out of the big ones. Have seen Crane but have not met him yet, also saw Land.

On January 6 there was to be a raid on several different places led by Jim Goodhart, City Chaplain, and Ed Young, the copper, but Abe got the news at City Hall and called Champa 2, the taxis got busy and hauled all the women out of the district. I believe there were two arrests made. On Sunday the 8th, the same thing happened.

On January 7 a councilman named Bert Grub was in the A & B taxi stand gambling in the little balcony that is fitted up for this purpose and is also equipped with five high powered rifles and shot guns. Sergeant Hand comes in and if there is any money on the table he grabs it and keeps it and walks out. He is not very well liked, but the bunch is afraid of him. Len Cravens, a policeman, also hangs around here and watches the game, but doesn't bother them, the police are all afraid of Silver as he talks of sending them out to shoot jack rabbits, meaning by that a beat at the edge of the city. I am told Silver can see the chief of police and have any man transferred and I believe this to be true. I was properly introduced to a man that runs a bootlegging joint and a gambling house at 1119 17th Street. His name is Olson, I have not got his first name, his woman also has a few rooms for rent. I am welcome to take a woman up there he says, he spoke of Mark Tillery [a con-man]. They are good friends and says he is now in San Antonio, Texas. He pointed towards Blonger's office and said the Big Racket Store was right down there, says there will be over a hundred of the big fellows here this summer, but most all of them are in Florida or California now. He says he will get me 33 per cent to steer some big oil man to him, he says they are all brother Elks and that they hang around the Club House. He has been in the pen, I think it was in California. He also told me that his wife is a shop-lifter and one of the best in the country. I have been over and registered at the Elks Club and met several. I am told that Dean works with Land and Bacon on the big stuff and that they have a room about a block from this hotel, the Sears.

Today I was in the A & B office and Sergeant Hand and Dago Mike had a conversation. Was down to Olson's place and he spoke of a Jew named Greenburg of Tulsa, Oklahoma. Greenburg was one of the fellows that beat Nick the Greek out of $14,000, last summer here in Denver. Saw Blonger in Dawes' cigar store. I met all the gang at A & B. Dago Mike said he would like to grease the

D. A.'s hand up with about $40,000 but he is afraid to offer it to him. I suggested that he get some one of the deputies and he said that there were only one or two that had any sense and that they were afraid of the D. A.

On January 11 came Andrew Koehn, one of the ablest detectives whom any of the District Attorney's staff ever encountered. Quiet, unassuming, thorough, intensely interested in his work, and accurate to a degree, Koehn was a real find. More than any other man, he was responsible for the final results, and many of the most important decisions were based upon his suggestions. In addition to all-around dependability, Andy had a photographic mind. He seemed to register in an uncanny fashion the physical characteristics of those he was watching, and once he really saw a man that person was a marked individual from then on. Koehn's attention was always riveted to the main task — the con-men — and he refused to be diverted on side issues.

Andy had been in the navy, and exhibited the beneficial results of discipline. Later he served in the St. Louis Police Department where his record was excellent. He was about five feet eight inches in height, well built, dark complexioned, neatly dressed, and was never conspicuous. Whereas everyone knew Cooper, Koehn failed even to register with most people.

Andy's cog in the machine was to watch the big fellows, and get the facts from the top down. Excerpts from his reports show the development of the evidence.

Located Blonger's office today. From upstairs across the street I could see two men by the window in 309 but neither could have been him. Car drove up about 4.40, large, dark-haired woman got out and went into the building. She came back in about 10 minutes, and drove away. License 8079. Wish you would look this up and inform me if this is the party who calls for Blonger.

[Her name is Berna Rames.]

Had several very good looks at Blonger today. He stood by his window a long time waiting for his car which arrived at 5.10 —

I then saw him come down and get in. I have seen enough to know him forever. His woman also. I am striking up an acquaintance at the Marine office upstairs across the street. As I was in the navy 11 years, this is easy and without the least suspicion.

Also visited around Blonger's home to get the lay of the land.

I went into the building to see the doctor who has the office next door. The doctor was out. From the hall I got a very good view of the office. Not much there, telephone, typewriter, check protector, adding machine, long desk, and a few easy chairs. The man in charge was the same one who was there the day before. Can you identify him from this description? About 60 years old, 6 feet, 155, looks very slim and tall. Plenty of hair, dark, but pretty near all turned gray. Short stubby moustache, dark and gray. Wears nose glasses.

[The District Attorney telephoned, 'Party unknown.']

At 9.20 P.M. I saw Blonger. He was dressed up like he just came from a big dinner or board of directors' meeting. White stiff bosom shirt, and evening dress, white bow tie. I tailed him as he took a slow walk down 17th Street. He went in at 1119 17th Street. This is on the corner of the alley and only half a block from his office. It's a soft-drink parlor. The back part is partitioned off. Must of had a very interesting game in progress, as I could see numerous men looking on very eagerly. I watched from the alley from across the street until 10.30. A farmer is on the outside for a lookout, he smokes a corn-cob pipe. No one would ever suspect him. From all appearances the boss hasn't much confidence in him, as he came out about every ten minutes to look at the temperature, and then he would look up and down the street.

As per our conversation I am endeavoring to establish myself here as a stock-salesman, which becomes the occupation of reformed con-men. As I bummed with a stock-salesman for years I know the game from A to Z. I believe it advisable to try to sell our list. They will then recognize me as a stock-salesman. I can later on ask them who is this man, and who is that man, and they can't help but think the reason I am inquiring it, that I want to sell them stock. Sooner or later the dicks are going to get to know me by sight around the Brown Hotel and instead of wondering who I am, they will learn I am a stock-salesman. Should any ever question me I would tell them that anyway.

I got a job yesterday to sell oil stock on a commission basis.

All police regard stock-salesmen as good fellows, sports, and harmless. If I get the friendship of these birds, they will take me to places that I would never find otherwise, and I can call on anyone that you may want me to, and there never will be one thought of suspicion. If this does not interfere with any of your plans, I wish you would give it careful consideration.

As per your suggestion I called at the West Side Court today, and made myself acquainted with Hal Crane. As soon as I laid eyes on him I recognized him from the description you gave me. To simplify matters a man called him by name, so I am positive.

Visited around the leading hotels, and pool halls. I learned one is not welcome in the rear of cigar stores unless brought in by someone known there, so will stay out.

Mr. Martin the oil man, met the Chief of Police for a few minutes yesterday, and made an appointment for this afternoon. He took me over and introduced me. We were treated very cordial, and he listened very attentively, and assured us he would recommend our oil proposition to anyone that inquired about it. Martin told him that he was going back to Dallas, and that I would act as his agent here. I inquired if the Chief had any objections if I called on the men there and tried to interest them. He assured me that would be perfectly all right, and he asked me to come and see him again.

# XIII

## *Spies*

UNDER the Denver charter the police and sheriff's office are under one head known as the Manager of Safety. The sheriff's office has two branches, the civil office in the main courthouse, and the criminal department in the West Side Court where the criminal cases are tried. The latter was in charge of Hal Crane, as chief deputy. His two assistants were A. F. ('Doc') Dawson and Jim Marshall.

Crane pretended friendship, but secretly was bitterly hostile to the entire District Attorney's office, and was one of Blonger's spies. He attempted to watch the prosecutor and made reports to his underworld leader of what he thought might interest the chieftain. Unfortunately for that dual alliance, Crane was none too bright, and heard and saw nothing but what was actually intended for him, so that the information which he gave Blonger was carefully prepared for that purpose. On the other hand, Crane's assistants disliked both him and Blonger.

'Doc' Dawson was as square a man as ever held public office in this country. He had been city marshal at Cripple Creek in its palmy days, and was afraid of no one. Powerful, squat, and bull-necked, he was prepared to tackle any bad individual on a moment's notice. He believed in the enforcement of the law, hated Crane, and became the mainstay of the

District Attorney in the sheriff's office. Dawson backed the prosecutor to the limit throughout the latter's four years in office.

Marshall was an interesting character. Tall, distinguished-looking, with white hair, mustache and a goatee, he looked like a gentleman of the old school. In his early days he had been convicted of train robbery, but the case was reversed by the Supreme Court. He then became a gambler, and, deserting his early training, acquired a reputation as a square 'Knight of the Cloth.' He was a dangerous man to deal with, was said to have several notches in his gun, and had lost the index finger of one hand in a shooting scrape. Marshall also took a dislike to Crane, and supported Dawson and the District Attorney.

Along in January Crane went to the office of the District Attorney and said: 'Colonel, I wish you would do me a favor. I would like to be sent out to the Coast to get a couple of men whom you are extraditing, and I want to take Pete Land with me. If you approve I know we will get to go.'

Crane, the chief deputy sheriff, Pete Land, the crack detective, both Blonger's men. What was up?

The District Attorney did some quick thinking, and decided it might give him a good lead on the activities of the pair. He could have them shadowed on their trip and see who their associates might be. So he said: 'Sure, I will be glad to accommodate you,' and telephoned the Manager of Safety and Chief of Police, and asked that they be delegated to go, which they were.

Arrangements were then made for a California detective to cover their movements. So for the two weeks which they spent in that state, most of the time loafing on the taxpayers' money, their activities were carefully noted.

The detective's reports about Crane and Land were interesting as showing the character of the men and their associates. Shortly after arriving in Los Angeles they went to a soft-drink parlor which was operated by a well-known crook and confidence-game artist, who was at that time awaiting trial under a Federal indictment.

The rear portion of this den was partitioned off, and a lookout was on duty to shut out those not wanted. Crane and Land walked through without any difficulty, but the operative was stopped and told to get out and stay out!

But he reported that this joint was the Los Angeles meeting-place for bunco men. Here it was that this type of grafters could get facts about the activities of their criminal associates in Los Angeles, as well as the address of any con-men in any part of the United States. It was the information bureau for the underworld itself. And the Denver men spent most of their first evening there.

The next morning Crane went to Long Beach to an hotel, which was likewise a headquarters and rendezvous for crooks and buncos. Later, at the cigar stand in another hostelry, he visited with the girl attendant, who was known as the confidential agent of gamblers and crooks.

From then on Crane and Land spent the bulk of their time with questionable characters, with con-men or their associates. Land did most of the talking and wrote down a number of notations in his memorandum book. After their pleasant sojourn in the underworld, they finally returned to Denver with their prisoners.

The cover on their movements had yielded nothing of value. They were friends of the con-men in Denver, and they associated with them in California!

The investigation was now getting so large that it required the time of another deputy, so early in the winter Fred Sanborn was told to put in all his spare moments with the bunco situation. While he had talked to Nitsche a year before, just before Ballard jumped, and had brought Kanavuts back for the Colonel, Sanborn knew nothing of the other activities of the office on the con-men. So he was now given all facts to date, and was set to work checking up the stories of the victims, and trying to locate former stock exchanges, hotel registers, and witnesses. Fred was an excellent assistant because when he was given a job he could handle it well without annoying the prosecutor with questions. He became number four in the office to be in on the secret.

A short time before this the District Attorney had soliloquized: 'I am checking into the underworld, but isn't it possible that they have someone in my own office watching me? And if they have, who is their man and how does he work?'

The office staff was considered, and eliminated as above suspicion. The Colonel then decided that, as so far his prosecutions had only been routine, there had been no necessity for the law-breakers to pay any attention to him, but that, as soon as they found him actively stirring up trouble, his every movement would be reported. All crook hunters of any ability whatsoever know that professional criminals seek either to fix the chief or some of his subordinates, or plant men close at hand to act as tip-offs. The District Attorney had himself already been offered twenty-five thousand dollars, so ample funds would be available to corrupt his men.

'If there is going to be a spy, why not let the underworld plant him now? Then we will be safe if we know who he is and can feed him little scraps of harmless information such as we are giving Crane, so that his bosses will think he is on the job,' again said the Colonel to himself.

Thoughts were transmitted into action, and he reached for the telephone.

'Hello, Chief, I need a detective up here to act as an investigator for me.... Who do I want? Oh, you pick him.'

So the head of the police department sent up Oliver Smith. He was a tall, raw-boned fellow, one of the bravest men on the force, and could be depended upon when politics and gang activities did not interfere. Would he prove faithful to his new superior, or would he be the spy for the underworld? The

District Attorney devoutly hoped he was their man instead of his, otherwise some of his deputies might be corrupted and he would not know whom to trust.

So Sanborn was given particular charge of Smith. He was told to arrange petty raids and inspections with him, to drop certain information so that Smith could use it if he wanted to, and to do all in his power to make the underworld believe that the detective had access to the office secrets. But nothing was to be given to Smith which had any bearing whatever on the con-men. Then Koehn and Cooper were told to comb the town for information about Smith.

Meanwhile a special safe was installed in a fireproof vault, a large safety box rented at a bank, and all secret documents locked up where only the District Attorney and Robinson had access to them. The new man was covered! Was he the real spy, or were there others?

The first of February brought the initial report on Oliver Smith's contacts with the underworld. Cooper wrote:

> I took Vandine, who is an ex-policeman, but at present a pimp, to lunch, and he said his woman runs a house and that it costs him $200 a month to run it. It had been costing only $175, but now that Oliver Smith has gone to work in the D. A.'s office, he has to pay him $25.

But Koehn came back with this:

> Personally I would not put much faith in Cooper's report in reference to Oliver Smith. That may only be the collector's excuse for the $25 raise.

Then, however, Cooper sent in another bit of evidence:

> I met Smith, your city hall dick, with Abe Silver in Champa 2. Smith was going out of town to get a prisoner and Silver was giving him lessons on how to make up his expense account. My informant told me that Smith was working in the District Attorney's office and that Abe was going to manage Smith, then everything would be perfect.

Now came something even more sinister. Smith was known to belong to the gang. But here came some information from Cooper about one of the deputies!

> Have you a man working for you by the name of Brown? This man Brown, who Beers claims is one of the deputies out of the District Attorney's office, came into the A & B, and asked for Mat Blasky. Beers said that Brown wanted some whisky, he thought, as Blasky has sold him some before.

At once Cooper and Koehn were called into conference, and strict directions given them that Brown, as well as Smith, was to be carefully watched, and that any underworld information about any other member of the office force was to be reported at once. 'The District Attorney's office must be above suspicion, and obey the law itself, or it cannot properly function,' said the Colonel. He then told his investigators that he would put a test on the two suspects by telling Brown, and no one else, the date on which he would pull a raid on the row.

Meanwhile the reports tied both Brown and Smith closer to the underworld. Gene Rossi, a gambler, was raided by the District Attorney. His men had to go through a hidden trap-door in the floor of a soft-drink parlor in order to find the place. And the underworld swung into action to save the gambler from conviction. Cooper wrote:

> Smith was in Champa 2 today; he seemed to be trying to help Gene Rossi out with his case.

> Bill Brown was calling Harrie Coffin over the phone asking for whisky. He claimed he was sick. The gang agreed that there would be no whisky taken to him, as he worked out of the District Attorney's office. A couple of them said he owed them for taxi-cab hire, and that he owed everybody else in town, and that he would not pay them. The remark was made that he was the best one in the office, but he could not do anyone any good; that he was lucky to be working.
>
> Roy Gardner said 'when in the Hell is the raid on the row.' Abe said it was coming off soon, that Smith was in yesterday and

called him out of the card game and told him that there sure was going to be one in a few days. Smith is going to find out and let us know for sure. While he is getting the dope the most of the line is closed, except for Harrie Coffin and a few other places.

It might be a good idea to slip Brown the dope that we talked about at your home the other evening, and I will see if Smith brings it down to the office.

Coffin made the remark before me today that he was damn tired of giving up $300 a month and getting nothing for it. I think if this closed up business lasts much longer, you may have some of them down talking to you about who they are giving the money to.

Then the suspected deputy was called in. 'Bill,' said the District Attorney, 'I am going to raid the row February 28. Keep that date open, because you boys will be busy. And tell it to no one.'

Cooper's next three reports stated:

Well, Smith says your raid is to come off on the 28th of February. He got this information from Brown and gave it to Abe.

Your Mr. Brown is a very close friend of Harrie Coffin's. Coffin has had a tip-off to close up tonight and is going to take his cross-eyed woman and leave town, and be gone a couple of weeks.

Was out to Abe's tonight, and while there the telephone rang. Abe said, 'For Christ's sake, that's Oliver Smith!' He says for Abe not to connect with him, as they are watching every move he makes. Of course this cannot be mentioned, as there was only three of us there.

With definite data on Brown peddling information to Smith, and with a verbal report from Cooper that Brown was taking a girl places where even Abe Silver wouldn't take his own wife, Brown's time had come. Besides, he was drinking heavily, staying away from work on account of hang-overs, and had no place in a law enforcement office.

As a cover to the discharge, the District Attorney called in Smith, shut the door, and sat down for a confidential talk.

'Oliver,' he said, 'Brown's drinking like the devil; we can't prosecute bootleggers and drink their booze. I've got to fire him. What do you think about it? You are an old-timer and know this game.'

'Well, I'd give him another chance,' said Smith.

'Can't do it,' was the answer. 'I feel sorry for him, but he's too open about it; everybody is talking.'

So on Sunday morning Brown was sent for and asked, 'Bill, do you know of any reason why you should be allowed to keep your job in this office?'

Visibly startled, he said, 'Why, what do you mean, Colonel?'

'Does your conduct justify your being a deputy district attorney?' was the answer.

Brown thought a long time, then said, 'No, I guess it doesn't.'

'Then sign this resignation, and you can leave without any publicity,' was the order. Bill signed and left.

The next day came the prompt statement from Cooper:

> Gardner was telling me today that the District Attorney kicked Brown out of his office; he thinks things will be tougher now for Harrie Coffin.

Two years later Brown died in an Eastern hospital, friendless and alone, a fugitive from justice, leaving a string of bad checks behind him. A boy with a brilliant mind, but who couldn't withstand the temptations of public office, booze, and bad company!

Smith, however, stayed on. A known spy must remain, or another takes his place in the eternal warfare between law and crime. Crane was watching from the sheriff's office, Smith in the District Attorney's office. The possibility of others unknown was a sinister and constant menace.

# XIV

## *Fixing*

About the middle of February the Associated Press began carrying a series of articles about the arrest of a gang of organized con-men in Florida. They had become so bold that the Governor of the State, Cary A. Hardee, had been compelled to ignore the local officials, and had himself supervised raids in which twenty men were arrested in Fort Lauderdale.

Florida has always been, and still is, a mecca for con-men. Prosecutions in its State courts are almost unknown. Sheriffs, police, prosecutors, and reporters have been on their pay-roll, and even the Federal courts have seldom done more than to assess small fines.

But with the Governor personally on the job, the gang was temporarily unsettled. Several of the Denver bunch, including Tom Jackson, a particular friend of Lou Blonger's, were in the toils. So two days later Koehn reported that Lou himself had departed for the scene of action and was on his way to Miami.

Tate was ordered to follow Blonger, and located him at the Strand Hotel, where he seemed far more interested in two ladies than he did in his men. But Blonger knew his ropes, and in a few days all were released on small bonds. The only effect of the arrest was that the con-men moved over to an adjoining town and took their victims there, protected as before. Seven more gangsters were picked up about a week later at Mobile, Alabama, on the old pocketbook trick, for trying to 're-tie' (that is, catch again) Barney Knapke, of Ohio, who had shortly before lost $12,000 to an Orlando, Florida, mob led by John B. Rumer, of Indiana. However, all from both raids were released save two, who happened to be wanted by the Federal authorities in Florida for bunco swindles in which the United States mails were used.

Tate secured pictures and identifications of the twenty-seven without disclosing any of the Denver connections. All he could report, however, was that Blonger was in active contact with many con-men, but he did not get close enough to hear any of their conversations.

The Denver fixer then played around for about a month, and left for Hot Springs, Arkansas, accompanied by Mr. and Mrs. Adolph W. Duff, and went at once to the old Arlington Hotel (since burned down). This was an annual visit, made every spring by Blonger, for the main purpose of visiting with the head of a national detective agency.

That company had long earned and enjoyed an enviable reputation as first-class detectives; but their business was not that of law-enforcing officers, but of private agents protecting the interests of their own clients. Consequently, they had to deal constantly with underworld characters and get information from them.

Blonger and the president of the agency had been friends for years. They corresponded regularly, and met annually in Hot Springs, Arkansas, to talk over the criminal situation, the president to find out from Blonger and his friends the names of those who had attacked his clients, such as wholesale houses, hotels, or contractors; and Blonger in turn to get from the detective whatever information the latter had gleaned about the activity of police departments or victims against Blonger and his gang in Denver and elsewhere. It was a *quid pro quo* of mutual profit to the great detective and the great crook.

Tate reported long and earnest, but very private, conversations between the detective and Blonger, in some of which Duff participated. He also noticed a short man with small mustache and receding chin, and a heavy-set, stocky fellow with red face, who seemed to be much in their company, but he couldn't identify either. He was sure, however, that they were con-men.

Then Hugh J. Alexander, of the First National Bank of Denver, came back into the picture again.

'Phil,' he telephoned, 'I've got some more information for you. I overlooked it entirely when talking to you before, and the more I think about it the more puzzled I am.'

Another visit to the bank and Alexander called in R. H. McDonald, the bank policeman. He knew about Blonger and the Seventeenth Street gang, and was trying to keep them out of the First National.

McDonald had a tale about Victor E. Larson, of Ontario, California. In September, 1921, Larson deposited with them a check of $15,000, for collection.

A few days later, and before the check was paid, Larson's son came to the bank. He said he had not seen his father, but wanted to find out why he needed so much money. The California bank had heard of con-men and had advised young Larson to go to Denver and scout the facts before they paid the cash. McDonald was therefore assigned the job.

The officer immediately advised Larson, junior, to keep away from the police department. The two of them talked to some of the bank tellers about the father, but the only records concerning his transaction were the opening of the account and the depositing of the check.

McDonald and the son then went to the father's hotel, but found the latter was in the mountains with some friends.

That night Larson, senior, returned, a very mystified man. He stated that he was in a business deal, the nature of which he then refused to reveal to either his son or McDonald, and that, while waiting for his check to clear, his two associates had taken him for a drive in the hills. They had stopped at Idaho Springs for lunch.

'Then,' McDonald said, 'that's when the funny business began. Larson said they hadn't any more than started to eat before one of the men was called to the 'phone. He was gone about ten minutes, when happening to look up Larson saw him beckoning to the other fellow. The latter excused himself, said he had to make some telephone calls and would return shortly.

'But that's the last Larson ever saw of them. He had to pay for all three lunches, and as they had ridden up in those fellows' car, he had no transportation and had to come back on the train.

'They had previously agreed that all should get their money on Monday, so he came over to the bank on the chance that they might show up, but they never did. Larson then got burned up at the whole affair, and told us about the "business deal," which, of course, was the old stock-market con-men's transaction. He then returned to California, fifteen thousand dollars to the good, and mighty glad his son came to Denver.'

'Now, what I want to know,' said Alexander, 'is who tipped those crooks off that McDonald and young Larson were after them.'

'I'll try and find out,' said the District Attorney. 'We can at least trace the telephone call.'

The telephone company records showed a call from Blonger's office to the con-man in Idaho Springs. But the tip to Blonger was never found. Was there some leak in the bank?

About a month later a telegram was received from the District Attorney at Houston, Texas, asking when the statute of limitations ran out on confidence-games. And a few days later he sent a long letter about the manner in which his friend, Doctor W. H. Scherrer, had lost twenty-five thousand dollars to the Denver gang in September, 1920, in a fake horse-race.

Scherrer, however, had not been content to take it on the chin. He had obtained a picture of Goodrich, one of the gang which swindled him. Goodrich was the man who went to the Cañon

City penitentiary in 1912 — the only one of Blonger's men who had ever served a term in Colorado. Scherrer then learned of a con-man named Joe Furey, who was serving a twenty-year sentence in the Texas penitentiary for trimming Frank Norfleet, about whom Woolwine had talked to Kenneth Robinson. Norfleet, after Furey escaped from him in California by bribing the deputy sheriffs, had relentlessly tracked his man across the country, caught him in Florida, and taken him back to the Lone Star State, where he was quickly convicted. So Scherrer had called on Furey at the penitentiary and told him his story and asked for help.

Furey, after talking with Scherrer a few minutes, said: 'Well, Doc, you are a pretty good sport. I would like myself to have taken you on for about ten thousand, but they shouldn't have trimmed you for twenty-five thousand. That's too much.

'I used to work in Denver,' continued Furey. 'You go there and see the "Boss." He gets fifty-five per cent of the swag, and if you put the pressure on right, I think you'll get your money.'

'But who is the "Boss"?' asked Scherrer.

'I won't tell you that, but if you scout around Denver a little while you will learn his name. Ask anybody in Denver that knows anything at all. Why, just step up to the clerk at the Albany and ask him who the "Boss" is and he'll tell you. I know your man Goodrich, also, but you get him through the "Boss."'

So Doctor Scherrer went to Denver and employed Charley Fox, the then District Attorney, as his lawyer.

Scherrer started in by handing Fox Goodrich's picture. 'Do you know that man?' he said.

Fox studied it carefully. 'Why, yes, I do,' he answered. 'He's a golfer. I've often seen him playing on the City Park golf links.'

'Well, I've played golf with him myself,' said Scherrer, 'but that's not all I played with him. He also played me for twenty-five thousand dollars, and I played the sucker for that amount.'

Scherrer then told him all about the swindle, and ended by asking, 'Who's the "Boss" that Furey told me to see?'

'The Boss,' said Fox, 'is Lou Blonger, and I'll call him now.' So Fox picked up the telephone and talked to Blonger in Scherrer's presence.

'Lou,' he said, 'this is Charley Fox talking. A Doctor Scherrer of Houston is in my office, and he says some of your boys trimmed him in Denver last summer for twenty-five thousand dollars.... You say you'll look into it? What's that you say? ... Mmm... That's interesting.... All right, let me hear from you shortly.'

Charley turned to Scherrer. 'The grapevine is sure good. Blonger tells me he heard about your talk with Furey and that he's been expecting to hear from you. Now you go on home and I will see what I can do about it.'

Later he reported that Blonger said he was working on it, but claimed that he was having trouble with Goodrich over the matter of restitution; that once before Goodrich had been stubborn about a settlement and had served a prison term in consequence. Fox also stated that Blonger predicted the others of the gang would not be caught, as they had successfully evaded being picked up in the past and their identity would be hard to establish.

After getting no results from Fox, Doctor Scherrer called on G. A. Fuller, the superintendent of the Pinkerton Agency. Fuller was an able detective, and square, and at once advised Scherrer against using Fox. He also told him that Blonger was the head of the gang, and that, if the proper pressure was brought to bear, Blonger would settle.

Blonger later offered Fuller two thousand dollars if he would drop the case and tell Scherrer that nothing could be done about it. But when Fuller refused to accept the two thousand, Blonger said that if Scherrer would take ten thousand dollars, they would clean it up. This was on condition, however, that Goodrich would pay his share. Though Blonger apparently tried to make Goodrich contribute, the latter told the fixer to go to hell, and Goodrich never returned to Denver. And as Scherrer did not actively push his case, no settlement was ever made.

In talking to Fuller, Blonger told him that there were thirty good con-men ready for the winter resorts, and that there ought to be good picking; that Duff was plying his business between Omaha and Hot Springs, Arkansas, and doing pretty well at the game.

The old rascal was actively working behind the scenes, but nowhere was he under the spot-light.

# XV

## *Uncle Sam's Expert*

THE national operations of con-men and their misuse of the mails are so extensive that the United States Postal Department is compelled to devote the exclusive services of several specialists to this task alone. The Department's main expert, Herbert N. Graham, of New York, went to Denver in March, 1922, on his never-ending trail of the con-men.

Shortly after his arrival, Roy O. Nelson, of the local inspector's office, telephoned the District Attorney.

'Colonel,' he said, 'Graham, one of our men from New York, is here on the same kind of business you have been talking about to me, and if you're not busy he wants to see you.'

'Send him over at once, Roy,' was the answer. 'I'll be tickled to death to see him.'

And then in a few minutes Inspector Graham himself entered the prosecutor's office. 'I'm H. N. Graham, of New York,' he stated. 'Here are my credentials.' And like the careful man he was, Graham handed over his identification folder, showing his commission as Inspector in the Postal Department.

Kenneth Robinson was summoned, and the three of them went into conference behind locked doors.

Graham was a lean and wiry fellow, careful in speech and sure in his movements. Except on very rare occasions he shunned publicity, and then only in order to help victims get the gangsters. Unlike most city detectives and many Federal men, he never allowed his picture to be published, because he did not want the underworld to become familiar with his features. His job, not glory, was all that counted with him. And so this book does not describe him further.

Graham knew con-men. He asked a few questions about the District Attorney's plans, how far he had progressed and how much (in reality how little) he knew. The prosecutor told him very frankly that con-men and their operations were almost a new thing to him when he took the job, and that he wanted all the help that he could get. So he asked Graham to start at the beginning and give him as much information as he could in the time at his disposal, and that he or Robinson would interrupt whenever Graham struck a subject with which they were familiar. In consequence, for almost two hours Graham regaled them with the details of the con-men and their operations, and the nomenclature of the underworld.

'Tom Woolwine, District Attorney at Los Angeles, whom you have already seen, and Solicitor-General John A. Boykin, of Atlanta, are two of the all too few State prosecutors who have really gone after con-men in their towns,' Graham said, 'and both have cleaned them out in good shape. They have made splendid records and you can trust them in every particular. The con-men's gangs are now particularly strong in Denver, Toledo, New York City, and Florida.

'I don't know how far you have gone into this racket,' continued Graham, 'but the further you go the more you will see that it is a mine for the police. Every place where they operate extensively they have ironclad protection from the powers that be. Denver is the worst place in the country in the summer, but Florida is a paradise for them in the winter; there the racket is State-wide, and they have protection in almost every tourist town. Florida's governors have tried to break it up, but have been practically powerless.

'I work all over the United States, with headquarters in

New York City. The real reason I am here is that all the activities of these gentry seem to center in Denver. Nearly all the printed paraphernalia which they use is made in this town. Did you ever see this kind of bond used by them?'

And with that statement he took from his brief-case a document worded somewhat as Dixon's $100,000 bond, purporting to be by the 'Metropolitan Bonding and Security Company.' However, his instrument was a fine, engraved fiber weave, similar to that used for municipal securities.

'This bond,' he said, 'is being used pretty generally by these grafters, and it is made of a peculiar high-grade paper which comes only from Denver, and I want to find out where they get it and who prints it.'

'I've never seen that kind,' said the District Attorney, 'but here is Dixon's bond.' And the Colonel handed Graham the sheet which Williamson had given him about eight months earlier.

'Yes, I've seen that one also,' said Graham. 'It's a type which has been used for years, but they still continue to show it. But it's a crude piece of workmanship which appears to require no improvements for the con-men's purposes, because the victim is never allowed any more than a glimpse of it, and they get no time for reflection. But the new one is much better.

'You've a hard job ahead of you if you ever expect to get this bunch. They are smart to begin with; all of them. They are the brains of the underworld, and the cream of the criminals graduate from all other crimes into the pay-off game, where the biggest and easiest money lies. And when the "Big Store" is operating, you will have spies all around, ready to report your slightest movement.'

Graham next explained some of the details of the operations. 'The set-up,' he said, 'starts with the town where the confidence-men are operating. If they are protected, the town itself is known as the "Big Store." The man who runs the Big Store has what might be called the franchise, takes care of the police, and arranges for protection, and is called the "fixer." He usually stays in the background while the man who supervises the work and is out in the open is the "manager." He rents the offices used by the gang, hires and fires the con-men, subject, of course, to the superior wishes of the "fixer," and divides the money.

'The big-money play of the con-men now is known as the "pay-off game." It gets this name from the fact that the victim is twice led to believe that his winnings have been paid-off to him, although they actually were held back after he caught a glimpse of them or had them in his hands for a few seconds. The victim is variously known as "sucker," "egg," "boob," or "chump."

'The workers in the crowd are divided into three main groups. First come the "steerers" or "steers." The Big Store [town] may be full of them. They are the men who first contact or get in touch with the victim or sucker. The "spielers," sometimes called "second" or "inside" men, are the next crooks on the scene. The spieler has the inside information and leads the victim to the stock exchange or horse-racing betting-parlor. This is presided over by the "bookmaker" or "clerk." The con-men call themselves "grafters." In addition to the sucker and his usual three con-men, on special occasions other men may come into the exchange. They act as customers and are known as "boosters." The con-men in a town call themselves the "gang" or "mob."

'The pay-off game,' he continued, 'is handled in one of two ways, either through the "store" or the "play-to-the-wall."

'The "store," also known as the "joint," is a completely organized gang, presided over by the fixer. It has a headquarters, or central office, one or more stock exchanges or horse-racing parlors, with as many attached confidence-men, bookmakers, spielers, steerers, and boosters as are necessary to pick up all classes of victims in the town. These men cannot work for the Big Store unless invited to do so. In such a mob there often are men speaking various languages so that they can approach people of different nationalities. Some may be flashily dressed dudes, some may be poorly dressed tramps, and others men of the world who have traveled all over the American tourist lanes and often to Europe. All play their parts like actors on a stage.'

'We know the "play-to-the-wall,"' interrupted the Colonel. 'They cleaned a Pueblo man, Wurzbach, out of $6800 by that means down in Excelsior Springs, Missouri. That showed us that they never touch Colorado people in Denver.'

'No, and they never will,' said Graham. 'Con-men have an invariable rule never to pick up a sucker who lives in the State where they are operating. The reason is that he may have powerful political connections. If so, they face sure trouble, as they may blow the protection sky-high. In that event the mob either would be forced to disgorge, or would be prosecuted, and if they faced trial under those circumstances the police would help send them over in order to save their faces. So they catch the suckers away from home.'

The District Attorney then told Graham about the Duff letters in Kansas City and showed them to the Inspector.

'What do you mean by "nut" and "sale" and "tied"?' the prosecutor queried.

'Remember,' said Graham, 'these fellows operate a store, so they use store language. A sucker is a "customer." The crook who finds him is called a "steerer" or a "salesman." The successful con-man who trims the victim thereby makes a "sale" to him, and is said to "beat" a sucker. If he stings his man for $25,000, he makes a "score" of twenty-five "grand." The victim is like a package, he is "tied-up" when he starts in on the game to lose his money, and is "tied" when he falls for the scheme and sends or goes for his money. If a man has been trimmed once and is again picked up by the same or different mob and falls for it a second time, he is "re-tied." The "nut" is the expense incurred in running the game and includes all overhead costs.'

'While you're at it, Inspector, we wish you would give us as much of the underworld nomenclature as you can think of which is applicable to this case,' said Robinson.

'Well, here goes, then,' said Graham. 'A con-man has an "accident" when he is arrested; consequently when he is in jail he is "in the hospital."

'In handling the sucker the latter is said to be "entertained," while the steerer or spieler is trying to interest him; he is given the "convincer" when he makes his initial winning; the money package which he handles at the exchange is called the "boodle," and the "blow-up" comes when the victim gets wise and wakes up to the fact that he is in the hands of con-men and the play is spoiled.

'In order to find out how much money a victim can raise, he is given the "break-down" by showing him a fake telegram that the spieler's uncle is in Mexico or out of the country. When his money is finally stolen at the exchange it is called the "blow-off"; when the "chump" has been sent out of town, he is given the "blow-off wire," which is the last telegram he receives from the mob, and in it he is told to go home and await further developments.'

'Then that is the name for the second telegram in the Carnes case,' said the prosecutor, as he showed Graham Lowery's wire from Kansas City.

The Inspector read part of it out loud: '"Will wire you where to meet me as soon as I get back to work. Have your business arranged so you can meet me." Yes, that's the "blow-off wire." That's the "come-on" language to keep the sucker still interested or "conned" so that he may either be "re-tied" or that his awakening may be delayed as long as possible.

'The last act is the "kick," which is the complaint to the police department. Only about one in ten makes it, and it doesn't help the sucker any.'

'Who are the "Jack" and "Cooper" mentioned by Duff?' asked the District Attorney.

'Jack is Jackie French, the famous bookmaker,' answered Graham. 'He is the cleverest fake stock exchange clerk in the business and is in Denver every summer. In the winter he can be found in Florida or Cuba or maybe Mexico, where he sometimes acts as fixer, manager, or even steers if he goes after the big fellows.

'French had one famous week in Florida in February of this year [1922]. In just seven days he cleaned up P. R. Nicholson, of Dillonville, Ohio, for $120,000; George Pohling, a Philadelphia brewer, for $200,000; and John G. Scott, an Englishman, for $25,000. He also tied-up Albert Seurin, of Cleveland, Ohio, for $13,000, but later lost him. The mails were used only in the last case, and I want French for it. Nicholson has offered a big reward for French, and Jackie is sure to be in Denver this summer.

'French is also a clever "badger game" artist. He served a term at Atlanta for impersonating a United States Marshal. This was for blackmailing a wealthy business man in a badger game on a Pullman car between New York and Chicago. Buda Godman, his paramour, was his assistant in that scheme. I have his picture with me. He's smart, has a very engaging personality, and an attractive, well-bred appearance. He is a lavish spender when in funds, and the women fall hard for him at such times.

'Cooper is Arthur B. Cooper, alias "Tex," the spieler. He and Mark Tillery are two of the best in their line. Tillery was here all last year, and Cooper has been here for several years. Cooper will be here this summer, but Tillery may not make it, as we have him in jail on a Federal offense in El Paso.'

Robinson then produced the District Attorney's small gallery of confidence-men, at that time only amounting to about four hundred pictures. Graham looked them over quickly, then said, 'Let me get mine; I'll be back in a few minutes,' and went out.

In half an hour he returned with a suitcase loaded with his

private collection, all of which he lent to the prosecutor so that copies could be made. From him were secured enough photographs to make a total of almost a thousand pictures. Graham, as he exhibited his gallery, gave his auditors the criminal history of the leading and outstanding con-men, and their particular specialties and weaknesses. And among his photographs were about twenty of the men who, he stated, were known to be actively operating in the Denver group, including Jack French and Arthur B. Cooper.

Graham then left to hunt for the printer of the engraved bond and to continue his ceaseless follow-up on the illegitimate use of the mails by the sharks of the underworld, but he kept in touch by letter with the District Attorney, ready to help in any manner at any time.

The postal inspector's story about Denver printing con-men's literature was soon substantiated by a letter from Elmo Barnett, written from Los Angeles to Mark Tillery, whom Graham had just mentioned, and sent in care of Blonger himself, in Denver. Barnett is one of a very noted quartet of con-men who now operate extensively in the larger cities of Texas. He wrote that he had a prospect, but was unable to make a 'sail'; that he supposed there was quite a crowd in Denver, but that Blonger wrote him that there would be nothing there for him. Then Barnett said: 'Send me a few credit orders, some telegraph envelopes and transfer slips. I only want a few of each. I can't take a chance on having any stuff printed here.'

Denver protection was still rated high among the underworld élite!

# XVI

## *Blonger Smells a Rat*

Across Seventeenth Street from the American National Bank Building was a two-story structure, the second floor of which was a cheap rooming-house. Koehn rented a room ostensibly for an office as a hosiery salesman, got a desk, a few chairs, told the landlord that his eyes were weak and that he had to have the shades down, and proceeded to keep track of Blonger's office, which was directly opposite, but slightly higher.

Shortly after Blonger left for Florida, Tate wrote suggesting that a dictaphone be planted in the fixer's office during his absence. Consequently, the District Attorney, Robinson, Koehn, and Cooper met at the former's house to make plans. It turned out that none of them had ever seen or operated a dictaphone. It was decided that the District Attorney would get an electrician and study dictaphone installation, and that the wires should be run to Koehn's observation room across the street. This turned out to be a serious error, because such rooms should never be so close as to be easily detected by the enemy.

During the primary campaign a young electrician named Ben Eager had been very active in the Colonel's behalf. He had later sought the job of special officer, but had been rejected for lack of experience and because it was thought a young attorney would be preferable. But here was Ben's line of work, so he was given a chance.

Eager knew nothing about dictaphones either, but soon found out what they were and how to install them. At that time they were of two types, both used by the deaf, one a small disk similar to the radio earphone, and the other a flat rectangle, three inches wide by six inches long, with a double diaphragm. They required bulky wet batteries to operate them.

The dictaphones (later called 'dicks' or 'bugs' by the force) were ordered, and the detectives told to scout Blonger's office and the vicinity and report. Koehn spent all of one Sunday afternoon in the building and found it deserted. But at night the bank watchman made hourly visits.

Blonger's room was on the third floor, with a high attic over it. The passkey of Philip A. Zang, the former manager of the building, was borrowed, and he was asked to stay in his office during the time that the detectives were working in Blonger's quarters. Zang readily agreed to help in any respect.

Cooper and Koehn went in one night and made a map to scale of the entire office and its contents. The room, furniture, rugs, pictures, washstand, and electric light fixtures were all measured, and a complete picture obtained. Then another conference was held to determine where to locate the 'bugs.'

Cooper said, 'Put one behind a picture, that's the regular place.'

'No,' replied the District Attorney, 'that's no good; it can be found too easily. Let's get a burglar-proof location.'

And after careful scrutiny of the plans, it was decided that the smaller instrument should be located in the cup of the chandelier against the ceiling, and the other should be placed in the attic, adjacent to a riser on the steam-pipe where a small opening remained. A similar chandelier was taken to the prosecutor's house, the dictaphone was found to fit, and a test run was satisfactory.

The night set for the job, the janitor worked until nine o'clock, so Koehn and Eager had to kill time with Zang until he left. But in the meantime they had carried in a hundred pounds of batteries, a large suitcase full of tools, and a step-ladder.

As soon as they entered the room, they put an old bedspread on the carpet to catch all waste and plaster. Then they tackled the chandelier, and found that it was plastered flush into the ceiling. When they got it down, they also discovered that its base was solid, so they took it into Zang's office, where Eager cut a hole for the 'bug' and fastened a shaft, so he could swing it from the rafters.

As a mechanic and electrician he certainly knew his business. But as he had to make about five trips to the attic, crawl forty feet each time to reach the chandelier, and work under a constant nervous strain of possible apprehension, he was completely exhausted. So at 2 A.M. he had to quit before the line was hooked up. But the work in Blonger's office was finished, and it was never re-entered by Ben Eager or Andy Koehn.

The next day was Sunday, and Andy's reports for the next few days follow:

> We were lucky in getting out last night, the noise the hammering and sawing made in that building on a still night is awful. The watchman made one round on the second floor and turned on all the hall lights, and I am positive he investigated. If any noise is repeated tonight, I am sure he will call the police and if I am caught in the building on a Sunday night I will have to leave town. We had a good alibi this time. But there is no alibi for working in the attic of a bank building on a Sunday night.
>
> B. E. said he could make those connections in a few hours, and will tackle it in the morning. He could work up there all day long in the attic in the day time and not attract any attention. As soon as we get a test I will send you a special delivery and advise you of results.

From the attic over Blonger's room the wires were taken straight back to the alley in the rear of the bank building. But then the problem was how to get them across Seventeenth Street to Koehn's office.

Ben S. Read, president of the Mountain States Telephone

Company, when visited the previous fall, had told the District Attorney that when the latter wanted anything from his company to see Cheney Bagby, one of their engineers. 'Bagby will be instructed by me,' he said, 'to do anything you ask.'

So Bagby was called upon and he gave orders to the line foreman to string the wires across the street on the Bell system telephone poles and to connect them with the two buildings. The telephone crew did its job without asking any questions. Then Koehn and Eager concealed their wires behind the false front of the building, and dropped them down a partition wall to Andy's room. It had wainscoting around the sides, and the wires were connected to a plug flush with the top of that woodwork. This was camouflaged by a Western Union call box, which was also hooked up to loose wires which were already hanging in the room. Then to listen in all Koehn had to do was to unscrew the call box and plug in his earphones, and he had Blonger's room.

The connections were finished early in the day, and Koehn was ready for the first man to appear in the fixer's window. His new reports started that night:

> When the little old man arrived in Blonger's office this morning I put on my headgear and waited patiently for something to happen. I had my window shade down, and I heard someone blow their nose. I quickly looked over, and there was my friend wiping his nose with his handkerchief.
>
> Spent most of the day in my office, testing out the connections. These were completed at ten o'clock tonight, and then we had the conversation.
>
> B. E. made this from the attic while I listened in from my office. The tests from the attic were perfect. I did not miss a word and he spoke in a low tone near the bug, and in a whisper ten feet away. I could very easily distinguish the low tone from a whisper just the same as if he spoke in my presence, and could plainly hear him moving about in the attic. We tried out both bugs and in the attic they work perfect. He then called up Blonger's office and I could hear the 'phone ring very plainly. Then I called up Blonger's office and he listened in, and he could hear the ringing

very plainly. There is a buzzing sound in the receivers, and the street cars are heard very distinct. Ben hopes to overcome this by connecting something into the line and by building up the batteries. The terrible noises the cars made crossing other tracks did not however drown out the talk coming over the line.

The adjoining door leading into my neighbor's office, which had such large eye-holes, I covered with a heavy dark green paper, placed a curtain rod and curtains in front of it, a few hooks and hangers, and now it's a suitable clothes closet, and does not appear as if I were trying to hide anything. The glass in the door and the transom which allowed all the light to come in from the hall, I painted the inside with black enamel. I have a heavy green curtain across the lower part of my window, and with the shade up, I can get a splendid view. While the sun was shining bright I got across the street and looked up at the office and all that I could see was the green curtain and shade. I also nailed up all the other doors and transom, made them airtight, also made other minor repairs, and gave my linoleum a coat of valspar.

I called Charlie James, Lou's office man, on the 'phone in Blonger's room and asked for Mr. Blonger and he informed me that he was in Hot Springs, and would not return to the city until about April 15th.

I need a telephone. Can you use your influence with that friend of yours at the telephone office and help him to get me one? As I understand, it takes five or six months to get one.

The telephone was obtained forthwith, though it took a special order from the telephone company's president.

April 14, Koehn, Cooper, and Tate were sitting in Koehn's room when Eager came in to see Andy about some alterations. Tate and Cooper were introduced to Eager, but he became very angry, and a few minutes later rushed out of the place.

The dictaphone was in, the connections were adjusted — all it needed was Blonger and his gang to start talking. And the District Attorney particularly wanted Blonger's story about Florida and Hot Springs and the boys.

But the next day came Andy's cry for help. The dick was

dead, Eager couldn't be located, Blonger, all sunburned, was in an animated conversation with Charlie James, Lou's office man, and not a word could be heard!

Eager was ambitious to be a detective himself, and when he left Koehn's office had gone at once to the District Attorney and demanded a full-time job in place of Tate or Cooper. The prosecutor refused to employ him or to tell him who they were, or the details of the investigation. All he agreed to do was to give him some work when he needed him. So Eager left in a huff.

But now Eager held the upper hand. Either he had to be placated or he might go to Blonger with all the details, and then the investigation would be at an end. When you investigate the underworld, the danger of a tip-off is so great that a prosecutor is not free to say or do what he wants. In any other situation Eager would have been fired; now he was to be given a job to keep his mouth shut. So swallowing his pride, the District Attorney tried to reach Eager. The latter, however, was ugly. First he refused for some time to answer his telephone; then when he did would only sulk and not answer questions. But finally he came to the District Attorney's house early the next morning and they had quite a talk.

The prosecutor flatly accused Eager of pulling out the wires, but Eager neither admitted nor denied it. Finally the District Attorney told him that if he would fix the lines at once, he would give him a detective job in a few days as soon as he could arrange the work.

An hour later the dictaphone was in order, but Blonger did not return for two or three days. Koehn reported that thereafter he would call unidentified visitors as X on the first visit, and thereafter, if from the underworld, as XA, or XB, etc., until their identity was established.

The next day Andy's first XA appeared. He came in at 10 A.M., spoke to Charlie James, looked over the mail, rushed out to a taxi, came back in an hour, and went to work at a desk sorting out letters and papers. Later he came down and waited for a car. Koehn described him as five feet five inches, one hundred and thirty-five pounds, age forty-five to fifty, very active and quick, deep lines over his entire face. A later report from Koehn stated:

> Eager arrived at my office at 9 A.M. with the toner attached to the receivers, it has improved the machine considerable. He told me that you said I should put him to work when I needed him. I stalled him off until the first of the month as you wanted me to, by telling him I couldn't use him until I had an operator, and that I expected to have one by the first.
>
> Couldn't see who was in the office on account of the snow. I could hear him writing on the typewriter, the slow one-finger system. It was so distinct that I could distinguish the difference between the sounds, when he hit a letter, or the spacer. While he was writing, the doctor who has the office next door to Blonger came in and said, 'Oh, good morning, when did you get back?' He said 'Friday night.' Weather and general talk.
>
> I am satisfied that XA is a local man, the Doctor knew him from last season, and he shook hands with an expressman at the office corner. I will probably make him in a few days. Got a better look at him today. He has long black hair, but does not fit the photos you sent me. — K.

The District Attorney telephoned Andy the next night that XA was Duff, and Koehn's report the next day showed:

> I was so thoroughly convinced that XA is our Number One [Duff], that I went up to see Goddard this P.M., showed him the side view of this bird and compared descriptions and he agreed that this was Duff.
>
> Very glad to hear from you tonight. I was going to tell you that XA was Duff as per above, but you beat me to it. Glad to know him. I could find him in the dark with my eyes shut now.

The 'manager' was in Denver. Things were about to happen. Koehn followed Duff to the Shirley-Savoy Hotel, and found him registered there with his wife. Later Duff went to his bank, where the officers all seemed very friendly to him. He had a big bundle of bonds and papers, and discussed them with a teller. To read some of them he put on nose-glasses, which were attached to a wide black ribbon, strung over his ear, giving him quite a dandified effect. But he gave a casual observer the impression of an alert, successful business man.

The dictaphone worked well for about two weeks, but gave little of value because Blonger was away most of that time. But early one morning Koehn was sitting in his observation room with the shades pulled down and the ear-pieces of the dictaphone clamped on his head, listening to what he could get over the 'bug.'

Suddenly he was electrified. Blonger rushed into his office, grabbed Charlie James by the arm, took him to the window, pointed excitedly across the street, and said: 'See that room across the street where the shades are down? The District Attorney has two detectives over there. They have a tap on my telephone and hear every word we say. I just went up to the telephone company and saw my friend Gus Peterson, its attorney, and he agreed to send down some men right away to examine my wires, and, by God, if that fellow has tapped them, I am going to file a criminal case against him and put him where he belongs. The Federal authorities are also going to help me find out what that District Attorney is up to.

'You know, Charlie, some fellow saw me last night, a little fellow with squint eyes, and he told me if I would give him $500 he would give me the information about some wires that were put in my office by the District Attorney. I pumped him. I got that much and then told him he was a cheap grafter and to go to hell, and I am going to get the dope for nothing.'

Koehn grabbed his telephone, called the prosecutor's private number, luckily caught him, and in a voice trembling with agitation said:

'Colonel, Blonger is on to us. I just heard him tell his office man that you have men over here, and also that you have a tap on his telephone wires. He has been to the telephone company, saw their attorney, Gus Peterson, and the lawyer promised to send men down right away to look over the place for him. What do you want me to do?'

'Steady in the boat, Andy,' replied the prosecutor. 'Hide your wires and clear out. Get your stuff out of the Adams Hotel and lay low, but telephone me at the house this evening. I'll do what I can to block him.'

# XVII

## *A Western Front Observation Post*

BLONGER was now out for blood. He hoped to find his telephone tapped, because someone had told him that it was unlawful to have this done. And the great fixer hoped to involve his adversary by invoking the aid of the very criminal laws which he had so flagrantly flouted for over forty years. Unfortunately for his plans his telephone was not tapped and Colorado passed no law making interference with telephone lines a crime until 1929.

However, if ever fast action was needed, it was now. John H. Mooney, the office man, was called in. 'I'm locking my doors and want no telephone calls or interference from anyone,' the District Attorney told him. Then, using the secret line, a call was put in for Cheney Bagby at the telephone company, and once again the god of chance looked with favor upon the Law, and Bagby answered the telephone.

'Bagby,' said the District Attorney, 'I've got a rush job for you, where I want the fastest and best action you ever gave in your life. Our friend, where the wires are located, has been tipped off that something has been done around his office. He thinks his 'phone is tapped. It isn't, so start with the fact that your lines are clear. But he's been up to your place, has seen Gus Peterson, and the latter has agreed to send some men down at once to look over his 'phone connections.

'Cheney, if your crew goes down there without instructions, they will find our wires, and there will be the devil to pay. Can't you give Colonel Young that assignment and have him hand-pick his crew? Tell him what we are trying to do. Get him quickly and ring me back.'

'I'm right after him,' said Bagby, and hung up.

Alexander W. Young had been a major during the War, and had been in command of a signal corps battalion in France. He made a splendid record there, and upon his return became a lieutenant-colonel in the Officers' Reserve Corps. Back with the telephone company he was the superintendent of its plants in Colorado.

The telephone rang again. 'Bagby talking. Young's here, no detail has gone out yet, and it's all up to him. I have given him the high spots. Now what do you want?'

'Thanks, you've done a swell job. Now put Young on the line. Hello, Young. Bagby tells me you understand the lay-out and I don't want to go into particulars over the wire. Your job, as I understand it, is to search for a tap on a certain telephone, remove it if you find it, and report the facts. I want you to go through with that very thoroughly, and you won't find any taps on that 'phone.

'But your job is neither to interfere with nor to report any other wires or other things that you see. Please leave them alone and pick that wire crew of yours with the greatest care, so that no one talks. Let me hear from you. I appreciate your co-operation.'

Colonel Young did an excellent job. He selected men whose mouths could not have been pried open with a pickaxe. They went up in the attic, crawled around its dingy corners, found the dictaphones and wet batteries, and rearranged the whole lay-out. But they found everything out in the open, so promptly concealed all wires and apparatus. After that was finished, they examined the telephone line, and found nothing wrong with it.

Then Young called in: 'That fellow's wire was clear and we so reported to the office. But your electrical job was rotten. So we did it all over for you, lugged those batteries back in a dark corner, covered your little ear-pieces, and we hope it will stand up. Anything more?'

'Not a thing, Young,' answered the D. A. 'My, but you're a brick! I'll thank you fully when I see you in person. Good-bye.'

Kenneth Robinson came in during the first talk with Young. 'Get Cooper for me,' he was told. A ring at the A & B taxi-stand produced results. 'Cooper, this is Reeves. 'Phone me at once.'

In came his response from another telephone. 'Cooper,' said the prosecutor, 'Nine [Blonger's number] is wise to Andy's room, and he had to pull out. Cover it and let me know who goes up there and what he finds. Don't let them spot you.'

Cooper reported that the fixer's emissary was none other than Billy Aarons, an agent of the United States Department of Justice, an unusually shrewd ward politician who had landed his job on the recommendation of a United States Senator and a Colorado Supreme Court Justice. Aarons had searched the rooms at about the same time Young was working on the wires. But all he was able to report was that some black-haired fellow with a dark complexion, who claimed to be a hosiery salesman, had rented the room about a month before and had left rather suddenly that morning. The room, he said, contained a desk, a few chairs, some socks samples, and wires to a Western Union call box. The curtain had a small slit in it.

Then the Federal agent traced the room occupant to the Adams Hotel, where he showed his United States credentials, and by means of them obtained further information from the clerk. The latter told him that his man was registered under the name of A. Kane, but had checked out that morning and said he was going to San Francisco. He had no friends nor associates, spoke to no one, and no clue was obtainable as to where he had gone.

Aarons stopped his work with this report. But was Blonger through? The relocation of the earphones might tell the tale. The dictaphones themselves and the wires leading from them were in better shape than ever. Where could the outlet wires be taken? Andy's opinion was needed, but he was still under cover.

Late that night Koehn appeared at the D. A.'s house, very much worried over possible damage to the case. He was sure that they had been sold out, and thought he should be discharged and some new man put in his place. He was afraid he had been recognized, and that his service to the cause was at an end.

The great strength of Andy Koehn was that he was never thinking of personal gain, but was working and planning at all times for the success of the assault upon the con-men. Andy was persuaded that he was needed, so stayed on the job.

Koehn was then told to scout the vicinity of Blonger's office for a new room which would be out of the fixer's sight. He soon reported that the Railroad Building, just south of Blonger's office, would be the best place to go. So he rented a light-housekeeping room on the top floor, and one night, with Eager's assistance, carried the wires out of the American National Bank Building and across the roof and into the new quarters, and once again the dictaphone was at work.

Blonger had saved his five hundred dollars and Colonel Young had saved the 'bug.' But the gang chieftain could now only be heard, and not seen. A place had to be found from which everything which occurred in his office could be constantly observed.

About that time Roy Samson, agent in charge of the Rocky

Mountain Division of the Federal Department of Justice, and the immediate superior of Billy Aarons, had resigned that job to go with the Denver prosecutor. So he was told to locate a place for an observatory. In a short time Samson recommended the building occupied by the Cassidy Hicks Wall Paper Company. It was two hundred and fifty feet north on Lawrence Street, and was the only place which afforded a direct view into Blonger's office. Luckily this structure belonged to Oscar Cass, a friend of the District Attorney. The latter told Cass what he needed, and Cass asked his tenants to give the prosecutor whatever he wanted.

Accordingly, Roy examined the building. The top floor was a huge wallpaper loft, with a twenty-foot ceiling. The D. A. called on his experience in France and told Samson how observation posts (called O.P.'s in the War) were constructed. The latter then employed carpenters and built a regular Western Front Observation Post close to the roof. It was reached with a ladder, and had double doors at the entrance, the entire cubby-hole being painted black on the inside. Any person entering or leaving shut one door behind him before opening the other, so that no ray of light would go through from the back to be visible from the front. Then Samson punched a hole through the brick wall, and found that he was directly in line with the center of Blonger's office. Telephones, with secret numbers, were put in the lookout and the O.P., and a powerful telescope installed.

It was now late in April, and the detail work of the investigation had again become too heavy to handle in connection with office routine. So Samson was given the job of writing to all victims, assembling the evidence, and identifying the members of the gang.

Roy's training for this task was excellent. He had been admitted to the bar, but had never practiced. He loved details, and because of his Federal work he was the only man in the office who had police training and was accustomed to making

BLONGER'S OFFICE (A) THE OBSERVATION POST (B)

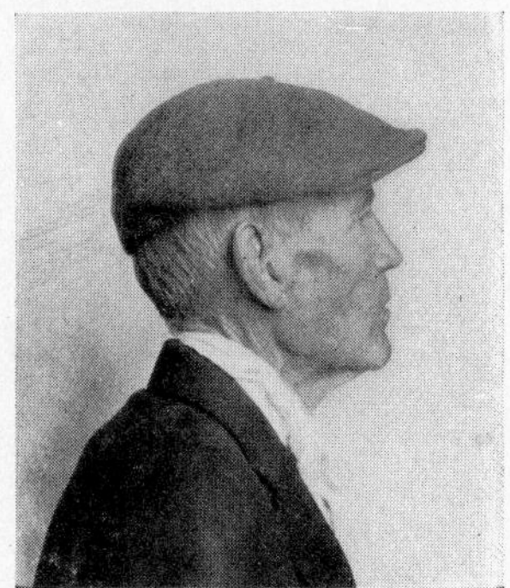

JACK HARDAWAY
(Steerer)

ROY FARRELL
(Spieler)

A. H. POTTS
(Steerer)

WILLIAM STURNS
'The Painter Kid'

arrests. He could not have been used as a detective, because bad facial burns, in a fire in his youth, had made him easy to identify. But he could be used in an office.

Samson was fed-up with the Department of Justice. His men, in the main, were political appointees, like Billy Aarons, and he could trust few of them. His job itself was political, and if he crossed powerful interests he could be fired in a minute. So, though he knew nothing of con-men, he eagerly grasped the chance for a job where all that was demanded was exact facts.

The main problem with Samson was to camouflage his work both to the office force and outsiders. A big steal made that possible. Some sheepmen had perpetrated a million-dollar swindle involving most of the Denver banks, and the District Attorney had conferred with the bankers about it. Their losses were so large that they feared prosecution would cause runs and wreck the institutions. The local papers knew all about the crime, and had stories set up in type and ready to run if the story broke. But they had promised the banks to keep quiet unless the men were prosecuted.

So the courthouse reporters were given the tip that Roy was working on the sheep case, and, knowing the dangers in it, they let him alone. With his movements thus disguised, Samson was able to work in private, without interference from the office or outsiders. Occasionally he was given some deputy district attorney's work in court to help conceal his job.

Fred Tate was then called upon for a third detective to man the O.P.

Shortly afterwards the District Attorney's doorbell rang. On the porch stood a lean, swarthy individual, hat pulled down over his eyes, with an air of mystery about him which he always assumed. 'Mr. Reeves?' he said.

The District Attorney said, 'Yes, come in.'

'No,' he answered, 'better read this first.' And he handed in a letter of introduction from Tate, stating that the bearer,

Robert Maiden, had served on the Kansas City police force with a fine background. After the prosecutor read it, Maiden accepted the second invitation and entered the house.

Maiden was not afraid of hell and high water, and it was doubtful if he knew what fear was. He had shot his man — a burglar — while on police, and was always looking for the next one. He was a good soldier, took orders well, but needed to be held in check and definitely guided. Whenever he let his imagination run riot, there was the devil to pay.

Maiden's job was to man the O.P., 'tail' or follow the bunks, and work under Andy. The lay-out was thoroughly explained to him and he went to work with vigor.

Maiden had an almost instant complaint. 'The worst feature about the O.P. is the damn pigeons. They think the hole in the wall is a swell place to light, and when I poke them out, I am afraid Blonger will get wise.'

The big mistake that was made was that the dictaphone was not carried up to the observation post and a first-class court reporter put on the job. Instead of that, because of shortage of funds, Andy was told to get the cheapest girl stenographer he could, but to be sure she could guard her tongue. He found one who could do the latter all right, but she must have put a padlock on both her ears and fingers as well, as the reports received from her were meager in the extreme.

The worst of it was, when important data occurred she didn't understand it, or couldn't write fast enough to get it, and all that she ever got were broken fragments. To make bad matters worse, the dictaphone itself was continually going out of commission. Ben Eager, who had installed it, had to be eliminated, and an electrician, who was thoroughly reliable, substituted in his stead.

Where could such a man be obtained? The problem was presented to Arthur L. Jones, the assistant general manager of the General Electric Company for the Rocky Mountain area, who was an old friend of the District Attorney.

Arthur sat for some time, thinking over the matter, and finally said, 'Phil, I will do it for you myself.'

The prosecutor said he would not allow him to; that it was a dirty job, and one in which, if Jones were caught, might be serious for him, and at the best would be very embarrassing; but Jones said no, that he thought it was a job that called for citizenship, and he wanted to do his part.

From that time on, for about a year, Arthur L. Jones, a business executive, went down to the American National Bank Building, and in old clothes crawled through the dirt and dust of the attic and carried up water and zinc for the wet batteries. Under the greatest difficulties he kept the dictaphone in operation, all without any pay, glory, or notoriety, but simply as one of the members of the team that was attempting to make a successful drive on organized crime.

And what a problem the maintenance of the dictaphone proved to be! An amplifier was installed, to catch the frequent whispers of Blonger and Duff, but it built up the noises so much that the earphones almost screeched. When Blonger's window was open, as it was during warm weather, the operators heard kids whistling, automobiles roaring, and the rattle of the street cars.

Four new batteries were put on the line and it went dead. Two were disconnected and sound came through. Once the dictaphones were burned out with too much current, and new ones had to be obtained. Often the line would become silent for no apparent reason whatsoever. When the wet batteries were recharged, it took twenty-four hours to build them up before voices could be heard. Then the zincs would be eaten up and the current die down. It was a continual electrical problem to keep them in order, complicated by the fact that Jones's work took him out of town a large portion of the time. But even with all these interruptions, the dictaphones furnished indispensable information, even through inefficient Mrs. Steno, as Andy Koehn called the stenographer.

But the enemy was active, one of the secret numbers was found, and an attempt was made to locate the O.P. telephone. Maiden reported:

> As I picked up the 'phone today I heard the operator tell some man that Main 6647 was a silent number and that she could not give him its location: I immediately said hello, and the man inquired if this was Main 6647, and I told him that it was. He said that he was the telephone man and that they were working on the line and that he wanted its location. I asked him if there was any trouble and he replied that unless there had been that they would not be working on it. I told him that the service suited me and that his wire chief could give him the desired information. I also asked him for his name or number with the telephone company and just where he was working at the present moment.
>
> He refused to answer saying, that it made no difference, that if I did not want the 'phone worked on it was all right with him. I told him that he was not fooling anyone, and rang off. I immediately called Koehn's place and repeated the conversation to Mrs. Steno. I then called Information, who told me that someone had tried to locate this 'phone, but she had no trace of the inquiry. I then talked with the wire chief who told me that unless a service complaint had been made that no one from the Company would be inquiring for the location and that the call was probably a stall to locate the 'phone.

That call, however, was the last time that dodge was tried.

At last the District Attorney had the equipment, a stenographer of sorts taking snatches of the conversation over the dictaphone, Maiden watching from the O.P. to identify the persons in Blonger's office, secret telephones from the observation post to the dictaphone room, and in the District Attorney's office, Koehn free to 'tail' anyone going to or from Blonger's office, Cooper in the underworld, Samson and Sanborn on details, Robinson for the high spots, and a working team.

The evidence now showed that twenty-four of the Denver gang had been identified by victims. Pictures and physical characteristics of all of these grafters, except Blonger, were in the District Attorney's rogues' gallery. Made into a table the known mob assumed this form:

| | | | |
|---|---|---|---|
| | The fixer | Lou Blonger | |
| | The manager | Adolph W. Duff | |
| *Victim* | *Bookmaker* | *Spieler* | *Steerer* |
| Backus | | Mead | Beach and Kinsman |
| Bergstrom | | | Irving and Lewis |
| Carnes | Randle | Tillery | Kelly |
| Gray | Randle and French | | |
| Griffith | French | Richards | Randle |
| Henson | French | Kennedy | Randle |
| Kanavuts | French | | Scott |
| Larsen | French and Randle | Cooper | Filger and Miller |
| McGrath | French and Randle | McCord | Filger |
| Menaugh | | | |
| Nitsche | | | Ballard |
| Scherrer | French | Goodrich | Grey |
| Tilton and Cobbs | | | Byland |
| Unzner | French | Anderson | Byland |
| Wurzbach | | | |
| Arrested on dope charge | | | Dixon |

Glancing at the evidence from another angle, the prosecutor found that Gray was picked up at a fly-casting contest, Tilton and Cobbs in a hotel in Colorado Springs, McGrath in a tourist shop in Manitou, and the others in hotels or on the streets in Denver. The crooks seemed to be able to get their victims under any and all circumstances. But they were now being watched.

# XVIII

## *Prostitutes, Bootleggers, and Police*

For several weeks Cooper, getting in with Silver and Beers, watched the varied life of prostitutes, pimps, bootleggers, and gamblers, as police and officials fattened at their expense. Koehn checked the police, and the reports made by these two unfold the drab facts of city graft:

I spent the day hanging around the joints and our cigar store. Saw Bacon and Land, and a number of other smart-looking dudes including Dean. Mike Rossi had a very heated argument over the place at 19th and Arapahoe, it seems as though they are having trouble. Mike says that G—— d——ed District Attorney knew all about the gambling at this place, that the landlord had called him up and told him that there would be no gambling there. — C.

I met Sammie Abrams today, he seems to be a pretty smart fellow. Abe Silver is selling whiskey that is confiscated by the police. — C.

I was with Beers and a bunch of pimps at the A & B when a police sergeant came in. Beers got change for $10 and put his cap on and walked out with him, and came back and said, 'Now that's settled.' — C.

I met the most important man in the City Hall, Abe Silver, everybody that came in greeted him with a 'Hello, Abe.' He had business with half of the people that came in. Everybody bowed to him but the Chief of Police. He greeted the Chief with an over-courteous bow and 'Good morning, Chief.' The Chief walked past him with a very snide nod of the head. Had I been

Abe, I would have felt insulted. It impressed me as if the Chief hasn't got much time or use for Abe. — K.

Visited around the City Hall this morning and met some more detectives. — K.

I was out to supper this evening with Vandine at his woman's whorehouse. She only has one girl. Vandine mentioned Land as not playing with any petty larceny stuff, that he only played the millionaire stuff, but that Abe played the petty larceny stuff. He also said he would show me a bunch of these con-men. He walked me past Dawes cigar store, here is where all the big birds hang out, he said, but that the most of them were out of town.

Abe remarked last night that the Mayor would do anything he said for him to do. He mentioned a number of policemen and detectives that he was holding on the job. He told Vandine that he would go to work on the first of the month. Abe said to Vandine, 'You got 84.3 in your examination, but you know you can't spell "it," "was," or "and." ' — C.

Abe asked me today to join the Eagles. He and Beers signed my application. I am to go in Wednesday night. The law was down to 19th and Arapahoe and looked the place over yesterday morning. The bunch is trying to find out who the snitch is, they think it's a fellow named Walton. — C.

This afternoon at 3.50 the Manager of Safety called Mike Rossi and gave him orders to close the place at 19th and Arapahoe Streets until after Friday, when Gene Rossi's case comes up.

The whores and pimps are all wild, the line is supposed to be closed up on account of some government men. About 11.30 this evening I dropped into the A & B, and three prostitutes came in and asked Petie Beers if it was all right to go down and start working tonight. Beers told them to go ahead as it was after 11 o'clock and he did not think there would be any raid. — C.

Beers was trying to sell the gambling paraphernalia from the place at 19th and Arapahoe, said they would never be able to open up the downstairs again, but they may get the upstairs open. He says that Gene Rossi and Dago Mike had too much notoriety to try to do any gambling.

Sergeant Reed came in for a great share of criticism today as usual, for being so hard on the boys. — C.

I see the police are giving their benefit ball on the 28th. I believe it would be a good place for me to go so I can spot all the detectives. — K.

I believe a number of your witnesses in the Rossi case were run out of town last night. — C.

I went to supper with two cops last night. I don't like to feed policemen but they handed me their checks. — C.

Pinkie seems to be having a lot of trouble, his whore has been arrested three times in the last week. He told me that he got instructions to pay the coppers on the beat $10 per week or leave town. He insinuated that he got these orders from Abe Silver. She hustles on Welton between 14th and 20th. — C.

Met detectives Mayfield and Wisdom in Champa 2, Beers is scared to death of Mayfield, said he was the king — — — ——, meaning that he could not be reached. — C.

I was in the A & B last night when a fellow named Red came rushing in and stated that four carloads of policemen had just left for Larimer Street. The pimps got busy getting their women out of the neighborhood. Then a detective came in and eased all our minds by telling us it was a shooting scrape and not a raid. The dick took this Roy Graham, the pimp from California, outside, and Beers remarked he was putting the bee to Roy for about twenty. — C.

The police ball proved a great success from my point of view. I think I saw everybody that amounts to anything from the Chief, Bacon, and Land, on down the line. Even Abe Silver was there with a big white badge. Also saw the District Attorney. I learned the name of many detectives, that I had known by sight. — K.

The police raid on the women has caused quite a rumble. Beers said he got 28 of the women out on bond. He gets $12 per head, so Vandine tells me. His woman's house was raided and his woman pinched and he was crying about it. Says they just got done paying $150 for protection, $20 apiece to three sergeants, $10 each to the coppers on the beat, $10 to the city doctor, for not examining his girl and another girl inmate. — C.

Spent the morning around the City Hall, so as to see the associates of the women who were locked up the afternoon before. The system is really amusing. They had the court doors locked and outsiders were excluded. But the pimps, fixers, etc., were all in the hall. That's where the Chief overlooked the biggest part of his raid; he should have grabbed all the pimps that were in the corridor patiently waiting for the verdict. Every so often Patrolman Baker would come out and tell Abe Silver what was going on in the court room, and then the pimps and interested ones would come to Abe and get the news from him. — K.

It seems like Sergeant Reed is making it tough for the women. Abe was very busy trying to square things up with Reed, but I don't think he got anywhere. — C.

There were a couple of girls arrested this evening, charged with robbing some fellow. It took Abe about an hour and a half to spring them out of jail. He had to go so strong as to go to the Chief of Police himself, but he succeeded in getting the victim locked up on a charge of drunkenness. Abe said, 'We will give him hell in court in the morning.' — C.

The two girls that I spoke of in yesterday morning's report were turned loose this morning. — C.

They tried to make a chaplain out of me over at the Eagles last night; I bucked and they then made me the bartender. — C.

Nothing happened until about five o'clock this evening, when Abe was supposed to have tipped the boys off and told them to go ahead and open up the line, and from what I could hear the most of the places were reopened this evening. All the pimps are trying to get upstairs places, or rooming houses, it seems as if these places are not bothered so bad. — C.

The women are all very busy hustling the streets. — C.

Had the pleasure of seeing Roy Graham slip a policeman a five-dollar bill tonight, to let his woman work the streets. Roy says he has to give this up once a week. — C.

Abe gave all the boys orders to get all their girls off the street tonight; said he got the news straight from the Hall, that they were going to clean up the streets, tonight.

Red remarked today that the gang would be in between now and the 20th. — C.

Your men Smith and Sanborn stirred up an awful commotion yesterday, when they made the raid on the gambling joint at 19th and Champa. Everybody was trying to get the boys out on bond. Abe was to meet Smith this evening and see if Smith can talk to Sanborn in order to spring these fellows on bail.

I took a ride down through the red light district this afternoon and noticed quite a number of places running. — C.

Your men Smith and Sanborn very near made me have a nervous chill this evening. They came in Sammy Abrams place and I had a quart of Canadian Club whiskey in my pocket, that Graham had just given me. Earlier in the day Reed had fanned Sammy's place, but found nothing. The clerk told Smith to come back that night, that Sammy wanted to see him. Smith went in the little office, that you know sits in the middle of the building and I am positive in my own mind that Sammy Abrams paid off, the remark was made after Smith and Sanborn left, that Sanborn was a good fellow; that he will do whatever Smith says. — C.

Beers told me this evening that you asked questions about him, about what he charged to get the girls out on bond and all the other questions I imagine, that was asked. Hogan and Beers told me this evening that you had gotten $10,000 from a bunch of bankers to clean up the vice and it sure looks like you are going to do it. They say that you have four dummies working for you that get $125 per month, but they are not on your payroll. — C.

If you keep razzing these pimps you are going to get a squawk who they have been giving this money to, some of these days. As they say, it is a hell of a fixer that can't stop a vag charge. — C.

I have been staying at Roy Gardner's place in the hills, but it must never be mentioned to Oliver Smith or anyone else, as it would only get me in a jam. He has an old-time confidence man staying with him named Ed Ginney. He talked of Blonger, Duff, and Land, who he said was the detective for the big mob, and looked out for the Big Store interest. But that he did not have any guts, and he would holler if the District Attorney ever hemmed him up. — C.

# XIX

## *Information on the 'Big Store'*

KOEHN wanted an excuse to walk by Blonger's door and to talk to his neighbors. So he called on the Italian doctor in the adjacent room, and, on the pretense that he was not feeling well, had the physician look him over. Charlie James was in the doctor's waiting-room, and Andy struck up an acquaintance with him. Then he called at the apartment house where Blonger lived, and looked over the neighborhood around Berna Rames's and Land's houses.

Then Beers, Olson, and Silver made arrangements for Arch Cooper to meet Duff personally. They thought Cooper had wealthy connections, and suggested that he steer some rich oil man into him. If he did, they said, Duff would split fairly, as the big mob would be in Denver during the summer, and all would make money. Olson claimed that in twenty years Blonger never had a man settled (that is, sent to the penitentiary), but a fellow had to see him before he started to work.

Next Morris Freeman, of Denver, was picked up in Denver and taken to Little Rock, Arkansas, where he was trimmed for $6000, and the same three laughed and told Cooper that one of the boys was Kent Marshall, a con-man with a Van Dyke beard who looked like a Count; that it was only a small take-out, but they needed the money.

As soon as Samson went to work, Cooper got it from the underworld. The gratifying report was that Samson was on the square and couldn't be reached.

After Lou returned, quite a number of the gang drifted into town, but left in a few days, as the 'Store' didn't open.

Mrs. Steno reported that Duff and Blonger talked about education and what they could do if they had one. And Blonger lamented that two or three gamblers and saloon-keepers blackballed him so he couldn't join the Elks.

Duff received a telegram from Kansas City:

> ARRIVE SUNDAY BRINGING CONTRACTOR WITH ME, CAN MAKE ARRANGEMENTS THERE

And Samson remarked, 'Two con-men are on the way here for jobs.'

The 'bug' heard Blonger 'hollering' because some dirty crook passed a bum check on him for a hundred dollars. And then he panned the District Attorney — 'What business does he have to run around and arrest people and look for whorehouses and gambling-joints, and interfere with other people's business. He should enforce the law and prosecute the cases the police bring him.'

Then the 'dick' gave the District Attorney something of more interest. Blonger told Duff to see Officer Strike, and to find out if he knew an electrician by the name of Eager!

'Eager was in this building and did the electrical work for that fellow's detectives while we were away,' said Lou.

And Duff answered: 'Don't you remember that I told you long before you went away that this fellow Eager was working and was here for no good purpose?'

'Those bastards are simply jealous of us,' responded Lou.

'Say, I got some dope from George Lusk [the city dick]. Ryan [Koehn's landlord where the first wires ran] told him that any time he saw that long, lanky fellow that was in that room, he would point him out.' And Koehn added in his report:

'Blonger would have dropped dead if he knew the long tall fellow was listening to every word he said!'

Lou wound up by saying: 'That fellow ought to be run out of town. He's making a hell of a mess of things.'

Sam Abrams told Cooper that Duff had a new car which would make plenty of fast trips to Colorado Springs and different places when the Big Store opened up.

Then the 'dick' gave a story of old times. A visitor came in to call on Lou, and these two were good friends of a man named Ed. Blonger admitted that he was quite a rough-neck in his early days. When he and Ed and the visitor were in New Orleans in the seventies, and all broke, they decided to get some money somewhere. Ed ran into a cattleman with cash, and as the three rascals were good card men, they framed up to beat him at poker.

They strolled in one at a time and hung around the barroom; then Ed casually accosted them, separately, and got all in the game. Lou won all the money and skipped out while the boy from the plains was reaching for his gun. Then the three pals met and split up. Blonger and his visitor got a great laugh out of it.

Then Lou said: 'I met that cattleman a year later. He was sore as hell and demanded his money. I said, "All right, step out in the hallway here." When he got in the hall, I put my hand in my back pocket. I didn't even have a toothpick. And I said, "Now, you damn old — — — ——, if you don't get out of here I'll blow your damn heart out." And he beat it.

'Ed told me that night that all the police in New Orleans were looking for me, so I skipped to Hot Springs.'

Then Lou regaled his visitors with stories about his gambling-house in Salt Lake in '71.

J. W. Lakeman, a con-man, wrote in asking for a summer job. The District Attorney already had his picture, so was ready to identify him when he showed up. And then a letter came to Duff from J. H. Fuller, of Excelsior Springs, Missouri.

Samson, wildly excited, came rushing in. 'That's J. H. French. He's going to be here this summer. There's a $5000 reward for him for that Nicholson job where he stung him for $120,000 in Miami.' So all were told to watch for French.

Lou and Duff had a visitor. Lou received a telephone call from Hal Crane, and said, 'All right, Hal,' and then stated:

'There was a young fellow here who got in bad for intimidating a witness, and for fixing one of the jury, and he ducked to Kansas City. They had him located there and I did not want him to get pinched, so I wired $150 to get him out of town before he got nailed.'

'Beers said that you know more about his place than he does himself. He left orders for all the pimps to stay away from there.'

'Dick' reports:

A man named Mack from Colorado Springs, a gambler probably, called today. He spoke of a smart lawyer down there that was elected to office some time ago. Mack said, 'I went right to him and said, "Well, if we all vote for you what are you going to do if you get in?" and he said, "Everything will remain wide-open just as Blackmer had it." Well, he got in and closed us up tight, and I went to him again, and said, "I thought you were going to let us run," and he said, "No, I can't. I got fourteen hundred church people behind me and I want a higher office." He ran again and he was snowed under.' Duff said, 'Yes, he is the one that had me in the jug down there.'

Mack wanted to know what's doing — Duff: 'Everything very quiet right now. It will pick up about the middle of July. I had a wire from French, but he says there is nothing doing either.'

Someone mentioned Tom Jackson, and Lou said, 'I got him out of that mess in Florida. I went down there to get him out.'

While Duff and Blonger were alone, Lou said, 'Find out how many fellows he has working' — this was before a long silence. Duff said 'All right,' and that was all.

Lou told this story to a caller: 'You know, before I went away there was a woman who kept coming up here annoying me about some mining stock, and when I left I thought I was rid of her. I wasn't back in town two days when she came up here again, and had a whole bundle in her arms, her mining stock, some oil stock and a lot of papers, and I told her to put her stuff down and sit down.

'Well, she started about selling me her oil stock, and I said, "Now listen, we won't talk mining stock, or oil stock or lots or any other junk — let's speak of love," and I went over and grabbed her by the arm. I knew I would either get rid of her this way, or I wouldn't want to get rid of her.

'Well, she went all up in the air — no man had ever talked to her like this before, etc. "What, in all these years?" I asked. You know, she was damn near forty. She said "No," and she wouldn't stand to be insulted, and she rushed out mad as hell. Well, I thought I was rid of her for sure, but now I will bet a hundred dollars to one cent that she is going to try and cause me trouble.'

Visitor to Lou: 'Was this the time that the detective was in the room across the street?' Lou said 'Yes,' and they both laughed.

The old man must have some dope on what she did do, or what she intends to do, as he said, 'I got a date with the Judge at noon today, and I am going to tell him all about it before she starts something, or tells that fellow. She is liable to tell him that I tried to tear her clothes off of her. I never did know what her game was, and it looks damn funny'; and he continued, 'You know you can't tell what a damn woman is liable to do.'

Blonger telephoned Berna Rames — 'Well, I went to see the judge. I went right to him as he was on the bench, and told him the whole story. He said he was very glad that I came to him and that I should not worry — that everything would be all right.'

Met Blonger on 16th Street in company with a short heavy set man. Fellow he was with had on a black fedora hat, and had all the earmarks of a lawyer.

Letter to Mrs. J. R. Farrell at the office shows that Roy Farrell, a big spieler, is on the way in. His picture is in the gallery.

Sammy said that Duff told him a few days ago that they would not make the big spread until June 15th or later, and that there was not a thing doing now.

This A.M. one of the real boys came in. Lou told him about the tap on the 'phone. ''Phone, hell,' he said, 'I'll bet it was a dictaphone.'

'Where do they put those things?' asked Blonger.

'Oh, they generally hang them behind pictures.'

So they took down the pictures, turned over the desk, the rug and all the furniture, and found nothing.

Duff: 'I wonder who French is doubled up with at the Springs?'

X: 'I think Alec.'

Duff: 'Oh, say, Abe Silver got a letter from that grafter, and he wanted him to ask me if he could get in on the Big Store. I told Abe not to even answer his letter.'

X: 'Oh, the hell with him. He is the one that tried to get me out of the Big Store that time. And he wanted to double-cross me.'

Duff: 'That fellow has Roy Samson, a Government man, working for him now.'

Lou: 'Who is he?'

Duff: 'Roy Samson — he used to be with the Government.'

Blonger: 'Is he from here or out of town?'

Duff: 'He worked here right along.'

X: 'What's his graft?'

Duff: 'Oh, he has that kodak stuff; he is getting pictures of everybody.'

Sammy Abrams introduced me to a man named Arch Corrich, who has been a steer for the Big Store for the last twenty years. He also has a brother working in a bank, that Sammy says is a steer for the big mob.

Very quiet today, excepting your raid on the Greek joint on Market Street, and the arrest of Dago Mike. You got plenty of criticism, but of course that is not interesting to you. I hear that Petie Beers came to see you twice, but did not have any luck.

The sum and substance of the entire conversation today was panning you continually. Your name was mentioned forty times, and one loud-mouth bird I guess I could have heard without a dick.

This X came up with Lou this morning. Duff also came in a few minutes later.

Lou: 'Some lousy copper pinched some niggers, and the D. A. filed charges against three houses for running a house of prostitution. I told the judge that the men worked, and sometimes they paid their rent and sometimes they didn't. Well, they all got fined. There isn't any justice in these courts — I guess they will have to pay it. I told Bacon to get busy and do what he could. That fellow wants to close up all those houses. Why don't he nail the doors shut and be done with it? He makes me sick, now he went over and raided a crap game. He can't keep his damn nose out of anything. He also started something on this Ku Klux business — he better be careful or they will get him.'

This X must be a lawyer that works for Blonger. He knows all his business, and the way he spoke he must of defended the negroes. You will probably know him; he talks continually, and awful loud, and he laughs long and loud at everything that Lou says. It's all a huge joke with him. He laughed at everything they said, and he laughs while he talks.

Then they got on you again.

X: 'He will have you in jail yet.'

Blonger: 'Yes, that time he sent for me, that was just a stall. He didn't say a damn word to me about the big store.'

X: 'It's a wonder he doesn't get after Art Duff. I don't think he knows you are living, does he, Art?'

Duff: 'The hell he don't! Didn't he try and get me pinched in Kansas City, and wanted them to take my picture? Christ, didn't he write them and tell them where I was stopping, and where I was getting mail, and all about me, and a friend of mine come and showed me this letter?'

This X knows Samson. — X: 'He has this fellow Samson working for him now. He used to get $4200 a year from the Department of Justice, and now he is getting only $150 a month. The D. A. can't pay him any more unless he pays him out of his own pocket. He has two men for investigators and they are lawyers, and they are allowed $3000 a year for the two.'

X: 'Oh, you know Samson — one of his ears looks like it is half-chewed off. How did that happen — he was struck by lightning, wasn't he?'

Duff to Blonger: 'There is a dandy place out there and I sure would like to buy it, but I haven't enough money. If things were as good here as they were two years ago, I sure would buy the place.'

Visitor to Blonger: 'The District Attorney doesn't bother you, does he?'

Lou: 'The hell he don't. Didn't he have my telephone wires tapped and have two detectives in that room across the street watching me?'

Duff received an interesting telegram:

CHICAGO, MAY 31

A. W. DUFF

LEAVING HERE BY MOTOR SATURDAY FOR DENVER. WOULD LIKE TO KNOW IF YOU WILL BE READY TO GO FISHING WHEN I ARRIVE. IT IS A LONG TRIP BY AUTO.

WILLIAM SNYDER

And he answered it this way:

DENVER, JUNE 1

WM. SNYDER, CHICAGO.

WOULD SAY JULY FIRST.

A. W. DUFF

# XX

## *The Red Lights Put Out*

FROM early days commercialized vice had flourished on Denver's Market Street. That 'red-light district' was an established institution, and was one of the show places of the town until 1912, when public sentiment forced the authorities to close it up. After the War, however, a lax city administration allowed many of the old establishments to be reopened in the twelve-block area bounded by Eighteenth, Twenty-Second, Champa, and Larimer Streets.

The new system differed entirely from the frontier plan of blazing red lights and half-naked hussies openly soliciting from crib windows and doors. Instead of a wide-open 'row,' the houses were now required to be kept darkened at night and heavy shades were placed at all the windows to keep the lights from showing, as was done with all towns in the war zone in France. A colored maid usually sat inside the door and opened it on a rap from any man who wanted to get in. Abe Silver, the constable, ran the district, and in order to open or maintain a house the madams, *maquereaux*, and inmates all paid tribute to him, in addition, of course, to the stipend to the copper on the beat.

Crime and disease were rampant in the area. Many tourists were being 'rolled' — that is, stripped of their wallets — by the girls, and venereal troubles were materially on the increase. In fact the situation became so critical that the United States Department of Public Health sent investigators into the houses and published a very adverse report on the conditions.

Early in the year Blonger had purchased an old 'parlor-house' known as the 'Anna Gould Mansion,' which from 1880 to 1912 had been a celebrated Western resort. It had been idle for several years, but the approval of the Broadway extension project placed it on a triangular corner, and the fixer, with a shrewd eye for a real estate bargain, and, with early information on the success of the project, had snapped it up.

Arch Cooper reported to the District Attorney that Red Hogan, the bootlegger, had rented it from Blonger for a hundred dollars a month, and intended to start a beer-garden and old-fashioned 'honkey-tonk,' and, with the exception of the District Attorney's office, was all squared with everybody, including the United States Prohibition officials.

'Let Red alone,' advised Cooper. 'Hogan's place will be a good resort for Blonger's grafters, and will make it easy for me to find and identify them. Hogan knows Lou so well that he describes him as the "old born fixer."'

But Cooper simply saw the situation as one to make his own job easy. The case itself was Blonger, and whatever he did had to be studied in connection with the entire attack. Lou had secured entirely too much information about the District Attorney's activities against him. He had read the letter to the Kansas City prosecutor, he had located Koehn's room across Seventeenth Street, he had tried to find a tap on his telephone, and he had heard that the District Attorney had raised a fund of ten thousand dollars to fight crime, most of which he believed was to be spent in investigating himself. Blonger was getting too hot on the trail and had to be thrown entirely off the track and, if possible, be made to believe that the prosecutor was after different game. The rental of the Anna Gould house to Hogan offered the opportunity.

If the churches could be aroused to wage a righteous crusade against vice, funds might be raised through their efforts and Blonger and the underworld attacked from that angle. Accordingly, invitations were sent to all Protestant denominations in the city to send representatives to a meeting at the First Universalist Church, of which the District Attorney was a member, to discuss the prostitution situation.

About one hundred men attended. After giving the general picture of the condition, the Colonel stated:

'The way to attack vice is to hit it in the pocketbook. It is not the girls you want, it is the property owners. If these people, many of whom pose as respectable members of your churches, are sure that their places will be locked up for one year under the abatement laws, they will not tolerate prostitutes in their buildings. When that happens the row will shut up, regardless of grafting politicians.

'To do this we need money, money to get exact evidence of the ownership of the places and the knowledge of the owners as to the character of their use. When we have these facts a raid and an arrest of the girls will be just the incidental step to driving protected prostitutes out of town. The round-up will give us a list of all the girls in each house and their individual police records. Then we can file our cases against the landlords and board up the district.'

Although his auditors agreed to present the situation to their respective groups, the District Attorney aroused little interest in the matter, as all the churches in Denver raised only two hundred dollars. However, one of the ministers, when he mailed the donations from his denomination, unwittingly solved the problem. He forwarded fifty dollars in checks of one or two dollars each, there being about forty checks in the envelope.

As soon as this money came, the District Attorney telephoned Petie Beers, the head of the underworld 'grapevine,' at the A. & B. Taxi Company, and asked him to come to the office.

'Petie,' said the District Attorney, 'you are the center of the tip-off system in this town. All the crooks, bootleggers, pimps, and whores pay tribute to you and your gang. They pay you a fat price for information as to what is going on, and for the use of your taxis in hauling them back and forth from the City Hall, and I am going to smash you and your whole bunch. You and Lou Blonger own a lot of whorehouses, and I am going to put them out of business.'

'Why, Colonel,' said Petie, 'you are all wet. I don't own a house; neither does Blonger, and there is damn little going on in this town. It is just as quiet as they make them. All I do is to have taxis for hire. If some of the girls want my cabs instead of the other fellow's, that is just business and nothing else.'

'That's fine, Petie,' said the District Attorney, 'but now let me tell you something. To show you that we mean business in this matter, here is one letter that just came in this morning from the little Boulevard Congregational Church in North Denver, and you can see the number of checks that it has sent in as a starter. I am raising a fund to investigate the row, and when I get it, I will lock up every joint down there.' And Beers was casually shown the pile of checks in such a manner that he couldn't see the small amount that each one represented. After a few minutes' conversation, Petie left.

That afternoon over the dictaphone Blonger was heard to tell Duff: 'What do you think that G—— d—— fool is up to now? That fund that we thought he was raising to attack me with he is getting from the churches to shut up the row, and a fat chance he will have. These G—— damned reformers make me tired. They do a lot of talking; they may arrest some of the girls, but they won't get to first base. Petie Beers told me he was called over there this morning, and the District Attorney shot off his mouth to him and told Petie that he was the center of the tip-off. Now, how did he find that out about Beers being the tip-off? That fellow is funny. I can't make him out. At times he is right; other times he doesn't know anything, just plain dumb.'

The following morning the District Attorney sent for Blonger. Printed forms had already been prepared for the abatement cases, and among them was a notice to landlords that their houses were being used in violation of the law and that, if they did not correct the situation, their places would be shut up.

Lou came in poker-faced and pleasant as usual.

'Hello, Blonger,' was the greeting.

'You 'phoned for me,' said the fixer. 'What do you want?'

'Well,' said the prosecutor, 'I understand you purchased the Anna Gould house over at Twentieth and Market and are renting it to Red Hogan for a parlor-house and beer-joint.'

'Why, you're crazy,' said Lou. 'That place has been shut for years, and I bought it as an investment to put something else there because of the Broadway extension.'

'Well, Blonger,' said the District Attorney, 'I don't fall for that story. I know exactly what you bought it for. You intend to open a "honkey-tonk" and you can't get away with it. I am going to shut up the row in this town. I am more interested in stopping that kind of stuff and booze than anything else. But to be fair to you I am going to serve you with a notice right now that your place is being used for immoral purposes, so that you can't say that you didn't have full warning. After that notice, if a single girl opens up at that joint, I will close it for a year.'

'Aw,' Blonger replied, 'I will take your notice, but you don't know what you're talking about.' And grabbing the papers he slammed on his hat and stamped out.

Again the dictaphone was interesting, this time in a conversation between Blonger and some unidentified police officer. 'That crazy fool over there thinks I am going to open a whorehouse! Why, I never was in that business. He served me with a notice he was going to lock me up for a year, and made me go all the way over to his office just to tell me what he was going to do.'

For some unexplained reason the police officials seemed to be willing to co-operate in a raid on the red-light district. The Chief detailed two officers, Luther Harding and George K. McWilliams, to assist in the investigation. The District Attorney stood to win whether the scheme fell down or was completed. A failure would make the gang feel more confident, while a success, with police help, would not only convince Blonger that the prosecutor would take no action against criminals without police assistance, but might also make him believe that the District Attorney had decided to drop his investigation of the con-men.

The officers were instructed to locate every house used for prostitution in the downtown district. Next they were to obtain the name of the madam and the name of the people who owned the property, and then go to the landlords and try to rent the places from them. When talking to the owners, they were to try to ascertain from them the present use of the houses, and in that way to secure the positive evidence that the landlords knew that their places were being used for purposes of prostitution; in other words, the evidence was to be obtained before the inmates or owners were molested.

Harding and McWilliams were careful, and obtained the proof on the owners of about sixty pieces of property. Some of the landlords were from the underworld, but many were among the so-called 'respectable' people of Denver, including some women of the 'holier-than-thou' type who were active church workers on Sunday.

After all the evidence was assembled, the matter was gone into in detail with the Chief and the raid set for four o'clock one afternoon. Because of the tip-off system, the Chief revealed his plans to none of his force, but ordered the off-duty shift to be on hand at the Auditorium, three blocks from the City Hall, at a quarter to four to hear a lecture.

When the officers had reported, the doors were locked, and raid orders issued. Lists of all places were furnished and the details instructed to get all inmates in the houses assigned to them. In less than half an hour, girls in all stages of dress and undress were being tumbled into the patrol wagons and taken to the city jail. About one hundred and fifty women were rounded up, abatement actions instituted against the owners, and over fifty houses padlocked and closed for a year. Abe Silver's power was badly crippled.

Cooper's reports of April 22 and 24 were interesting:

> You sure stirred up an awful commotion with your raid, Saturday afternoon, and did you have an interesting conversation with the Chief at nine o'clock that evening? He is supposed to have told Abe that you would. Then we would know whether the girls could get out on bond or not....
>
> We got the tip, but were too late, as you folks were already down there before the A & B cars got there. From what I can hear you got everybody that was working....
>
> It looked like a pimp convention around the A & B today. They were all trying to get their women out. Somebody gave Beers the information that the Klan was going to run all of them out of town. If they do this, the population of Denver will sure go down.

The women were prosecuted by the City in police court, and fined, as usual. Then the Mayor refused to pardon any of them, much to Abe's consternation.

A few days after the abatement cases were filed, a former Denver judge called on the prosecutor. He was in high dudgeon, and claimed that his client, who he said was a most respectable woman, had been insulted by being made a party defendant in an abatement case; that she was absolutely innocent of any wrongdoing, had not the remotest idea of the character of the people who were in her house, was a prominent church worker, and that the outrage had to be rectified at once, the case dismissed, and an apology made to her.

The District Attorney was very sympathetic with the judge, told him that of course it was quite possible a mistake might have been made, and that if the judge would bring his client to the office so that the prosecutor could talk with her, the entire matter might be disposed of. The judge said that they would appear at two o'clock.

Harding and his partner were asked by the Colonel to attend

the conference, but to remain in an anteroom until called for. They had already informed the District Attorney, however, that they had had a personal conversation with the lady, had asked to rent her house, but that she had at first refused to do so because she was getting one hundred and fifty dollars a month for it, from a woman who ran a red-light house. The officers told her they would pay much more money than the girl would who was running it; that they had some girls of their own they wanted to put in there, and that they would pay her two hundred dollars a month, and she had agreed to rent it to them at that figure for that purpose.

The judge and his church-member client appeared on time, and if ever a lady showed indignation, she exhibited all the traits of it. She would hardly speak to the District Attorney, and she was going to have a public apology for this insult to her character. She was asked if she knew the kind of people who were occupying the place, and she said she certainly did not; she would not think of having people like that in a house of hers. And her attorney was even madder than she was. When he reached the height of his emotion, the District Attorney interrupted and said he wanted them to meet two men.

The police officers entered the room, and the woman stiffened in her seat. 'Harding,' said the District Attorney, 'did you ever see this lady before?'

Harding took a notebook out of his pocket and said: 'Yes, sir; we called on her on March 23 at her house on Humboldt Street. We offered to pay her two hundred dollars a month to run a house of prostitution, and she agreed to rent it to us, saying that the girls who were there were only paying her one hundred and fifty dollars a month.'

'Judge,' said the prosecutor, 'are there any questions you and your client desire to ask these officers? Do you still want the public apology to this lady, or would you prefer to contest the case in court? Of course it is possible you will let the matter go by default.'

The judge was strangely quiet. Then he said: 'You can do as you damn please with your case. We are not going to have a thing to do with it.'

The District Attorney stood up. The judge changed his mind again. 'I'll do this much,' he said. 'I will stipulate that you can lock the place up for a year, if you will agree to produce no testimony!'

# XXI

## *Feints*

DECEPTION of the enemy is one of the great arts of successful generals. It is just as important in the constant warfare of Society against the underworld. Two men had to be deceived as to the main attack of the Law, Lou Blonger for one and Ben Eager for the other.

While Eager had helped Koehn carry the lines to the rooms later occupied by Mrs. Steno, he could not be relied upon. But in order to get the dictaphone restored, he had been promised permanent work. Some job had to be found for him where he would not come in contact either with Blonger or with the prosecutor's detectives. It was a puzzle which gave a lot of grief to the prosecutor and to his chief assistant.

Finally Robinson said: 'I have it. Let's put Eager to work on prostitution. Turn him over to me and I'll keep him busy until Blonger is disposed of.'

So Robinson sent for Eager and said, 'Ben, we have a good job for you, and we will put you on the secret pay-roll from funds paid in by the church people. We have shut up most of the red-light district, but some places are still open. We want you to find out all the houses that are operating, who the madams are, the number of girls in each, the owners of the property, how much protection they pay, and to whom. It is to be a very confidential proposition. You are to report to no one but me.

You are never to come near the District Attorney's office, but you are to mail your reports to my house daily, and every so often I will consult with you and go over the situation to see how we are getting along.'

So for weeks, from May until the end of August, Robinson had to think up one excuse after another to keep Eager busy. He had to read his reports and keep in touch with the situation which Eager thought he was developing, all to prevent another flare-up and possible exposure of the main attack.

Eager was easily disposed of, but could Lou Blonger be fooled?

As mail came to Lou's office for the various con-men, Roy Samson would write H. N. Graham to see if he wanted any of them, and what was the latest information about them. Early in June a letter came for Walter Byland, and the Postal Inspector said he wanted him badly on a 1918 job, and would grab Byland when the latter appeared in Denver if it could be done without injury to the District Attorney's plans.

'I will have Roy Nelson, one of our local agents, make the pinch in connection with your office,' said Graham. He forwarded a recent picture of Byland and said: 'Look out for his wife, Gladys. She is a college graduate, good-looking, and as smart a "moll" [woman of the underworld], as there is in the business.'

After a conference it was decided that the arrest of Walter Byland might be a wise move, as the Federals could do it without the prosecutor appearing in the matter in any manner. Nelson could give out the publicity so that the confidence-game end would be well played up. Then the District Attorney's men would pay no attention to Byland at all, and make no effort to see him or anyone connected with his case. Thus some dust might be thrown in Blonger's eyes.

A few days later Walter Byland arrived and promptly called on Lou Blonger. Robert Maiden had studied his picture, and spotted Byland from the observation post. Descending at once, he followed Byland to his home on South Sherman Street, and thus obtained his address.

Maiden then telephoned Roy Samson, who drove up shortly afterwards with Roy Nelson. Maiden reported to them, and then, with Samson, faded out of the picture while Nelson arrested his man.

That afternoon Duff, wildly excited, rushed into the fixer's office, and the 'bug' gave this:

> Duff: 'Byland's arrested. I don't see how in the hell he got pinched down there.'
>
> Blonger: 'Neither do I.'
>
> Duff: 'I wonder who tipped them off.'
>
> Blonger: 'Damned if I know.'
>
> Duff: 'How in the hell did they get onto him, and how did they find out where he lived?' Duff was moving around the office pretty lively, and talking loud and fast. 'There were four fellows on the corner, and when he got on the street car two of them also got on the car; I don't know where the other two went.'

The next day Blonger expressed his opinion:

> Jesus Christ, he is a big ninny; he had the easiest chance in the world to get away and then he lets a Post Office Inspector pinch him!

And the grapevine news came to the District Attorney through Cooper:

> Went in Hogan's place, and Hogan remarked about Byland getting arrested. Also that he and Byland had worked together a great deal, and that they were real partners. They can't figure out how the Government got wise that Byland was here. Hogan said this was for a job that happened two years ago.

For several days neither Lou Blonger nor any of his men paid any attention to Byland, but left him alone in the county jail. And as far as the District Attorney's office was concerned, Byland didn't seem to exist. Duff and Blonger talked a good deal about what they should do with him, but when two weeks had elapsed, Duff said: 'Hell, the District Attorney is dead from the neck up. If he wants any con-man, he wants Walter. And he doesn't even know who he is. Let's spring him.' So they put up the collateral for a bond, Tom Ward went into court, and Walter Byland came out and rejoined the gang.

However, the arrest made the few con-men then in town very scary, so that it was difficult to follow any of them. A new scheme had to be devised which would bring the prosecutor himself face to face with some of the mob.

Arch Cooper had reported that one of the main rendezvous of the gang, and a place where some of them could always be found, was the Black and White Cigar Store at the head of Eighteenth Street, across from Trinity Methodist Church. That store was a bootlegging joint run by Sammy Abrams, whose underworld activities had been described both by Cooper and the anonymous letter-writer. A raid on it was simple to stage.

Edmond Young, the old Quincy Club raider, was again asked to help, and one evening the District Attorney, Ed Young, Roy Samson, and Fred Sanborn visited Sammy's joint. They parked their car about a block away, walked over, rushed into the back room, and found Abrams himself pouring drinks to two customers. In one of the pockets of an old coat on the wall was a bottle of 'moon.' They arrested Sammy, and then made a vigorous pretense of searching the place. But they found no more booze. So the customers were lined up and examined. Luckily both were con-men — Audley H. Potts and William Sturns, the 'Painter Kid' — and their pictures were identified in the District Attorney's private gallery the next morning. Each was wanted by victims for Denver swindles.

The Colonel searched them personally. From their wallets came the regular grafter's traveling paraphernalia — the Metropolitan Bonding Company bond, the clipping of the young man who made the killing on the stock exchange, cards for various aliases, etc. The District Attorney looked at all this stuff, read it carefully, some of it aloud, showed it to his associates, and then said: 'Why, these seem to be respectable business men of rather large means. I see no reason to arrest them.' And returning their property, he added, 'Young, you can turn them loose.'

Half an hour later, when the District Attorney's party returned to their car, Sturns and Potts were sitting on its running board, and two much-wanted con-men had to be politely asked to sit somewhere else instead of being promptly arrested. But their capture at that time would have been fatal. Sturns left town a few days later, and was not seen again by the prosecutor, but Potts kept his headquarters in Denver.

Cooper's report the next day had this:

> I hear that you raided Sammy Abrams but did not find the plant, which had about twenty-four pints of moonshine in it. This is in the same room where you found the bottles in the coat. They think they know who tipped you off, and claim it was a woman.... I wanted to help get Sammy out last night, but they said there was nothing I could do as he was being held for the District Attorney.

A later report said:

> Abe Silver told me that we had a lot of hard work to do to keep Sammy Abrams out of the pen. Said the jury would be drawn September 12th, and it is going to be very necessary to check them....
>
> Audley Potts told me about the raid. Said the District Attorney himself searched them, looked at all their papers and turned them loose.

And Mrs. Steno sent this in from the bug:

> Blonger: 'That fellow don't know anything. The damn fool had both Potts and Painter, and read all their stuff, and doesn't know a con-man's lay-out when he sees it. He's just a big bag of wind, and will never get wise to anything!'

The big fixer himself was falling into the traps. The feints were making headway.

# XXII

## *The 'Big Store' Stays Closed*

June skies were bright, the days were sunny, Colorado's famous tourist weather was at its best, the mountain resorts were filled with visitors, but the great emporium of Lou Blonger and A. W. Duff failed to open. Plenty of 'customers' were on hand, but few 'salesmen' had appeared to offer them their alluring wares. Scattered reports of the month's investigation revealed that the gang chieftain was uncertain what to do.

> I was told today... that there had been a real fast confidence-man in town known as Doc Robinson, but that Duff and Blonger had the chief of police call him to the station and give him orders to leave Denver... I imagine he is one of the boys who don't split. — C.

The mail cover listed a new steerer getting his mail through Blonger — William H. Loftus. His picture was on hand in the District Attorney's picture gallery awaiting his appearance.

A telegram — this time from a bunk who was not wanted:

CHICAGO, ILL. JUNE 7

A. W. DUFF

DENVER

CAN YOU USE GOOD SALESMAN THIS SUMMER?

JOE PERICH

Followed by Duff's curt reply:

DENVER, COLO., JUNE 8

JOE PERICH
CHICAGO
DO NOT COME.

DUFF

I met a fellow this morning named Saul; a big gambler of St. Joe, Mo. He told me the place where the big boys hung out last summer was in the Iron Building.... Saul says that most all the real con-men are at the races in Erie, Pa. Says there is nothing doing here yet as everybody is scared to death of the D. A. — C.

A. H. Potts, the con-man searched at Sammy Abrams, seems to have left Denver. He writes letters to Duff and Byland from Salt Lake City, and sends them, as do all the rest, care of Lou Blonger. — C.

Someone called Blonger on the 'phone and wanted him to 'fix it' for the deputy sheriff that got in trouble here for padding his expense account. — K.

The case couldn't be fixed, and the deputy pleaded guilty to petty larceny and was sent to jail. In 1932, however, he was appointed deputy warden of the very jail in which he had served his time ten years earlier!

I had a talk with Gene Rossi, the gambler, and Duff today. Gene was talking to him about opening up another joint. I imagine that Duff is going to be interested in it.... They are going to open up a taxi stand, bootlegging joint, and gambling house on West Colfax. Will get the address later. — C.

Blonger arrived early. His windows were open part of the time and the outside noises made it very difficult to hear. — Mrs. Steno.

Duff went to the Brown Palace and made straight for the elevator. Greeted Pete Land, the smart city dick, who arose at his approach. Both entered the elevator, and went up. — M.

Hogan tells me that Duff lost $18,000 in the shake down in Miami, Florida, this last winter. Hogan said that during the month of July all the big grafters would be in town and that he would make plenty of money. — C.

Duff and Blonger spoke of the ability of some man to 'pick up' somebody. Duff said, 'I don't know if he can pick up anybody, but I know damn well I am not going to do business with a greenhorn.' Blonger, 'Why, hell, all he has to do is to tell them that he knows everybody between here and New York, and that he corresponds with everybody.' They both laughed. Duff, 'Well, if he comes up here, be G—— d——ed careful what you say to him.'

Duff to Blonger: 'He lost $60,000 on that deal — I really feel sorry for him.' — Mrs. Steno.

At 1.30 there was a Dodge car in front of Dawes' Cigar Store. Hal Crane and a city dick in front seat. Lou Blonger and city dick in rear seat. — K.

Duff showed up at Champa 2 this afternoon. Had a very confidential talk with Beers. — C.

A letter for Les Randle arrives at the gang chieftain's office, from Salt Lake City. Randle's picture is in the gallery. He's a steerer and bookmaker.

Duff was around today talking to Beers and Dago Mike, and Councilman Bert Grub.... Duff spoke to me again today, and said, 'Hello, big boy,' but before this called me by my right name. I imagine they are fixing up something about this new place that they opened on Colfax. They are all interested in it. — C.

Blonger and Duff had quite a talk this morning. Both of his windows were open and the outside noises interfered with me, and I lost considerable valuable dope.... Lou said, 'Every rich man that comes here will want to go to Colorado Springs.' In this same conversation Duff mentioned the Utah sheriff and something about the gang at Salt Lake. Duff also said, 'That bunch won't try to pull anything here. They are too damn afraid of the Government. — K.

Duff: 'I was out to the crap game last night at Mike and Gene's, and I won $200. They only had a bank roll of $1000. It's a five per cent game. Anybody can walk right in there. All the damn cops are around there already trying to collect.'

Lou: 'You ought to stay away from there. You can't be too careful around those places, and that's a swell place to get a reputation.'

Duff: 'That's right.' — Mrs. Steno.

'Phone call... Duff: 'Yes' — 'Who?' — 'Oh, George Belcher' — 'No, there won't be anything doing for a week, over a week.' — 'All right, good-bye.' — Mrs. Steno.

I met Billy Maurice this morning, and he was asking Abe all about Lou Blonger and Hal Crane. He understood that the D. A. was a very tough customer, and that he could not be handled. He remarked that Duff told him that there was nothing much doing yet. Says that some more of the boys would be down in a short time.' — C.

... Later the visitor said: 'I wonder what the S—— B——'s did last night. Did anybody follow you, Lou?' Lou: 'No.' — Mrs. Steno.

Blonger said, 'Hal Crane is trying to get him out of town for me.' — Mrs. Steno.

I was down at Sammie Colby's place this evening. He talked about Mark Tillery getting nine years in El Paso, Texas. He explained that Tillery and his partner were spielers the last two years. He remarked that the Big Store was on Seventeenth Street. 'My God, that conviction will make it tough on Duff,' he said, 'as he will have to get some new store men.' Said that Tillery and his partner, whom he referred to as 'Dutch,' were considered the best in the business. I don't know who Dutch is, but may find out. — C.

More mail at Blonger's office, this time for J. H. French and Roy Farrell, the latter a spieler. Robinson wonders if Farrell is to be the new man in place of Mark Tillery, who is still in Uncle Sam's custody at El Paso.

Visitor: 'What do you think of that deal that was pulled on me?'

Blonger: 'Can't tell what is liable to happen now. That fellow had a detective stopping over at the Adams a couple of months ago, and he was out getting dope on the women and booze, but he left town long ago.' — Mrs. Steno.

'That report sounds good,' said Robinson. 'They haven't discovered Koehn so far.'

3.35 — Woman came up. Judging from the talk she must be a Madam. 'Hello, Lou, what's doing anyway?'

Blonger: 'Not a damn thing. That G—— d—— District Attorney has everything closed tighter than hell.'

Woman: 'What good is it going to do him?'

Blonger: 'He has my place nailed up. I didn't know they were hustling there.'

Woman: 'Of course not.'

Both laughed. Woman: 'Oh, the D. A. is just trying to make a name for himself.' They talked whorehouse and booze for half an hour. — K.

I am satisfied that the man I saw with Duff and at the William Penn Hotel is Jackie French. Will watch the El Tovar apartment, across from Blonger's apartment. — K.

'If French is here, opening time must be near,' said Samson. 'I'm going up with Koehn and look at that fellow myself. You know I was instrumental in sending him to the United States pen at Atlanta, Georgia, for a badger game a few years ago, and I'll know him anywhere.'

So Samson and Koehn hung around the El Tovar for several days, but failed to locate French.

Visitor: 'Duff did pretty good last year, didn't he?'

Blonger: 'Yes.' — K.

A woman came in, no doubt another Madam, and said, 'I came up to say "hello" and "good-bye."'

Blonger: 'Are you going away?'

Woman: 'Yes, there is nothing in this town.'

Blonger and the woman then had a long talk about the D. A. closing up these houses, and so forth. It was brought out that Blonger owns a number of them that were closed up, but he has them leased and says he will hold the parties for the rent. — Mrs. Steno.

I was up at Red Hogan's place this evening, and Walter Byland was there, drinking beer. I only got a peep at him through the door, but Red told me that he just got out on bond. Hogan remarked that he was going to go out of the beer business, that he was going to get him good clothes and go down and see Duff and go to work. — C.

... Gene Rossi and the crap game, and so forth.

Duff: 'I told him to his face I wanted square dice.' Someone won $500. — Mrs. Steno.

July came, and still the con-men mark time.

# XXIII

## *The* 1922 *Fishing Season Opens*

THREE detectives were on the job, and they and five persons in the District Attorney's office were delving into the activities of the con-men. Evidence had been assembled against about thirty of the Seventeenth Street gang, but the whereabouts of most of them were unknown. The Big Store was closed, and only Lou Blonger, 'Kid' Duff, Walter Byland, and two or three steerers were in town. All the other grafters stayed away.

Cooper reported: 'The bunch are all complaining that they never saw the town so dead, that only a few con-men are in town, when ordinarily at this time of the year the place would be lousy with them.'

One of two things appeared to have happened: either the enemy had slipped away and was attacking the Law elsewhere, or it was forming for a quiet attack in an unexpected manner. The wise old fixer was playing a very cautious game.

When Blonger had returned from the South in April, Cooper's reports showed that some of the mob drifted into town a few days later, but had left almost as soon as they came. Mail had arrived for several gangsters at Blonger's office, but, with the exception of Byland, the crooks had failed to claim it. Underworld talk had set the dates for the opening of the Big Store for various times in June, and Duff himself wired that it would open about July first. But the middle of that month arrived and the joint was not even established.

The only thing to do was to eliminate the District Attorney from the picture. He had made an unpopular move in prosecuting a murderer for insanity rather than for murder, and this gave the Ku Klux Klan, which was then beginning to come into the picture and which the District Attorney had fought a few weeks before, a chance to attack him. So it had instituted recall proceedings against him, which were enthusiastically joined in by Blonger, the City Hall crowd, and the underworld, and petitions were actively circulated. But they never obtained enough names to file the recall. However, the threatened attack was a blessing in disguise to the District Attorney because it braced up the con-men.

About this time the prosecutor held a conference with his men, and they decided that it was necessary for him to get out of town, ostensibly on a long vacation, so as to give the mob a chance to come to Denver.

Accordingly, he announced in places where it would carry far through underground circles — to Hal Crane, the chief deputy sheriff, to John Drake, the warden of the county jail, and to the police — that he had not had a vacation in a year and a half, and that he was going to the mountains where he could not be reached by telephone, and that he intended to forget all about the office for the rest of the summer. He stated that Kenneth Robinson would be in charge of everything, during his vacation, and that whatever Kenneth said would go.

Robinson quite actively followed around after his chief, and, among others, called on Hal Crane. 'Hal,' he said, 'the boss is going away for the summer and is leaving me in charge. Last summer we raised hell all through the hot weather. We raided the Quincy Club and Julius Epstein, and several other gambling-houses and bootleg parlors, and this spring we cleaned up the row, and, if he thinks I am going to go on the rampage while he is gone, he has another guess coming. I am going to take it easy and am not going to look for any evidence of any kind against anybody. If this office does any business while I am running it, it is going to fall in my lap; if possible my lap won't hold it.'

These conversations were promptly repeated by Crane and others to Blonger, and a lot of them were heard over the dictaphone, showing that the tip-off system was in excellent working order. An underworld rumor, reported by Cooper, stated that the District Attorney would be out of town for thirty days and that it had cost the gang five thousand dollars to get rid of him. Cooper wondered if Crane had shaken someone down on the claim that he was responsible for the vacation, and ended his report with the statement, 'The mob expects to make its winter money during the month that you are gone.'

A few days later the Colonel left for his vacation, accompanied by his family, telling no one except Robinson and Samson where he was going. The place was a little mountain resort near Mount Audubon, some sixty miles in the hills. It had a telephone, and he was in constant communication by mail and wire with Denver. Kenneth Robinson also drove up two or three times a week, in the big Packard of one of the subscribers to the investigation funds, to deliver the written reports of the detectives, while anything requiring immediate action was handled over the telephone in code. Robinson had all the worst of the bargain, as the Packard owner had a hobby that Bacon wrote Shakespeare, and he used these trips to prove his points.

The District Attorney, to the underworld, was out of Denver, but he knew what the con-men were doing, and he gave them rope for a month. The only question was, Who was the rope going to hang, the con-men or the District Attorney?

No sooner had the prosecutor left town than letters and telegrams went out from Blonger and Duff to the fraternity, telling them that 'the fishing season would open' in a few days, and that they would be glad to have 'fishermen' and 'salesmen' come to Denver for the season — and they came by the scores.

Four days later Mrs. Steno picked up a telephone number which led Koehn to Room 316, Shirley-Savoy Hotel. Here he found one George S. Dover, of Kansas City, a short, heavy-set, florid-complexion fellow, who was very much on the job. Dover answered the description of one of the men seen by Tate with Blonger and Duff at Hot Springs.

Con-men soon began to make a rendezvous of the place. Duff was there frequently and telephone calls were numerous. Dover likewise had many conferences with the fixer himself, at the latter's office. The main forces of the enemy were rapidly concentrating for the summer campaign.

Dover's real name was soon found to be George Belcher. He had already served three penitentiary terms for picking pockets and grand larceny, and in addition had been tried and acquitted for the killing of a policeman.

Cooper saw that many con-men were hanging around Sammy Abrams' place, although they carefully avoided Phil Dawes's cigar store, which was the hangout of the big fellows — Blonger, Duff, Crane, the deputy sheriff, and Land and Lusk, the two city dicks.

One of the steerers in Sammy's place was overheard to say, 'G—— d—— Duff, he don't own the whole circumference, and if we had a bank roll we would work anyway.' It looked as if Duff were ordering some more out of town.

Then Jackie French, the chief bookmaker, and the big shot of the con-men, who personally met the suckers, called upon Blonger, and was greeted with loud cries of delight, and warmly congratulated upon his big clean-up of over a quarter of a million dollars in his big week in Florida during the winter. French was dressed in the height of fashion, and exuded prosperity.

'There's a hitch to that, however,' said French. 'Because of the big reward offered for my arrest, I'm going to lay low this summer, and play around in the mountains and have a good time. But if you need me on a big case, I'll book for you, otherwise use Randle.'

Samson and Koehn again checked up on French, and found him living in an expensive apartment with Buda Godman, whom Inspector Graham had mentioned as French's accomplice in the Pullman-car badger game. She had the alias of Helen Strong, and when not with French was the mistress of the owner of one of the Big League ball clubs.

As soon as Samson found French and Buda together, he wanted to arrest both, and get the big reward for French. 'We'll need a lot more funds before this is over, and that money will help a lot,' he told Robinson. But the latter absolutely forbade French being molested at that time.

Sammy Abrams said that the Big Store would open on the twenty-sixth. Police captains and Crane were in frequent meetings with Blonger, and Crane was very much relied on by the fixer, who telephoned him every morning at the West Side Courthouse to make sure that the District Attorney was still away. Oliver Smith drove to Sammy Abrams and gave him some information about the contents of affidavits on the District Attorney's desk. Both Crane and Smith were doing their best.

And then, July 28, in answer to a telephone call, came these words from Blonger: 'Do you know where to find anybody... 729 17th Street is the "Lookout."' Later that day Blonger called the telephone office and ordered a telephone put in Room 5 of that building in the name of A. L. Long, to be installed at once.

This was the 1922 headquarters, the 'Lookout,' whatever that term might mean. But the Big Store was now going full blast. George Belcher seemed to spend most of his time sitting in the window watching the street, just as W. S. Patterson, the Federal narcotic man, had seen a man doing a year earlier. A short, slender fellow, with a slight mustache and little chin, was frequently seen to be carrying a small suitcase in and out of the building. He answered the description of the other man seen at the Arlington Hotel in Hot Springs. Numerous men, rapidly identified as members of the mob, were coming in and out.

Roy Farrell, a spieler, whose mail had preceded him by weeks, rented an apartment near French, and lived there with his wife. The con-men, as they came to town, stopped at hotels, apartments, or boarding-houses, or even rented furnished homes, dependent upon their financial means of the moment. At night ten or fifteen would meet in the Civic Center and talk things over.

One day Koehn watched a con-man trying to pick up a man and his wife, but after half an hour the steerer gave it up in disgust. Andy asked them, 'Who was that man who spoke to you?' And the old fellow answered: 'I don't know. He just came over and talked and talked, and was so inquisitive and wanted to know everything about me. But I have met his kind before and didn't tell him anything.'

Blonger made several calls upon the Mayor and the Manager of Safety, Koehn getting the time of the appointments from the dictaphone, and going over to the City Hall to see that they were kept. And they were kept, to the minute, in all cases.

Lou talked daily to his visitors about the District Attorney, though mostly about the detective who had been across the street.

And the District Attorney's assistants got a real kick from Lou's complaint that some cop was getting too big a rake-off from him — but he paid it.

On August 9, Koehn spotted twenty-three con-men. Three he followed to their hotels and located their rooms by watching the key numbers given them by the clerks. The proprietor of one of the hotels was an old friend from St. Louis, and through him Andy located five at that hostelry.

But one man, whose automobile license was issued to one J. D. Brady, turned out to be a real find. Six of the men had been sitting on a bench in the Civic Center, and then walked to the Melton Hotel near-by. All went up the steps, and in a few moments Koehn saw a window light up at the end of the hall. So he went in and paid for the nearest room.

In a few minutes another visitor came up, gave three light taps on the door, and was admitted. So Andy got partly undressed and went out in the hall close to Brady's door, where he heard this:

> Brady: 'I rang up Duff and he told me it was all right with him if it suited us.'
>
> Another said: 'There ought to be a reserve fund for the steerers.'
>
> Brady: 'I bet you nothing like this ever happens again, that we have to wait for a District Attorney to go out of town before we open up.'
>
> Another: 'Stanley last year got an easy $25,000 deal at Manitou.'
>
> A third man: 'What do you think of that fellow I had two days and he committed suicide.'
>
> Brady: 'The steerers are sure getting the tough breaks this year. We had the same trouble down in Florida also.... It's discouraging, but I'll ring up Duff and let you know tomorrow.'

The next day Andy identified as Brady the picture of A. B. Cooper, alias Tex, a big spieler, one of the men mentioned by Inspector Graham.

Duff and Belcher were seen in front of the Denham Theater Building, handing out what appeared to be blue checks to several con-men. Later it was found that these were money orders sent by Charles F. Dixon from Salt Lake City, the man whose box of paraphernalia Harry Williamson had seized in the summer of 1921. Dixon had just made a $25,000 killing, and was paying his debts to his fellow gangsters.

And Koehn saw Steerer Stephen J. Olsen pick up a sucker at the station — a farmer with a cheap suitcase, and take him to an hotel. Andy got both names and addresses from the register.

Con-men were rapidly overrunning the city. Steerers, sizing up the tourists in their search for suckers, were walking up and down the principal business streets, loitering on corners, and sitting on the benches in the Civic Center and State Capitol grounds. A particular hang-out, where large numbers of them gathered daily, was the stoop of the Albany Hotel at Seventeenth and Stout Streets. Here they sought to intercept out-of-town visitors when they purchased their home papers at the street news-stand. Victims were being picked up right and left, under the eyes of the detectives and police, and with no molestation.

The O.P. for Blonger's office was no longer needed, the dictaphone was enough to cover him. The fixer was not now important. What was needed at once was observation of the main forces of the enemy, the army of con-men on the streets. Their names, personal descriptions, and residences were imperative.

The Crest Hotel, across from the Albany, offered possibilities for a new O.P., so a room was secured on its third floor. Koehn, from behind drawn curtains, put the field-glasses on the con-men, and, aided by the pictures, rapidly made identifications. Another O.P. was then secured in a house across the street from the apartments of French and Farrell, and Maiden manning it obtained definite data on that important pair and their associates.

By this time Roy Samson had compiled from the detectives' reports a list of sixty-three known and suspected con-men then operating in Denver. About half were called by their correct names; where these were not known, some were described by letters, and still others by physical classifications, like 'Slim Blacky,' 'Blind Man,' 'Thick Lips,' and 'Artist's Cap.' A few of the names were duplicates, but it was the best list that could then be made.

Samson, without eliminating the descriptive names, which were valueless outside the office, with the same thoughtlessness that had characterized the District Attorney's early action in sending the Duff letter to Kansas City, mailed this list to Irvin

B. Bruce, the Captain of Detectives at Colorado Springs. That city was then having its annual rodeo, and Samson believed that a large number of the Denver gang would be there to pick up suckers among the spectators, so that they could bring them to Denver for a killing.

Samson asked Bruce to arrest any of the men on the list and to mug and finger-print them and get their personal identifications, and then run them out of Colorado Springs. Captain Bruce, of course, would have to turn them loose, anyway, because he had nothing on them, and that treatment at Colorado Springs would not alarm them, as they were accustomed to being kicked out whenever they were picked up in that city.

However, Bruce posted the list on the Colorado Springs police bulletin board. Pete Land and George Lusk happened to be two of Denver's 'friendly' detectives who were in the group of outside officers called in to help guard Colorado Springs from foreign racketeers. They and all the others were given copies of the list, and they soon found out that it had been prepared in the District Attorney's office in Denver.

Pete at once got 'sick' and returned to Denver and rushed to Blonger's office. Maiden had gone back to the old O.P. for a few minutes and saw him enter the room, and the dictaphone spluttered this much:

'Hey, Blonger, here's something you had better look into. It's Van Cise's list.'

Blonger carefully read over a sheet of paper which Land handed him, and said: 'What of it? You fellows are still with me, and that fellow can't make an arrest without using the police.'

Land said, 'You know us, Lou.'

Just then Duff came in and the three of them sat close together, and their whispers were inaudible over the 'dick.'

But all the District Attorney then knew was the conversation in Blonger's office; the other facts were developed later. By that time seventy-five con-men were at work in Denver.

Then Kenneth Robinson sent in a hurry call for his chief in the mountains.

'Return at once,' he said, and intimated that there was danger of a tip-off unless the attack was made immediately.

# XXIV

## *Orders for the Attack*

Daniel Webster is said to have planned many of his cases while on his fishing trips. The District Attorney spent the larger portion of his vacation studying the public enemy, Blonger's underworld gang, and the details of the final attack against it.

In the army before a battle order is issued, the commander makes an estimate of the situation, in which he first considers the plans open to the enemy and attempts to determine the one which his antagonist most logically will adopt. Then he turns to the plans available to himself, and tries to select the one which offers him the most promise of success.

In fighting the underworld the army system is a big help in solving the problem, particularly when the antagonist is organized.

Only two plans were open to Blonger's gang, to close the store at once, or to keep running until things became too dangerous to operate. The fact that, in the face of all the information which Blonger possessed about the District Attorney, the fixer had assembled his men and commenced operations was proof that he was not going to close unless some unexpected development occurred. Therefore, it was safe to assume that his plan was to run throughout the summer, and that the Law could await the proper time to strike.

The plans available to the District Attorney were numerous:

1. To use the city police.

This was not to be considered for a moment. If they were called upon, one of two things would happen, either no arrests at all would be made, or two or three young steerers would be locked up in order to put up a front, while the rest of the gang would be allowed to escape.

2. To use either the regular city or county jail, maintained by the taxpayers, to incarcerate criminals.

Equally preposterous. The first batch of prisoners would be duly locked up, but the tip-off system would prevent any further arrests.

3. To use only the six younger deputy district attorneys, Kenneth W. Robinson, Roy O. Samson, Fred W. Sanborn, Lewis D. Mowry, Bernard A. Gates, and Andrew J. Reynolds, together with the three detectives, Koehn, Cooper, and Maiden.

This was unwise because the investigators had to be kept under cover for future developments, while six deputies were not a large enough force for the task. These six had had some experience with criminals, but Samson was the only deputy who was trained in making arrests. They might be used, however, as the directing officers in the raid.

4. To use former officers of the World War.

This was also rejected, because they lacked experience in handling prisoners. But they might be used as car drivers in the patrol cars to carry the arresting forces.

5. To use the State Rangers.

This offered real possibilities.

6. To arrest the gang at once.

This would insure the arrest of the mob and avoid any danger of a slip and of the gang jumping out. But the conviction of the crooks, not their mere arrest, was the objective, and more evidence must still be obtained.

7. To arrest the gang while they were swindling a sucker.

If the exchange was raided when a victim was only in the initial stages of winning big money, he would be so sold on the game that he would accuse the District Attorney of interfering with his business, would be hard to convince that he was the victim of a crooked deal, and would be a poor witness at best. If the attack was delayed until the boob took his cash to the Store, he might even lose his money despite the best efforts of the District Attorney's men to prevent it. To plant a phoney sucker on the con-men, have them pick him up as a victim, and then arrest the mob in the act, and with that as the immediate excuse for the raid, seemed far more practicable.

There was so much about the manner in which the Blonger gang had to be attacked that was unusual, there was so much that at first might even be deemed outrageous by both the ultra-conservatives and the liberal elements, that the evidence had to be overwhelming, and the round-up, at least of all the leaders, completely successful. No halfway result would suffice.

The plan of attack had finally been settled when a sleet storm immured the District Attorney under a projecting rock on a precipitous peak near the Fair Glacier in Boulder County, Colorado. The plan was to plant a phoney sucker on Blonger; to arrest the gang while the play on him was in progress; to use the State Rangers in plain clothes, directed by the deputies, all of whom were now to be let in on the secret; to use former World War officers as car drivers; to secure a centrally located building as a private jail, and there hold the gang incommunicado until all were rounded up.

Two men were found who agreed to act as dupes. One, J. W. Bryan, a well-to-do Nebraska farmer, and the other, Hoxie Thompson, a prosperous lumber dealer of Houston, Texas. The latter was an intimate friend of Doctor W. H. Scherrer, of Dallas, who had lost twenty-five thousand dollars to the mob in 1920, and who later figured in Fox's and Fuller's dealings with Blonger.

They were told to visit all the haunts of the con-men, to buy papers at the Albany news-stand, to sit on the benches at the Civic Center, and just to act naturally, except to be willing to talk to strangers. They took up the task with vigor.

Meanwhile, the major problem was to find a jail. No ideas about its location came to the District Attorney while in the mountains, except that it must be located in a neighborhood where the movements of men would not arouse suspicion, and in a section where no con-men lived.

Upon the Colonel's return he scoured the town for warehouses or large buildings which might be suitable. Finally the solution came. His church, the First Universalist, on the corner of Colfax and Lafayette, had no minister, was temporarily closed, and was ideally located for a jail. It was on a main street, and was set back on the alley in the rear of a large lot. On the north side of it was a passageway about three feet wide, blocked off by a high fence. The patrol cars carrying the gangsters could drive down the alley from the north and stop in back of the church. Then the Rangers could conduct their prisoners west on the narrow sidewalk, and before reaching the front of the church drop out of sight down the outside basement stairs and deliver the gangsters to the guards below. Then the car and Rangers could drive off after a delay of only a few moments.

The basement was deep in the ground, and contained a large room, with high ceiling and barred windows. By blocking all but one door, it made a good cell room. A stairway led to the first floor, where there was a small study, with bookcases and cupboards. The second floor, at the same end of the church, was the kindergarten. The church auditorium itself was locked up and was not to be used in any manner.

The arrangement was almost made to order. The prisoners could be herded in the basement room, and a rope blockade built to keep them twenty feet from the door. The first-floor quarters were fixed for clerks and the storage of evidence seized during the arrests, while the third floor became attack headquarters, where the telephones were installed, and the gang records and pictures kept.

The first thing to do was to secure the Rangers, a partially trained organization of State police with which Colorado was then experimenting. They were stationed at various places around the State, but were handicapped by being called on to enforce the Prohibition Law. In the membership were some excellent men, former soldiers, who had plenty of nerve, and who knew how to take orders.

As the District Attorney was a State officer he called upon the Chief Executive of the State without whose command the State police would not operate in Denver. Governor Oliver H. Shoup was given the inside story of the gangsters and at once issued an order to Colonel Patrick J. Hamrock, commander of the Rangers, that his men were subject to the orders of the District Attorney, and that they were to obey his instructions without any questions. Colonel Hamrock was asked to have fifteen of his best men under marching orders, ready to move at a minute's notice, all of them in plain clothes, but to have their uniforms with them.

Three meetings were now necessary to organize the attack and issue the proper orders; one with those on the force who were in the secret, in order to get their suggestions and advice for the raid; one with the six deputies, three detectives, and volunteers for duty at the church; and one with the car drivers. Then all that would be necessary would be to flash the day and the hour, in army parlance called 'D' day and 'H' hour, and the attack could start.

The first of these meetings reviewed the evidence to date, and brought suggestions from all, but the best were given by Andy Koehn as to the actual manner of arrests on the streets.

After a session of several hours the meeting broke up so the District Attorney could prepare and issue final orders at a later gathering. When this convened, the three deputies who had just been admitted to the secret were present for the first time. They could hardly believe that an investigation had been going on in the office for so long a period without their knowledge.

The detailed orders for the attack were then given by the Colonel:

'This meeting and all that is said here is secret, and is to be revealed to no one until our operations are completed.

'Lou Blonger is the head of Denver's protected underworld. For eighteen months this office has been investigating his activities. He has about seventy-five con-men operating in Denver with the knowledge of the authorities. The police force is involved, and neither they nor the regular jails can be used in any manner. We lack evidence, however, to arrest any officials or police.

'Koehn, Maiden, and Cooper are the detectives who have been working on the job, Robinson has been on the high spots, and Samson and Sanborn on details.

'In a very short time, at a date and hour to be later fixed, but in daylight, we will round up this gang and hold them incommunicado in the First Universalist Church as a jail. You are not to leave town or be out of touch with a telephone until this work is finished.

'The attack will be led by you six deputies, Robinson, Samson, Sanborn, Mowry, Gates, and Reynolds. Robinson will be on special work early in the day and the rest of the time at the church. Samson will arrest Duff and clean up the con-men's headquarters at 729 Seventeenth Street and then the stock exchanges; Sanborn will arrest Blonger, and the others will have special details as later assigned, generally picking up con-men at apartments, hotels, and on the streets.

'Koehn, Maiden, and Cooper will scout the town, followed by patrol cars, and point out the con-men, but must not allow the gang to identify them.

'Harold Healey, L. W. Linville, Harold Webster, and Cheney Bagby have volunteered their services for duty at the church. Linville and Webster will thoroughly search all prisoners, take all documentary evidence and identify it to each prisoner by the initials of each. They will also take all money and jewelry, and give complete receipts for the same, and have a duplicate signed by the prisoner, if possible. The data from each man will be securely kept in a canvas bag, and turned over to Healey, who will keep all under lock and key. Bagby will man the telephones and direct the patrol cars.

'The State Rangers will participate. Some in uniform will guard the inside of the church and allow no one to enter without a pass from me. Six in plain clothes will be paired with the deputies and will make the actual arrests. The remainder of the Rangers will be held at the church as a reserve.

'I will be at the headquarters on the third floor.'

Two particular warnings were also given to the men.

'Look out for the "office,"' continued the District Attorney. 'That is the underworld's high sign for an officer, is a warning that an arrest is imminent, and when it is given is a request that the associates of the criminal and his lawyer shall be notified immediately that he is in jail so that steps can be taken to get him out. The "office" is given by opening and closing either half of the coat, meaning that there is an officer's star on the vest underneath.

'Watch your prisoner's hands all the time so that they neither flash the office nor tear up documentary evidence. Do not let them throw away anything, even a newspaper.

'You will find these gentry easy to handle. They are accustomed to fixing and will not resist capture. Koehn suggests that, where street arrests are made, the Ranger step up on one side of the man and the deputy on the other. Then show him your badges, tell him the District Attorney wants to see him, put him in the car, and bring your man to the church.

'Watch out for the women. All their "molls" are in this racket, and are the worst grapevine we face. If you arrest a con-man in a room with a girl, telephone in and we will send some woman back to stay there with a Ranger to guard her, until we are through. If the women get wise, the arrests are over.'

Other details kept the meeting in session until after midnight.

Robert G. Bosworth, a lawyer, and Paul Loughridge, a bond man, both very prominent Denver citizens, selected the prospective car drivers. They assembled fifteen outstanding men, former officers in the War, at Loughridge's house. All that their guests knew in advance of the meeting was that they were to drive automobiles, when called upon to do so, in rounding up gangsters. The same instructions were given to them that had been announced to the deputies.

'In addition to these orders,' said the Colonel, 'you are to park your cars a block from the church, and show no activity of any kind around that building. I want no more than one car at a time delivering prisoners. Hold the others back.'

Enthusiastically these men agreed to help in the work. Their names appear with the personnel in the Addenda, and they rendered wonderful service on the day of the raid. All promised absolute silence and to be ready on an instant's notice to join in the attack on the gang.

Here was a hand-picked group of men, carefully selected after much thought by Bosworth and Loughridge, and yet one of them talked! John Green, one of the men, a bachelor who lived with his parents, had no car of his own, but always secured his father's when he wanted it. He went home and told the latter that he had a business matter coming up in the next day or two on which he would want to use the car the entire day, and just wanted to make sure that it was available.

The father, for some unaccountable reason, demanded the details. The son refused to give them. The father then said unless he knew what the car was going to be used for he could not have it. The son then told the father what the plan was, and at once an explosion occurred. 'That G—— d——ed District Attorney!' said the father. 'I wouldn't help him in anything. I wouldn't give him anything. You can't use my car for any purpose of his. I know Blonger and I am going down and tell him all about it.'

The old man was stubborn. The boy begged and pleaded

with his father that his honor was involved, that he had promised to keep his mouth shut, and that Blonger must not be told, and the old man just as vigorously stated that he had signed and was circulating a petition for the prosecutor's recall, and that he was going to block anything he tried to do.

The attack was almost ready to start, the enemy were in utter ignorance of their impending doom, and now a venomous old man was bent upon the utter destruction of months of effort. The success of the Law hung in the balance.

# XXV

## *The Three-Time Sucker*

THE first thing the next morning, Green went to Bosworth's office and told his troubles. Bosworth promptly notified the District Attorney of the danger to their plans. Here was a nice kettle of fish. The trap was all set, almost ready to spring, the con-men were busily plying their trade, and now a hitherto unknown enemy threatened to ruin the entire situation.

Very shortly, Bosworth thought of a friend of the old man, located that party, told him the situation, and put it up to him that he should take the fellow out of town for a day or so and get him out of the way until the raid. Luckily Green's father had not yet seen Blonger, so the scheme worked, and another barrier was jumped.

In the meantime J. W. Bryan and Hoxie Thompson had been hanging around for days, trying their best to arouse the interest of the con-men, but with no success whatsoever. It began to look as if the plan of a phoney sucker was to fail. Then, entirely by chance, and with the greatest kind of luck, came J. Frank Norfleet, of Hale Center, Texas, a man who had been twice trimmed as a sucker by confidence men, who had then turned detective and followed his crooks all over the country, landing them one after another in the penitentiary, the man who was the nemesis of the bunco-steerers. Frank Norfleet, trailing the last man of the guilty gang which stole his $45,000 in Texas in December of 1919, reached Denver about the twelfth of August.

If ever there was a he-man, Norfleet was it, but he did not look the part. Instead of the steely gray eyes of fiction, he had watery blue ones. Instead of the powerful, crushing grip of the man-killer, he had a soft and flaccid paw. Instead of being tall and broad-shouldered, he was a little fellow about five feet six inches tall, weighing about one hundred and twenty-five pounds, and had a soft, drawling Texas voice.

He was the kind that fooled you, one whom you would pass on the street without noticing, and yet he was as brave and fearless a man as ever rode the Western plains. He toted one gun in a shoulder holster under his left arm; he had another one stuck under his trousers in front, and he carried a pair of handcuffs in his right-hand hip pocket. He was quick on the draw, a dead shot, and knew how to put the handcuffs on his man and take him along. Hated and feared by the con-men, he would have been instantly murdered by any of them at the least possible opportunity, and whenever Frank started after them, he took his life in his hands.

That the mob would unhesitatingly kill a known enemy, and especially Norfleet, was revealed to the District Attorney by Walter Byland some six weeks later.

'We picked up Norfleet as a sucker for the second time in Jacksonville, Florida,' said Byland. 'We started to take him out to the Everglades, where we had a swell Southern home all fixed up as a pool-room for betting on horse-races. We thought Frank was a real boob, but Joe Furey, the man Norfleet was after, was sitting on the piazza of one of the hotels as we went by, and recognized him. He sent us a note, stating that the chump was Norfleet, and to grab him, tie him up with baling wire, rap him over the head, and throw him in the lake during the night. We intended to do it, but Norfleet beat us to it and got away.'

In January, Thomas Lee Woolwine, District Attorney of Los

Angeles, had told Kenneth Robinson about Norfleet and the office had then communicated with him, as it did with every victim of the con-men whose names were obtained. This had been of material assistance in getting identifications and fixing the personnel of the Denver gang. Norfleet had given all the information he possessed and promised to visit the District Attorney if he ever came to Denver.

The Texan found that his last man, W. B. Spencer, alias 'Whitey Harris,' was at Albuquerque, New Mexico, trailed him there, and was told he had come to Denver, and he then started for Colorado's capital city. Luckily he stopped off in Colorado Springs. There he saw 'Dad' Bruce, the square captain of detectives, who told him about the prosecutor's plans and to be very careful when he came to Denver and to stay under cover until he saw the right man in the District Attorney's office. Consequently, Norfleet dyed his mustache and hair, which were white, a dark brown, and registered at a little hotel under the name of Mullican. Bruce told him to see the District Attorney, Robinson, or Samson. He went to the office, found the two former away, and was taken down to Samson's room in the basement.

Roy said: 'Glad to see you, Norfleet, but for God's sake keep out of sight. If the con-men find you are here, you will spoil the work of fifteen months. We will help you locate your man Spencer; we will help you take him back to Texas; but don't go out-of-doors in the daytime, and if you go around at night, keep off the main streets and out of leading hotels.'

Frank agreed that he would, and kept his promise for a week. Then he heard that a Texas friend of his was stopping at the Brown Palace Hotel, and the urge of one longhorn for another brought him trotting up the street early in the morning to say 'Howdy' — and how he said it!

As he started into the Brown Palace Hotel, Denver's best hostelry, two of the gang happened to be inside its portals looking for a sucker, and here came one made to order. Frank looked like the type that would never know you a second time. He was still a countryman rubbering at the sights, enjoying the big city, and so, on the nineteenth of August he was braced by Leon Felix, alias Jew Felix, under the name of R. C. Davis, and picked up as a sucker for the third time in his life.

Norfleet was easy to approach because he was looking around in the lobby, trying to find his friend, and Davis said to him, 'Are you looking for someone?'

Frank said, 'Yes.'

Davis wanted to know if he could be of any service to him.

Frank said, 'No, my party is not here.'

Another con-man, an ex-safe-blower, named Robert Knowles, was with Davis. The two of them talked for a little while, asking him where he came from, and who he was. He told them his name was Mullican and he lived at Farris, Texas, thirty-seven miles south of Dallas, and that he had a farm of three hundred and fifty-five acres.

Norfleet, of course, at once recognized that he was in the hands of a gang, and decided to play along awhile and see what happened. And he certainly told some yarn about that farm.

He said he could lease his farm for oil, which was a lot easier than raising a crop on it. Davis told him that he was lonesome, that his wife had gone home, and said he was from the South, that he was glad to meet a fellow Southerner, and if Mullican would like to go for a drive, he would be glad to take him for one. Norfleet did not want to go for a ride, but desired to get rid of him, so told Davis he had to go down to the Western Union Telegraph Office to send a telegram, and to the railroad office to get a ticket to go home.

Davis said, 'Well, you know, I am really fixing to go home myself and I want to go to the general ticket office also, so I will take you down there in my car.'

So they went outside and Davis got into a big Cadillac which was standing at the curb, and they drove to the Western Union

Office, and then to Frank's hotel, the Columbia. First, however, Davis took him for a short ride around town.

He said, 'Money comes in pretty slow nowadays unless a man happens to get into some speculation.'

Frank said, 'Yes, I guess so; it is pretty slow in the farming business.'

And so they talked over Norfleet's land proposition, and Davis wanted to know how much Frank could get for it. Norfleet's shrewdness now becomes manifest. He said he had one hundred acres leased for one hundred and fifty dollars an acre and his wife was offered a lease on two hundred and thirty-six acres at two hundred dollars an acre. That would leave nineteen acres of his oil land; he thought he would keep that.

Norfleet asked Davis how speculating was done, figuring that he would see how well Davis knew his part. So the latter said that a few days ago he had talked with Judge Brady, of Kansas City, one of the Supreme Court Judges down there, and Brady told him about a young friend of his who got quite a write-up in the newspaper, the paper saying that some rather mysterious young man had cleaned up $125,000 in the stock exchange, and had set out to break up the bucket shops, and had done it. Davis said, 'I sure hope I can meet that young fellow sometime and get him to help me make some money.'

At the Western Union Office Frank wrote a telegram to Mrs. Mullican at Farris, Texas, telling her not to sign the oil lease on the balance of the land, that he thought he was going to get far more for it in Denver, and to wait until she heard from him. He showed the telegram to Davis, and sent it. Norfleet had a hard time shaking Davis until he told him he had to write some letters and tend to business, and made an appointment to meet him at the Brown Palace Monday, August 21. Norfleet's next statement to Davis was a consummate bit of keen thinking.

'Davis,' he said, 'when I go up there to the Brown Palace on Monday, I won't know you again. You know I am nothing but a cowpuncher, and I am not used to city fellers like you with your creased pants and white collars; you all look alike to me. So when I get there and look around, you will have to come up and find me.'

As soon as Norfleet reached his room he telephoned Kenneth Robinson, and shortly afterwards was closeted with him, telling him the whole story. The result was that that night at the prosecutor's house Norfleet, Robinson, Samson, and the Colonel decided that Norfleet was the man; that he should stay with the gang, and lead the way to the inside of the stock exchange, and that the arrests would be made there while the crooks were in the act of trimming Norfleet.

However, there was great danger that the Denver police might arrest Norfleet for carrying a gun. It would be most unwise to try to get a permit for him, and hence he was stripped of all his artillery, and Norfleet, without his guns, without his handcuffs, without his personal means of protection against a bunch of desperate crooks, was a different individual. Afraid of no man who walked the earth as long as he had his trusty weapons for protection, Norfleet was as helpless as a child when they were taken from him, and more or less timid in consequence, but he was game.

He was assured that he would be covered every step he made by gunmen who were as fast on the trigger as he was, and he said, 'All right, boys, I will go through,' and he did. That night Norfleet said: 'Do you know, boys, when I got the Colonel's first letter I didn't know whether to answer it or not, as I wasn't sure I could trust you to help me get Spencer. I have had so many dealings with crooked police and sheriffs that I am afraid of every man whose job it is to catch or prosecute criminals.'

When Norfleet left the District Attorney's house, he was told to come back Monday night, when further plans would be made.

# XXVI

## *Norfleet Fixes 'D' Day and 'H' Hour*

THE next day Andy Koehn, in covering Norfleet as he walked around the town, saw Duff meet William H. Loftus, a prominent steerer, by the stoop of the Albany Hotel. Duff at once called Loftus aside, and unfolded a two-column typewritten list and showed it to him. They had quite an earnest discussion about it, and beckoned to several other con-men, who seemed somewhat excited when they read it. But Koehn could not get close enough to hear the talk or see the writing and had to move on to keep the Texas cowpuncher in sight.

Monday morning Norfleet strolled into the Brown Palace Hotel, rubbering around like the veriest rube, and in a few minutes was picked up by Davis, who took him on a drive out to the park and around town, and up over Lookout Mountain. They talked a lot about Norfleet's finances, and how much money he had in the bank, and whether he could raise money quickly, and Norfleet told him that was easy, any bank in Texas would lend him money on his farm and his leases.

'In order to get it,' said Norfleet, 'I told Davis all I had to do was to take the train home and go to the bank. Davis seemed to like that idea, and kept me out until dinner-time, when he took me back to my hotel.'

That night Norfleet attended the conference already referred to, where the preliminary plans for the attack were made. The 'mysterious stranger' was due to show up the next day, and there was a possibility that Norfleet might not be able to get away Tuesday night. He was given special delivery envelopes addressed to 'M. Reeves,' the name used by the District Attorney for all special mail sent to his house. He was told that if he wished to communicate with the District Attorney to use one of those envelopes, or, if it was imperative to telephone, to use the secret number, and in any event to telephone from the office of the Smedley Dental Group at 10 A.M. Wednesday.

The head of this office was Doctor William P. Smedley, one of the finest and squarest professional men in Denver. It was the largest dental office in Denver, occupying most of one floor of a large building, and offered an excellent chance to shake off an accompanying con-man. Besides, a toothache is the best excuse to offer at any time when you want to get away from people. Norfleet was told that, if any of the con-men accompanied him, they would be required to stay in the anteroom, and that he would be taken alone to the dentist's private office. Will Smedley was then communicated with, and agreed to do anything that was asked of him, and he certainly co-operated magnificently.

The next day Davis took Norfleet out for a walk, and the mysterious stranger turned out to be P. J. Miller, in reality A. B. Cooper, Koehn's J. D. Brady, of the Melton Hotel, an accomplished spieler, and a slick and clever rascal, who, though frequently arrested on con-game charges, had never graced the inside of a cell for more than a few days. They then took Norfleet to a stock exchange in the Denham Building, and played it for $303,000, which they won — on paper. From there they went to the Metropole Hotel, where Norfleet took a joint room with Davis, who signed the register for both Norfleet and himself, putting the latter down in his alias of L. A. Mullican.

Norfleet, minus his revolvers, in a room with a con-man with a gun, was in an unhappy predicament. He did not know whether the con-men had recognized him. If they had, that night might be his last, and so he told Davis that he was going to take a bath, went in the bathroom and locked the door, took off his trousers, shoes and stockings, sat on the edge of the tub, splashed his feet in the water, and wrote the District Attorney the following letter:

THE HOTEL METROPOLE
DENVER, COLO. 23–22

Room 310. They are going to play me for what money they think I have — and abandon the Trip home. I will wire my wife — on the Dallas County Bank — Just as soon as I learn the exact Plans. If you get the wire to wife, you will understand. I will try and talk again. If not to late to get in. We are in Room I dont feel well.

I have met the misterious man Mr. R. C. Davis my first man Mr. P J Miller the misterious man M A B Zachery the Broker in office. We took 303,000 dollers moved to this Hotel will Finsh to morrow I may need help Room 226 — Denham Bldg — I cant be at Columbia to nite I am being watched I am in Toilet now Watch after me

MULLICAN

Then Norfleet finished his bath, came out, sat down and openly wrote a letter to his wife, Mrs. 'Mullican' of Farris, Texas, read over part of it to Davis about how he was going to make a big sale of his interest to the Texas Company, and then walked over with Davis to the post office and mailed both letters.

The District Attorney received Norfleet's letter late that night. Everything now depended on the way the Norfleet matter was handled, as an error meant that the work of months would be lost. But nothing could be done until the telephone call came from Norfleet from Smedley's office at ten o'clock the next morning.

Wednesday morning Pete Land, the close associate of Blonger, the Denver detective who a few days before had delivered 'Van Cise's list,' whatever that might be, to Lou Blonger, came to the

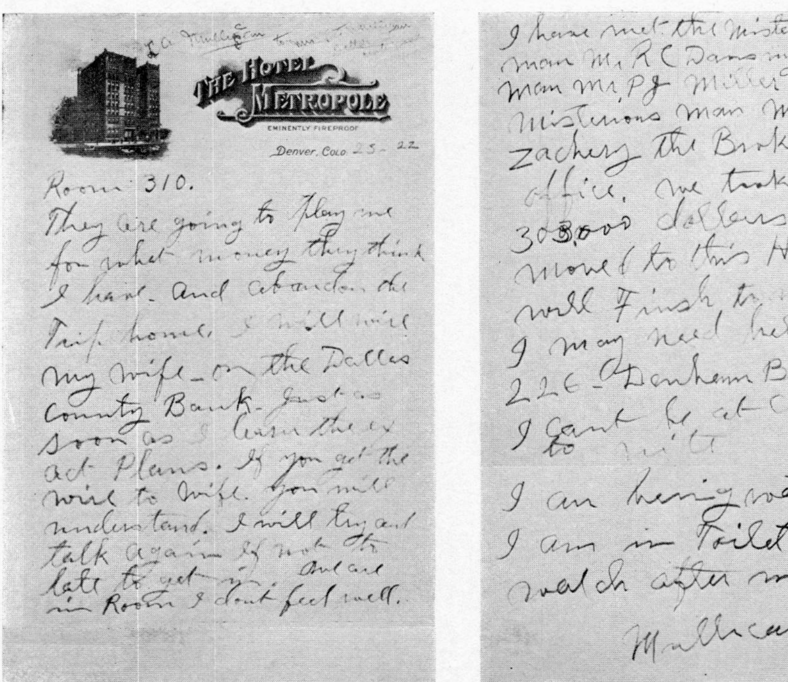

THE HOTEL METROPOLE
EMINENTLY FIREPROOF
Denver, Colo 25- 22

Room 310.
They are going to play me
for what money they think
I have. And abandon the
Trip home, I will wire
my wife—on the Dallas
County Bank—Just as
soon as I learn they
act Plans. If you get the
wire to wife. You will
understand. I will try and
talk again if not too
late to get in. and are
in Room I dont feel well.

I have met the misterious
man Mr R C Dans my first
man Mr P J Miller the
misterious man M A B
Zachery the Broker in
office. we took 300,000
dollars
moved to this Hotel
will Finish tomorrow
I may need help Room
226-Denham Bldg.
I cant be at Columbus
to [illegible]

I am being watched.
I am in Toilet now
watch after me.

Mullican

LETTER FROM NORFLEET (AS MULLICAN) TO
THE DISTRICT ATTORNEY
Written while the former was in the hands of the gang

District Attorney's office and insisted on seeing the prosecutor at once.

'Colonel,' he said, 'you and I had a falling-out over the Turley case, but I just dropped in to tell you I was wrong and you were right about that bird. And I didn't want you to feel sore at me about it.'

'That's all right, Pete,' was the reply. 'I have forgotten it.'

'Well, Colonel,' Land continued, 'I want to make a suggestion to you as a friend. While those recall petitions are being circulated around, I don't think they will get anywhere. But you need friends among the police and you have lost a lot of them. Do you know how to get them back?'

'Why, no, Pete, how would I do it?'

'Well, you're just returned from your vacation. Robinson has not stirred up anything while you were gone, and the town was quiet, anyway. But when you go out on the rampage and make a raid on your own, the papers bawl hell out of the police and they all get sore. Why don't you go down and see the Chief and tell him that in the future you are going to co-operate absolutely with the force, and agree to give your information to us, and have the boys make the raids and do the arresting for you? A little team-work will make a big man of you and we can all get behind you for Governor or Senator.'

The telephone rang — the secret telephone — with Norfleet on the wire. And here was Land directly across the table!

'Hold the 'phone a minute,' he said. Then: 'Pete, would you mind stepping outside a few minutes? I have some personal matters over the 'phone.'

Land left and the conversation was never finished, as Norfleet was holding the line.

He was at Smedley's office. He said: 'Davis is with me, but is sitting in the waiting-room. They told him only patients were allowed inside. But the plans are changed. I am to go to Texas on the midnight Colorado and Southern tonight, and Davis is going part-way so as to get his money. What do you want me to do?'

The Colonel told him that he would pick both of them off the train at Littleton, ten miles from Denver, and to go ahead with those plans.

Land was told that the District Attorney had an emergency call, and to return at 9 A.M. Friday. Then Robinson and Samson were called, and the three rushed for the District Attorney's house to hold a conference as to what should be done. On the way up, the Colonel said, 'We strike tomorrow; "D" day is now known.' The crux of fifteen months of investigation was at hand. The Norfleet incident at last had fixed the date for the attack. But the plan of the arrest on the train was wrong. Some other con-men might be there, and again the tip-off would go into action. Norfleet must be reached, and speedily.

So the District Attorney telephoned to the dentist's office, pulling Doctor Smedley away from a suffering patient who was left to writhe in the chair because of public pains more serious than his tooth. The dentist was told that Norfleet must be found as soon as possible, and called to Smedley's office to finish his teeth, and that they must get him. Then, when Norfleet came, he was to be taken to a separate room, and there telephone the District Attorney at the latter's home.

Doctor Smedley told his secretary to telephone the Metropole and get 'Mullican,' but she could get no answer. The hours passed, but nothing was heard of the Texan. To make matters worse, while Norfleet was being sought Robert G. Bosworth telephoned about Green's father being on the rampage. Not until about two o'clock was that threat wiped out.

Finally just before five o'clock Norfleet was located. The girl said, 'If you will come to the office right away, Mr. Mullican, we will finish the work on your teeth.' The prosecutor was notified that Norfleet was on his way, and the anxious hours were nearly ended.

Norfleet caught on, told Davis his message, and they went at once to Smedley's. Davis and 'Tex' Cooper remained outside in their big Cadillac car. Then Norfleet called the District

Attorney at his house. My, what a welcome voice it was to the latter.

'The plans are changed,' said the Colonel. 'It is up to you to have a terrible toothache, and be so darn sick that there won't be any question about it. Go back to your hotel after the dentist gets through with you, groan and ache and carry on, and keep Davis with you all night, and at seven o'clock we strike. Kenneth Robinson will make the arrest in your room at that hour. Put Smedley on the telephone.

'Will,' said the prosecutor, 'Norfleet must give all the appearance of a suffering patient. Dump everything in the shop on his tooth and mouth so you can smell it for a block and fix it up swell. Thanks, old man.'

Meanwhile, Norfleet's con-men sat in the automobile talking about him. Walter Byland later related their conversation to the Colonel. 'Tex' Cooper said: 'I am afraid of that fellow — something funny about him. I think we had better drop him. You remember how nervous he acted up there in the stock exchange, particularly when Farrell [a spieler] and Roy Coyne [a steerer] came through with that old farmer. He jumped every time the door opened. I don't like the looks of his eye, particularly the way he tried to get people's names. I say we let him go.'

Davis said: 'Nothing of the kind; he is my man. We have tied him for fifty thousand dollars, and he looks all right to me. I want to go ahead.'

Cooper said: 'All right, you're the doctor, but I'll bet you a thousand dollars there is something wrong with him.'

Davis said: 'I am broke or I would take your bet, for I want to play him.'

If ever a dentist did a good job on a patient desirous of convincing his friends that he had a toothache and was a sick man, Will Smedley holds the record. The doctor never told what he did, but he must have put on everything that dentists have, and added all the drugs in town, because when Norfleet went out of the office he was shaking in his boots. By the time he reached the car where his bunk friends were waiting for him, he was white to the gills, and before he had driven two blocks he vomited all over the Cadillac. There was no question in the minds of the con-men that they had a sick man. Davis and Cooper rushed their victim to the hotel, got hot-water bottles and warm towels, and a kidney plaster for his back, and nursed him till late at night. Then Cooper left, and Norfleet spent his second night, now really a sick man, alone in the room with Davis, an armed crook.

When the District Attorney hung up the telephone, after his last talk with Smedley, he turned to Robinson.

'Kenneth,' he said, 'notify the car drivers to be at the church at six tomorrow morning. Tell the others to be at Roy Samson's at eight tonight for final instructions.'

Then the prosecutor called the head of the Rangers.

'Colonel Hamrock,' he said, 'call your men. We want them at the church at six tomorrow morning. Enjoin all to absolute secrecy in every particular.'

And from north, south, east, and west, the Rangers jumped upon their motor-cycles and started for Denver, traveling through the night, the forces of the Law gathering for the attack upon the underworld!

# XXVII

## *The Attack Gets Under Way*

At five o'clock in the morning Thursday, August 24, 1922, the District Attorney opened the basement door to the church. Shortly afterwards the deputies, then Webster, Linville, Healey, Will Loughridge, and Bagby, constituting the headquarters force, and finally the Rangers, appeared upon the scene. Samson reported that fifteen cars, with drivers, were all parked within a block radius, awaiting orders. Captain O. L. Dennis of the Rangers was placed in command inside the church, and he and three of his men donned their uniforms.

Each of the six deputies selected his own Ranger. Then the entire group was assembled for final instructions from the Colonel.

'The first arrest will be made by Kenneth Robinson. He will go to Norfleet's room at the Metropole and there arrest Leon Felix, alias R. C. Davis, and wait for "Tex" Cooper and arrest him.

'Before the general round-up starts, Blonger and Duff must be in the church. Samson will arrest Duff and Sanborn will capture Blonger. When we have the fixer and manager behind the bars, the rest of you will move on your assignments.

'Use the telephones often, and report progress and your locations.'

At seven o'clock Kenneth Robinson, accompanied by Ranger Myron Donald in plain clothes, rapped on the door of Room 310 Metropole Hotel. Norfleet had been lying awake all night, while Leon Felix, alias R. C. Davis, had slept peacefully in the adjacent bed in utter ignorance of the identity of his roommate and impending events. Felix opened the door rather sleepily and looked into the muzzles of two guns.

'Put up your hands, you're under arrest,' said Robinson, and Norfleet sat up in bed, grinning with delight.

'Davis,' said Frank, who did not know that Felix was Davis's real name, 'do you know who I am?'

And the con-man said, 'No, except Mullican.'

'Well, for your information, my name is Frank Norfleet.'

'My God!' said Felix, falling back upon the bed.

Robinson and Donald put handcuffs on him, searched him, found considerable evidence of con-activities, including a fake telegram which he had shown Norfleet to impress the latter with the con-man's apparent financial responsibility. It bore the signature of an eastern bank, and authorized Davis to draw on it for fifty thousand dollars.

They then locked Felix in the bathroom and told him if he made any racket whatsoever it would be too bad for him. As his hands were fastened in front so he could smoke, he made himself comfortable and there was no disturbance or trouble from him.

'The weather's fine,' Robinson telephoned the Colonel. 'Everything going on schedule, and we are waiting for Number Two.'

Then he, Norfleet, and the Ranger spent the time examining Felix's effects while waiting for the latter's pal.

At eight-thirty came another knock, and this time while Robinson and Donald from inside the room held the guns on the caller, in marched their new prisoner, A. B. Cooper, the cleverest spieler of the gang.

Mugged at police headquarters or in the penitentiary

Cooper does not look like very much, but dressed for a victim, he was a classy-looking individual, and that morning he was ready for business. Wearing a straw hat, blue coat, white trousers and shoes, colored shirt with cravat to match, and a big diamond stickpin, A. B. Cooper looked and acted like a successful young broker. Robinson recognized him at once from his picture in the gallery.

'Cooper,' he said, 'we are going to search you. I will give you a receipt for all your money and valuables. First, however, have you met Mr. Norfleet?'

Never an eye batted 'Tex' Cooper. As far as anyone could have told from his demeanor, he had never heard of the Texan.

Ranger Donald made a thorough job with his search of the spieler, who yielded up a wealth of incriminating documents. 'Tex' Cooper was well fixed, and carried a lot of valuables on his person. Besides several hundred dollars in cash, he had an expensive platinum watch and considerable jewelry. Robinson started to write out a list of the separate items, when Cooper drawled: 'There is no need of mentioning that diamond stickpin in the receipt. You have included plenty without it.' And Cooper pointed to a three-carat stone taken from his tie.

'Tex' Cooper had been accustomed to dealing with crooked officers to whom such a bribe would have meant a speedy release, but Robinson merely smiled at him and said, 'Sorry, old man, but you had better take the receipt, and I will keep the jewelry for the time being so you won't offer any of it to some other person.'

Again Robinson telephoned. 'Number Two party ready to go to church.'

'Wait an hour for other worshipers, then come in,' was the answer.

Meanwhile, real trouble had broken out at the raid headquarters.

The last admonition of the District Attorney to all his men had been absolute secrecy. The raid had to be a surprise attack, and as carefully guarded as any movement in France. Many obstacles and leaks had already been overcome, but success depended entirely upon no information reaching the enemy.

At midnight Wednesday someone telephoned Forbes Parkhill, star reporter of the Denver *Post*, 'The Rangers are coming to town early in the morning,' and hung up. That was enough for Forbes. At eight o'clock he was at the Capitol Building, saw Colonel Patrick J. Hamrock, the head of the Rangers, and Lewis D. Mowry, one of the deputy district attorneys. Mowry was at the telephone. When he saw Forbes, he caught himself, and said, 'Well, never mind, I'll see you at the church.'

Parkhill asked both Hamrock and Mowry what was up; each said he knew nothing, and Mowry rushed out.

Parkhill hung around. He lost Hamrock, so telephoned his paper and told them where he was and that something was up with the District Attorney and the Rangers. He was ordered to stay on the job, and they would see what else they could get.

Joseph Cook, an exceedingly able and clever news-hawk, covered the West Side Court for the *Post*. He sent in word to his paper that the three old deputies, the clerical force and Oliver Smith, the city detective, were the only ones on duty at the office, that the information man said the District Attorney and the rest of the deputies had gone fishing!

This added to the mystery. All sorts of rumors spread about, and every guess was made but the right one. Cook had no leads, but Parkhill did, and he hung on to them.

Shortly after nine Hamrock returned, and at once Forbes Parkhill went after him.

'Look here, Colonel, there's something up and the *Post* is entitled to know about it. We've done a lot of favors for you in the past, have always supported you, and unless you give us the information we won't back you any further.'

Hamrock refused to talk, so the reporter sprung his trump card.

'Well,' he said, 'I know you are all up at the church, and unless you tell me which one it is we will comb out every church in Denver until we find the right one.'

Hamrock was stumped. Finally he said: 'I don't know anything about it. It's the District Attorney's party and I have sworn not to say a word. But I'll take you to the church and you can see him yourself.'

So the harassed head of the Rangers drove Parkhill to Fourteenth and Lafayette, one block from the gang's jail, and let him out at the Plymouth Congregational Church, to find his way as best he could, and then drove off.

Parkhill found that edifice empty, then went to the Universalist Church, saw signs of activity, knocked, and Captain Dennis of the Rangers came to the door in uniform. The quarry had been run down. Parkhill demanded admission; Captain Dennis denied it.

Parkhill was insistent, and said, 'I've got the story, anyway, and I want to see Van Cise or Hamrock.'

Captain Dennis replied, 'Wait, I'll see about it,' locked the door, and reported to the Chief.

'Colonel,' he said, 'Parkhill of the *Post* is outside, wants to see you, and says he has the story!'

Real trouble was again at hand, this time at the very inception of the raid. Some prisoners were already in the basement, but Blonger and the majority were still at large. Once an extra was on the streets, no other man would be arrested except Blonger, and when he was captured, nothing incriminating would be found on him or in his office. Would months of effort now be destroyed by the Denver *Post*?

So Captain Dennis was told to send in the man on whom the success of the entire raid depended.

'Hello, Forbes,' said the prosecutor. 'I wish someone would treat you like kittens — put you in a sack and take you out behind the barn and drown you. You and your tribe are about the last people I want to see. But now that you're here, I'll tell you all about it and let you see the whole lay-out, on condition that I talk to your editor before you leave.'

Parkhill wanted to use the telephone, but was told he couldn't use it, or any other, until he had the whole story, and until his chief was talked to. So the District Attorney had to give up the direction of the raid, go out of his headquarters, and around the church with the reporter, giving him all the minute details of everything, and consuming as much time as possible in order to save every vital minute for more arrests.

Parkhill was a keen reporter, and balked at restraint. Finally, bursting with enthusiasm, and an absolute scoop in his hands, he wanted to tear out and rush to the paper. But the prosecutor telephoned William G. Shepherd, the paper's managing editor, and finally persuaded him to come to the church before Parkhill left with his story. It was a big concession on the part of the managing editor of a large paper like the *Post*.

Shepherd was given the high spots on the raid, and then the District Attorney said: 'Shep, this means a lot to Denver. If you publish the story, we make no more arrests. If you suppress it, we will finish our work. You have a scoop on this so far, and we won't tip off any other paper. If you will help us out, you can send up your photographers and special writers and get anything you want for tomorrow's paper.'

Shepherd proved himself a real American, said, 'All right, nothing until the noon edition tomorrow,' and left. Shortly afterwards *Post* reporters and photographers were all over the place, with the secured right to anything they wanted. They earned it, and it was given, even though many of the photographs and interviews were later construed by defense counsel as publicity-seeking by the District Attorney.

Then the *Post* reporter himself lost his scoop. The Denver *Times* was also scouting around for the District Attorney. Parkhill was using a telephone to his paper at an adjacent fur store late that afternoon, when a *Times* reporter came in on him, as Parkhill did on Mowry. Parkhill closed his conversation abruptly — 'I'll be at the Universalist Church,' he said, and left.

And very shortly afterwards a *Times* reporter was knocking at the church door. But this was late in the afternoon and the day's work was nearly over.

So that evening the District Attorney and Kenneth Robinson called on William C. Shanklin, of the *News-Times*, and after a great deal of argument, persuaded him to follow the lead of the *Post* and to run nothing in his papers until the noon extra the next day.

For the first time in his life, Joseph Cook, the *Post* reporter, was scooped, and never got over it. For months he had been in and out of the office every week day, once or twice he had obtained an inkling of some strange investigation and had asked the District Attorney and Fred Sanborn some embarrassing questions, but he had never guessed what Roy Samson was doing, or the big secret of the office. But dodging Joe had long been a major task.

# XXVIII

## *The Gang Goes to Church*

Adolph W. Duff, the manager, lived in an apartment house at Tenth and Lincoln Streets, and was accustomed to walk to the office in the morning, sometimes going down Lincoln and sometimes going down Tenth.

Roy Samson was given the hard task of arresting Duff without his actions being observed. He picked William W. Grant, Jr., one of Denver's leading lawyers, for his driver. Cleverly parking their car east on Tenth Avenue so they could move down either street, they waited for the manager to appear.

About eight-thirty Duff came out, nervous and active as ever, and started north down Lincoln. Grant's car followed, shot over to the curb, and Samson called out, 'Mr. Duff, don't you want to ride downtown?'

And Duff, thinking it was some friend of his, walked over to the car, had a gun shoved in his face, was shown District Attorney's and Ranger's badges, and told to get in. He was then driven rapidly towards the church.

'By God,' said Duff, 'your District Attorney isn't going to get away with this! If he thinks he can pick up a reputable business man on the street and arrest him this way, I will show him what's what.'

'Aw, you'd better shut up and wait until you see what's

going to happen, Duff,' said Samson, 'before you shoot off your mouth too much. In the meantime just put on these little bracelets.'

And he slipped the cuffs on the bragging crook and brought him into the church, actually prisoner Number Three, but the first one to land in the private jail.

At once Samson started to search the manager personally. Putting his hand in Duff's inside pocket, he pulled out a type-written list of names, and a black notebook. A hasty glance at the former, and Samson turned to Harold Webster.

'Finish the search, and bring me everything you get from him. I'm going upstairs to the Colonel.'

Samson took the steps about three at a time, burst into the office, and shouted:

'Colonel, what do you think Duff had? Here's the very list I sent Bruce — it turns up in his pocket! Where did he get it?'

And he handed the District Attorney a sheet reading as follows:

James Allen
'A'
Walter Byland
— Barrett (see C's report)
Thos Beech
J. D. Brady
W. H. Burk
Blacky Slim
Blacky Shorty
'B'
'C' (Jew)
Art Cooper (?)
John Clark
Drucker, Chas (551)
Frede, Joe # 43 (Swiss)
Kelly Robert
'D'
'E'
Eddie
French
Filger
'J' (Jew)
Walter Kelly
Loftus (ST Regis)
'L'
Miami (Ma friend)
Maxey
Mooney (blind man)
Nole
'N' (Neal)
'P' Plaza Hotel
Petts
Pierce Geo
Pappy
'Q' (Cane)
# IE (Mous.)
Reynolds Jno
Red
Soloman, Fred
Sturns, Wm
Smith, J. R.
Smart (Chicken)

| | |
|---|---|
| Farrell, Jos. P. | 'S' St Regis |
| " Roy (?) | Specks |
| Frunkey | Sandy |
| Gates-Gorman | Tate |
| Goldberg, Harry, General Delivery | Thick Lips |
| 'G' (Lieut.) | Witting, White |
| Hogan, Red | Glenn Harlan W. |
| 'H' Harvey Hotel | & artists cap # 580 |
| Welch, Wm. Harrison | Klein, Frank C |
| Chas Keif, Chas. W. (# 101) | Davison, A. C. (?) |
| Dockerty, Tom | |

The District Attorney examined it as eagerly as did Samson. 'Well, we got Duff just the same. But the others may have flown. So shoot the works and don't wait for Blonger's arrest. Hustle on every con-man in town, before they light out on us.'

Deputies and Rangers dashed into waiting cars and raced downtown to the rendezvous with Koehn, Maiden, or Cooper, or to the various hangouts of the mob.

Fred Sanborn had as hard a job as Roy Samson. Not only must no one know of Lou Blonger's arrest, but it was imperative that he be captured in his own office so that his room could be legally searched. The plans called for covering Blonger from the time he left home until he got to the office, so that there could be no slip, and a car had been assigned to watch his house. But Blonger had spent the previous night at the home of his mistress, Berna Rames, and so reached his office unobserved. Mrs. Steno telephoned, 'Blonger has come in.' Word was flashed to Sanborn, who rushed to the office.

Blonger was seated at his desk, with his coat off, talking to Henry Mullins, a former Denver detective and ex-convict.

Fred Sanborn and his men, a Ranger, Paul Loughridge, the bond-man, and Fred's brother, Will Sanborn, entered the room. Fred said, 'The District Attorney wants to see you at once, Mr. Blonger, and this gentleman who is with you.'

Blonger said nothing. Two coats were hanging on a rack in the office. Getting to his feet he put on one, and started to pull down his rolltop desk. Sanborn interrupted, 'Don't close

THE UNIVERSALIST CHURCH, WHERE
THE GANG WAS IMPRISONED

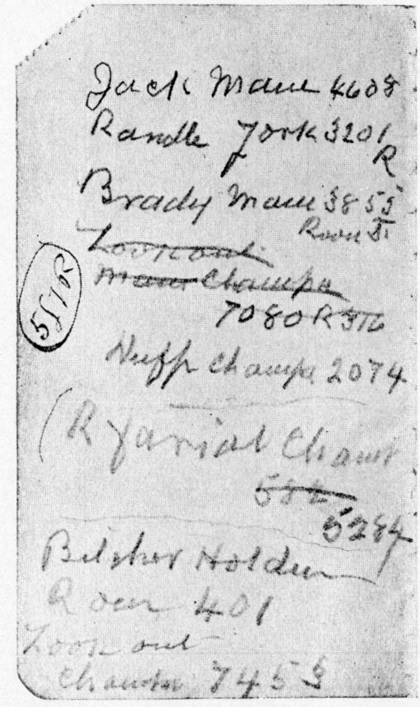


A PAGE FROM BLONGER'S BANK DEPOSIT BOOK

Giving the names and telephone numbers
of the principal members of his mob

that,' he said. 'And we want your desk and office keys, Mr. Blonger.'

Blonger took the latter from his pocket, handed them over, and said, 'Help yourself, you won't find anything,' and went out the door with Mullins, the Ranger, and Loughridge, while the two Sanborns remained to search the office.

Without waiting to examine them, all documents and papers of all kinds from Blonger's and Duff's desks were dumped into suitcases. Then Fred Sanborn examined the remaining coat, and it proved to be a gold mine. In one of the pockets was an old bank-deposit book in Blonger's own handwriting, in which he had written the names of the principal members of his mob, and their telephone numbers. Lou had also entered under the heading 'Lookout' the telephone numbers of the two which were used in 1922, also the one for 1921, and the confidence-men's club for that year. The name and telephone of Aarons of the Department of Justice also appeared. The wary old fixer was hopelessly enmeshed.

Blonger was brought to the church, which by that time housed fifteen or twenty of his men. He in turn protested his arrest to the District Attorney, but was told he could keep his comments until later, and that when he got downstairs he would understand the situation better.

Taken to the bull-pen in the basement, he saw Duff and others of his mob. For the first time in his long life of crime his equanimity deserted him, his head dropped, his knees sagged, and he sank into the nearest chair.

With Manager Duff rounded up, Roy Samson and a party rushed the 'Lookout,' and caught Louis Mushnick, the 'Thick Lips' of the list, coming out of the door. This man at that time held the all-time record in America for con-men, having trimmed an English sugar broker in Cuba and Atlanta, Georgia, for $245,000. Samson sent him back to the room, pulled his gun, and there arrested Les Randle the bookmaker, George 'Tip' Belcher the 'tailer,' J. Roy Farrell and George Kelley, spielers, and A. H. Potts. The latter was one of the two men the District Attorney had searched and turned loose at Sammy Abrams's bootleg joint a few days before.

This room was scantily furnished with cheap desks, tables, and chairs. A portable typewriter was on a small table by the window. In the rolltop desk were found settlement sheets with many recent victims who had either been swindled or were just about to be cleaned out. And in the desk drawer Randle had his complete bookmaker's outfit, all packed for instant use, in a small japanned tin suitcase, which contained a large folded-up oilcloth blackboard, and printed equipment of all kinds for a stock exchange or horse-racing club.

Concealed at the bottom of the suitcase was the prize catch of all, real money comprising the bookmaker's 'boodle.' This consisted of seven packages of currency actually amounting to only $2108, but which, with the bank wrappers then around it, gave every appearance of being $135,000 — hundred-dollar bills were on the top and bottom of each package with one-dollar bills between. Rubber bands were fastened around each end so that the victim would not detect the smaller currency. In addition Randle had in his pockets thirteen hundred-dollar bills, which were not then recognized as a part of the 'bank-roll,' and so were shortly afterwards returned to him under court order.

The gangsters seized in the Lookout were taken singly to the church and a Ranger and deputy left in charge. During the day five other grafters went to the Lookout for orders and were also arrested. One of them was lucky. He was rather hard of hearing, and dressed in old, slouchy clothes. He said he was a farmer from Louisiana, looking for a dentist. A dentist had formerly occupied the room and his name was still on the windows. The man was sent to the church, but when searched had nothing in his pockets but a small dictionary.

None of the prosecutor's force had ever seen this man before, his picture was not in the gallery, and a few hours later he was released. When last seen he was slowly meandering down the street. A few days later it was discovered that they had turned loose 'Puss' McCasky, a much-wanted con-man from Atlanta, for whose capture there was a large reward!

Roy Samson then went to French's apartment and found that he had gone to Estes Park, so he went to Farrell's quarters next door, and found Mrs. Farrell there alone. Samson then called in his sister-in-law and put her and A. J. Reynolds, the deputy district attorney, in charge. This was good head work, because in a few minutes Elmer Mead, the 'Christ Kid,' appeared, looking for Farrell. Reynolds hardly knew what to do with him or how to handle him, but pulled a gun and put him under arrest on general principles. Reynolds did not know that Mead was a con-man, but took a chance, and a good one.

Elmer Mead, as steerer, and J. Roy Farrell, as spieler, had a few days before tied up a sucker named C. H. Hubbell, of McPherson, Kansas, for $50,000. He had gone home, secured his money, and his cashier's check had been honored by the bank. He was then rooming at the Shirley-Savoy Hotel with Mead, and was ripe to be played that day! Farrell had not shown up at their room on schedule, so Mead had gone to get him. Though the arrest made Hubbell just $50,000 to the good, he wouldn't believe in their guilt for several days, and vigorously protested the arrest of his friends Mead and Farrell! He even tried to make bond for both of them so they could get out of jail! But his money was saved, and he was never initiated into the inner mysteries of the con-men's fraternity.

Roy Samson then visited the stock exchange in the Denham Building, but no one was in the rooms. The suite was admirably adapted to the pay-off game's purposes. It consisted of a private interior hall with three connecting rooms opening from it.

The stock exchange contained much better furniture than that in the Lookout. In the center room a rolltop desk and a long table stood end to end, and on top of the desk was a telephone. Roy Samson picked it up, gave it a slight pull, and the unconnected wire pulled out of the desk drawer. The fake telephone was found!

Some con-men's literature was on the tables. A Ranger and car driver were then left on duty, but no one appeared. Later it was discovered that the exchanges or racing parlors were never used except when the victim was being put through the play. A similar exchange was also discovered in the Kittridge Building.

Meanwhile, Andrew Koehn and Robert Maiden were busy combing the streets with the deputies and Rangers, pointing out their men all around town. Koehn was high man, with ten prisoners. Late that night Maiden arrested one of the mob right in front of the con-men's jail!

An ironical touch was given to the arrests. The first thing which greeted the eyes of the gangsters when they entered the church was a large Sunday School motto on the wall directly in front of the door. It bore two pointed quotations. One read 'The Way of the Transgressor is Hard.' The other said 'For the Lord Knoweth the Way of the Righteous, but the Way of the Ungodly Shall Perish.'

One of the con-men was heard to remark, 'I haven't been to church for twenty years, and by G ——, it will be another forty before I ever go again.'

Thirty-three men were now rounded up — Lou Blonger, the owner of the franchise and the hitherto successful 'fixer'; Adolph W. Duff, the 'manager'; Les Randle and William H. Loftus, bookmakers; J. Roy Farrell, A. B. 'Tex' Cooper, Walter Byland, and George Kelley, spielers; George 'Tip' Belcher the 'tailer,' and twenty-four steerers. All of the big men of the gang, with the exception of Jackie French, were in jail, even though their jail was a church.

It is a general custom in the underworld for crooks to keep in active touch with their molls. No news is bad news, and demands action. Early in the afternoon when the gangsters, who were in the church, failed to telephone their wives, many of

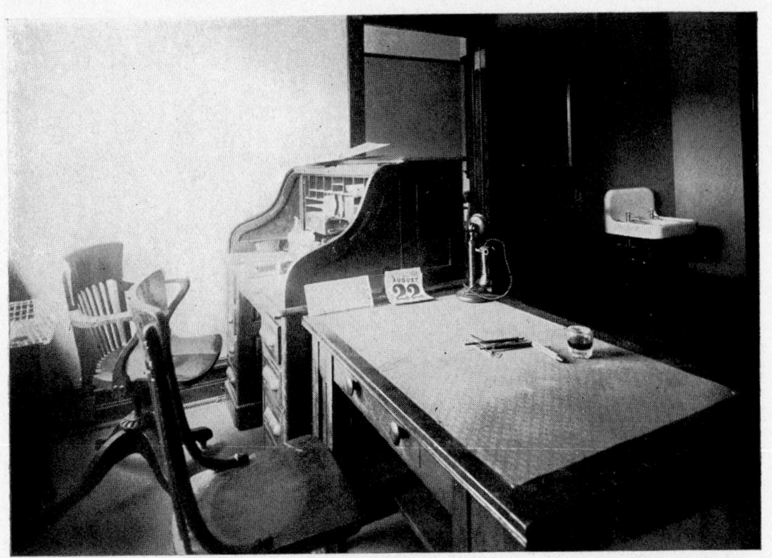


THE STOCK EXCHANGE IN THE DENHAM BUILDING

494 UNITED TURF EXCHANGE

Straight

Place

Show

V

105 SAN CARLOS CLUB

105 105

105

105 105 B

A. B. ORLANDO
SECRETARY

PASS BEARER
TO CLUB

No.........................

PARAPHERNALIA OF THE GAME

the women became suspicious. So feminine voices called the Lookout telephone. The strange answers from the deputy district attorney then in charge only enhanced their fears. They then called other wives, the alarm was sprung, and thus about forty steerers escaped.

Several suitcases belonging to the con-men were picked up at the railroad stations, through claim checks taken from the mob when arrested. Some were also found in their rooms. These were brought to the church to be searched for documentary evidence. As no previous preparations had been made to handle them, they were stacked in a corner, and about a dozen bags, contents and all, were stolen.

The attorneys for the gang later tried to capitalize on this, though the District Attorney, as soon as he found the bags were missing, paid each con-man the full value of his stolen baggage.

The Law attacks, and the underworld's thieves sneak in from the rear and loot. A world of crooks calls for constant vigilance.

# XXIX

## *Mopping Up*

EVENING came and the problem was, What should be done with the prisoners? French was still missing, and there was yet a chance to pick up a few more steerers. If the men were put in the city jail, no longer would the papers keep quiet, and the underworld would know everything.

Two adjacent counties had square sheriffs who were friendly to the District Attorney. They were telephoned to, their co-operation obtained, and the con-men, handcuffed and guarded by the Rangers, were taken in two groups, half to the Golden jail and half to the Brighton jail, each less than twenty miles away, where they spent the night.

Through carelessness, three men were arrested who were not con-men. Maiden had not checked them carefully enough before picking them up on the benches by the Capitol Building. One was a little fellow who wanted to see the 'Chieftain.' He was brought before the District Attorney and demanded to talk to him alone. At once he pulled out a wallet, exhibited a Klan membership card, and said that he recognized this as a Klan grab. He wanted to prove that he was a fellow Klansman from Chicago and in good standing, and was willing to assist in catching anybody that the Klan was after. He was released shortly afterwards.

Another was a man whom Maiden thought was Filger. Filger, however, turned out to have been dead for six months, and the prisoner was a devout Methodist and anything but a crook.

The third was an inoffensive salesman looking for a job. He attempted to resist when Maiden grabbed him, and Maiden hit him behind the ear with a revolver, cutting his head wide open. He was one of the most thoroughly scared men the District Attorney ever saw, and sat in a corner of the church by himself, afraid to open his mouth or speak to anybody. The con-men, of course, knew that he was not one of their number and thought he was a plant, but when they found he was not, Walter Byland, who was the 'kidder' of the crowd, began to work him over, and before long had him absolutely terrified.

Walter asked the man what he was doing at the time of his arrest, and he said, 'I was sitting on a bench on the Capitol lawn.'

'Oh,' said Walter, 'were you looking at the dome?'

'Why, yes,' replied the victim.

'Well, I know now why they arrested you,' said Byland. 'You are charged with conspiracy to steal the gold off the dome, and that's a capital offense in Colorado.'

So Walter told him that they had been seized by the Ku Klux Klan, which had been getting quite violent in Denver, and stated that it was quite probable that they were going to put all of them on crosses planted upside down on Table Mountain, and set fire to them, as an example to law violators.

On the way out to Golden that night, the salesman was not handcuffed, though the others were, and when the automobile had to stop at Colfax and Broadway for traffic, he made a wild dash from the car and rushed down a crowded street. But he was seized by Will Loughridge, the car driver, a former Yale football star, who made a flying tackle, threw the salesman to the sidewalk, hauled him back and put him in the seat.

And not a single word was said by any of the gathering spectators, none of whom could understand this altercation between men in plain clothes. Incidentally, there was no policeman present to interfere.

Later this man threatened suit for false arrest, and had a very substantial case. But he employed a high-class attorney and the prosecutor procured for him the best medical attention in town, paid him a small sum for loss of time, and secured him a job with a leading store of Denver, where he shortly afterwards became a branch manager.

The lawyers for the underworld, paid by the year, were early on the job. Henry Mullins, the ex-convict found in Blonger's office, had been brought to the church with Blonger. But about three o'clock in the afternoon he was turned loose by one of the Rangers without his presence ever having been reported to the District Attorney. Mullins promptly called on Blonger's lawyers, and the alarm was again spread through the underworld.

So about four o'clock in the afternoon one of these lawyers appeared at the church door and tried to get in, but was told to get out. Another went to the Brighton jail that night and demanded admittance, but had no better luck. But the next day, bright and early, they were on the job, seeking a writ of *habeas corpus* from the Denver court in order to get the mob out on bond. Gangsters always have certain types of lawyers looking out for their interests, so there will be no delay in getting all possible assistance marshaled at once.

An interesting sidelight on the powerful backing of Lou Blonger was that for two days after the first story was printed, no mention whatsoever was made in the Denver *Post* that the fixer had been arrested. Everybody else was written up, but not Blonger, the old friend of Harry H. Tammen, one of the two proprietors of that paper. Finally the case became so big that F. G. Bonfils, the other owner of the paper, ordered Blonger's name published. Then the *Post* swung over to the side of the

District Attorney and relentlessly pounded for the conviction of the entire gang, and the enforcement of the Law.

In that connection Forbes Parkhill tells this inside story on a conversation which he had with Harry Tammen:

> Unlike Bonfils, Tammen occasionally would chat with the reporters in the *Post* editorial rooms. The Saturday night following the raids, he sat on my typewriter desk and talked at length about the case. I mentioned that I thought it odd Blonger's name had been suppressed at first.
>
> Tammen said: 'Yes, that was done by my orders, because Lou Blonger was one of my best friends. I hated like hell to use his name, but the story became so big we couldn't possibly hold it out any longer. You know, son, Lou taught me the most valuable thing I ever knew. He taught me how to catch a sucker.'
>
> A moment later he added: 'I caught one.' He jerked his thumb toward Bonfils's office and finished: 'I've still got him.'

Ten days before the raid, William Sturns, the 'Painter Kid,' a nationally known con-man, one of the two men whom the District Attorney had chased off the running-board of his car after visiting Sammy Abrams's place, was arrested by a blue-coated policeman as a suspicious character. Painter stayed in jail overnight, was exhibited before the detectives at the show-up the next morning, and as no one claimed to recognize him, was released without even being mugged or finger-printed. But Sturns was one of Blonger's men.

Square detectives had little chance to identify a con-man, as the Denver Bureau of Identification had pictures of only seventy-six of this class of crooks, and most of the pictures were too old to be of any value.

Frank Norfleet wanted Whitey Harris, alias Spencer, and a circular giving his picture, identifications, and offering a reward for his capture had been in the Denver Bureau of Identification for many months. About the middle of August, two city detectives saw Harris loitering around a part of the town not visited by tourists, and arrested him. Harris was then passing under the name of Mitchell.

'You shouldn't arrest me,' he said; 'I am working for Lou Blonger, and he told me to tell anyone who bothered me to call him up and he would talk to you.'

Just then Sammy Abrams and Kid Duff appeared on the scene.

'Have you anything on this fellow?' asked Duff.

'No, only investigation,' answered one of the dicks.

'Well, he's all right,' said Duff. 'He's working for Blonger and me in our mines and is a pretty good fellow, but doesn't know much.'

So Mitchell, alias Spencer, was turned loose — the second 1922 con-man not wanted by the police.

The day before the raid, another notorious member of the gang, Harry A. Mueller, alias George Bradley, was arrested at the Kenmark Hotel on the complaint of a victim whom he was attempting to trim.

When taken before Detective Captain Bacon, he admitted he was a con-man, but no effort was made to locate his confederates or paraphernalia. He was released almost at once and was seen on the streets the morning of the arrest, but escaped capture. No publicity, however, was given to Mueller's arrest.

With this fresh record of these three con-men, Sturns, the 'Painter Kid,' Harris, alias Spencer, and Harry Mueller, in their hands, within ten days of the raid, and with all three released almost as soon as arrested, the police were now to find the main gang itself in the custody of the District Attorney. To rub it in they would now have to take charge of the mob themselves!

The morning after the arrest, Blonger and his men were returned to the church. Then the Chief of Police was telephoned and told to bring up his Captain of Detectives and several of the latter's men to look over Lou Blonger and his crowd. If ever there was an embarrassed group of police officers, who didn't know where the lightning was going to strike next, it was when they arrived upon the scene, were taken to the basement, and there saw thirty-three crooks who had been operating for years under their protection in the City of Denver.

The officers all protested that they had never seen or heard of any of them before, except Lou Blonger and Kid Duff, and that they only knew them as 'business men' in Denver! The prisoners were then delivered into their custody and the police hauled them to the city jail in the patrol wagon.

Even then special favors were attempted. George Lusk, the detective who had been with Pete Land at Colorado Springs, tried to take Blonger to the jail in his private car instead of in the patrol wagon with the others! But on protest this was given up, and the fixer rode with his gang.

However, neither Blonger nor Duff was photographed or finger-printed by the Denver police until nine months later, although the officials handled all the other con-men in regular routine fashion.

But Jackie French was missing, French for whom a huge reward was outstanding, French who had made the quarter of a million clean-up in one week in Florida, French, the clever ex-bellhop from St. Louis, the Beau Brummel, the smart con-man, the bookmaker, the badger artist. The only evidence as to his whereabouts was the janitor's report at the El Tovar Apartment that French had gone to Estes Park, but where he was in that wide expanse of territory was unknown. Then fortune favored the Law!

In the same apartment house where Adolph Duff dwelt with his wife was an Irishman, William I. Reilly, the labor member of the State Industrial Commission. Reilly had a well-developed bump of curiosity, which he put to excellent use the day after the raid.

The Friday afternoon editions of the papers came out with huge headlines about the arrest of the con-men, the *Times* and *Express* carrying Kid Duff's and Lou Blonger's names in bold print, and stating that they were expecting to be released on bond late that afternoon. Reilly knew that a man named Duff lived in the adjacent apartment, though he had never met him, and so hurried home, opened all the doors and windows in his apartment, and sat down to hear, if he could, if his neighbor was Duff the gangster.

The con-men's lawyers were successful, and, about five-thirty Friday afternoon, got both Blonger and Duff out on fifty-thousand-dollar bonds. The same amount was fixed for all defendants.

At once they started to gather their forces together and to see how much protection remained. Duff rushed home in a taxicab, grabbed the telephone, and put in a long-distance call for French at the Stanley Hotel at Estes Park. He was told that French was out and would not return until nine o'clock, and left word that he would call him at that hour.

His curiosity satisfied, Reilly did nothing further. Lady Luck had definitely set in against French, for at ten minutes to nine Reilly accidentally met Colonel Hamrock of the State Rangers on the street, told him that Duff had put in a telephone call for some fellow named French at the Stanley Hotel at Estes Park, and was going to talk to him at nine o'clock.

'Good Lord!' exploded Hamrock, 'why didn't you tell me before? The Colonel is trying to find him.' Rushing for the nearest telephone he called the District Attorney, and at five minutes to nine gave him the information that Duff would talk to French at nine o'clock.

Instantly the Colonel swung into action, called the telephone company, asked it to cut all conversations then going on between Denver and Estes Park, stated that he was hiring all lines at once, and that no conversation should be allowed to go through except his; then he put in calls for the Forest Ranger and town marshal at Estes Park, got them on the telephone and requested that they go to the hotel, arrest French and hold him in his room incommunicado until turned over to the District Attorney. He added that they would be held personally responsible for his safe-keeping.

Shortly after came the telephone message, 'We have French. Shall we bring him to Denver?'

'No,' was the response, 'I will come and get him myself.'

So that night the District Attorney and Roy Samson, driven by Ranger William Q. Howell, in 1935 lieutenant-colonel of the 148th Field Artillery of the National Guard, drove rapidly through the darkness to Estes Park for French.

When they got there, the District Attorney stated he did not want his name mentioned, and then went into French's room and said, 'Hello, Jack, I haven't seen you for some time. How are you?'

French replied, 'I don't place you, but I would like to know what this is all about.'

One of the local officers then spoke up and said French had an opium pipe and a jar of hop. The Colonel told the officers to leave the room, that he wanted to talk to the prisoner alone. He was curious to see if French would be as clever as Cooper in his attempt at bribery.

'I am going to take you down to Denver on a con proposition, Jack,' said the District Attorney. 'What have you been doing up here?'

'Oh, just playing golf and having a good time,' said French. 'By the way, I have a brand-new Studebaker car and three or four thousand dollars in jewelry and money with me, and you might just as well drive that car back and take that jewelry along with you.'

'No thanks, Jack,' said the prosecutor. 'That is exactly the reason I came along on this party. I am the District Attorney and you picked the wrong man to do business with this time.'

'Oh, hell! No hard feelings, are there?' said Jack.

'Not at all, but we might as well put the cuffs on right now, to make sure that we land you in Denver, and not let you get loose on a mountain road on the way home.'

So the bracelets were snapped on French's wrists and he was taken back to Denver. On the way he told a lot of his experiences as a con-man, gave many of the gangsters' phrases, and admitted his activity with the Denver crowd. Jack was a little 'hopped up' at that time, and somewhat more talkative than usual.

But the Law nabbed French in the nick of time. He was staying at the Stanley Hotel with his charmer, Buda Godman, alias Helen Strong, and the two of them had a very wealthy and gullible Episcopalian minister in tow, on whom they were planning to spring the 'badger' game the very next day. Instead Buda temporarily fled to New York, while French went behind the bars.

In case the reader may not be familiar with the badger game, it is the old proposition of a beautiful adventuress enticing the victim into a bedroom, getting him into a compromising position, then having the alleged irate husband burst in on the scene, and the victim pay to avoid publicity.

When not with French, Buda played fast and loose with the owner of one of the Big League baseball clubs. Two telegrams tell the tale:

NEW YORK, JUNE 15, 1922

J. H. FRENCH
1515 GRANT STREET
DENVER, COLORADO
LEAVING FRIDAY FEELING BETTER NO ONE KNOWS ADDRESS ALL MY LOVE

BUDA

DENVER, COLORADO JULY 5, 1922

CHARLES A. STONEHAM
15 WEST 60TH STREET
NEW YORK CITY
ALL MY LOVE AND BEST WISHES FOR HAPPY BIRTHDAY WILL CALL YOU THURSDAY NOON

BUDA

The telegraph company's notation on their records was: 'Sender's name Miss French, address 1515 Grant Street, Denver.'

This is the Buda about whom French told one of the con-men: 'She played her part like a queen in that badger game that landed me in the Atlanta pen in 1916!'

# XXX

## *Captured Documents*

BEGINNING the afternoon of the raids, and continuing for weeks thereafter, the huge mass of documents and papers of all kinds, taken from the gangsters, were carefully sorted out and studied at length. The search of the prisoners at the church had yielded memoranda of some kind from every con-man except lucky 'Puss' McCasky, who had been released too soon.

From these men came telephone numbers and addresses, or names, of different members of the gang. Those of the Lookout, Duff, and the stock exchanges were common among the steerers, while the big fellows had Blonger's number as well. When these were matched together, the whole gang interlocked.

Hence no paper with writing on it was so unimportant that it could be thrown away until the last clue to its possible significance was unraveled. Names with addresses were apt to be those of either suckers or members of the gang, and more of each were wanted.

Illustrating what a fertile field such things were, Adolph W. Duff's notebook revealed the name of Alfred Seurin, of Cleveland, Ohio. A letter sent to Inspector H. N. Graham with this information, resulted in the identification of Duff and Thomas Beech as the two other men who, with French, had attempted to swindle Seurin out of several thousand dollars in Florida in

# MARGINAL DEALINGS BRING FORTUNE TO STRANGER

R.O.S. 8-24-22 Store.

The above is a good likeness of the man who yesterday thru the uncanny manipulations of the stock market caused a great wave of grief in the local Bucket Shops.

For years these houses have reaped a golden harvest, operating for the benefit of a syndicate of wealthy men, many of whom once held seats on the New York and Chicago Stock Exchanges.

These branches of the International Exchanges (in reality Bucket Shops) have for a long time been a menace to the general speculating public, and in a number of states have found it difficult to do business. However, they manage to operate in such places by obtaining club charters.

Should this chain of exchanges scattered thruout the country meet with the same fate as several of the local branches did yesterday thru the speculations of an unknown, it is safe to say that it will be unnecessary to legislate against them. Rumor has it that this mysterious stranger procured about $200,000 in the last few days.

Everyone commented on the fact that every deal went exactly as he planned. So it was only a short time until the operators showed reluctance in accepting his commissions. Consequently, when he made his final plunge on one of the active stocks and cleaned up over $100,000 the managers of the various clubs were thrown into a veritable panic and refused absolutely to take further commissions from this wizard of finance.

NEWSPAPER CLIPPING USED BY THE SPIELER TO SHOW HIS PAST WINNINGS

The face is torn off so that any spieler can use it

the winter of 1922. This evidence formed the basis for their later Federal indictment in Ohio.

On the edge of a scrap of newspaper found in Beech's pocket, and in his handwriting, was an apparently worthless memorandum giving the following: 'John Emrich, 2703 Hardie Avenue, Fort Smith, Arkansas.' A check-up revealed that Beech had steered Emrich through Blonger's Store in 1921.

Duff's notebook gave the names of many con-men, and the telephone numbers of the Store and six or seven leading detectives, including Oliver Smith. The latter had worked in the District Attorney's office the entire day of the raid, in blissful ignorance of the incarceration of his friends.

And so the work went on — matching facts and documents and assembling the cases on the various defendants.

The working literature of the mob was in a different category from the individual documents. This literature was the confidence men's printed paraphernalia. It was used both in the Store and by the spieler. None of it was genuine, and witnesses had to be secured who could testify to its falsity. In law it would then constitute the 'false tokens' which make these swindles the crime of obtaining money by means or by use of the confidence game.

In their part of the 'pay-off' game the steerers use no literature. This is reserved for the spieler, and the first stock documents appear through him. One of the initial papers which this clever talker shows to a prospective victim is a newspaper clipping reciting the big winnings which he had made on the stock exchange. This is to corroborate the previous story of the steerer in which he had told the sucker about the great luck which a young man had on the stock exchange. The preferred form has a man's picture at the top of the column. This is then mutilated, either by tearing off the head, or by cutting it off above the chin. Then any spieler can use it as if the picture were his. Other forms have no pictures at all.

The next document shown to the victim is always some form

of letter from the spieler's alleged employer, reproving him for the publicity which he had received. One form was in the box given to the District Attorney by Harry Williamson of the Federal Narcotic Department, and set out in Chapter VI. Sherwood, Sheppard and Company is the favorite letterhead for stock-exchange transactions, while some form of Turfmen's Association Stationery is used when horse-races are invoked.

A second letter used by the spieler is that from the Metropolitan Bonding Company. It is shown to the steerer, and then to the sucker. The bonding company writes that it has received a letter from the spieler's employer that his bond will not be renewed at its expiration. It goes on to state, however, that inasmuch as his business transactions have been thoroughly agreeable to it, it will be glad to write his bond with any new employer.

The next step is devised to convince the victim that the spieler is a responsible business man of large means. So he is always shown a bond in the sum of one hundred thousand dollars, and sometimes for good measure a letter of credit on an eastern bank is likewise exhibited. The latter entitles the bearer to draw drafts up to at least twenty-five thousand dollars. When the pocket-book scheme is used, these are found when the sucker picks it up and examines its contents. When the spieler is intercepted on the street, he shows them to the victim in one of his early talks.

The bond of the Metropolitan Bonding and Security Company, taken from Charles F. Dixon by Harry Williamson of the Federal Narcotic Bureau, was matched by dozens of similar forms on the fine bond paper which Inspector Graham had traced to Denver in March of 1922. These bonds and letters of credit were found on the spielers and in the Lookout. Some were filled in with the names the spielers were using on particular victims, while others were in blank, ready for future use.

From the Lookout Roy Samson obtained the so-called 'Com-

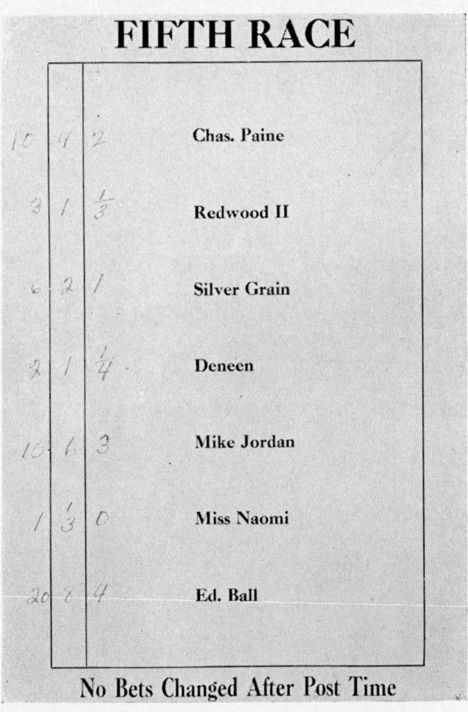

# FIFTH RACE

| | | | |
|---|---|---|---|
| 10 | 4 | 2 | Chas. Paine |
| 3 | 1 | 1/3 | Redwood II |
| 6 | 2 | 1 | Silver Grain |
| 2 | 1 | 1/4 | Deneen |
| 10 | 6 | 3 | Mike Jordan |
| 1 | 1/3 | 0 | Miss Naomi |
| 20 | 8 | 4 | Ed. Ball |

No Bets Changed After Post Time

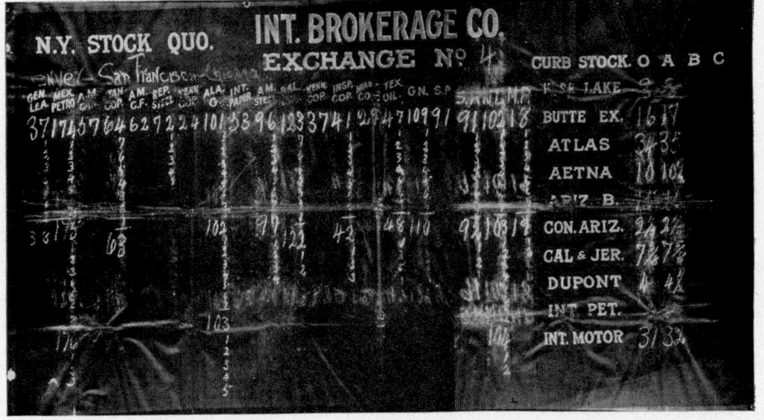


RACING SHEET AND BLACKBOARD USED BY BLONGER'S MEN

missioner's Code,' which was used by the con-men in their fake horse-races. This code forms the basis for a telegram later shown to the victim. This was on the stationery of a so-called American Turfman's Association, with a claimed capital of $5,000,000 and an alleged headquarters in New York City, New York. There were different names for each letter of the alphabet, such as A—'Bin,' B—'Bad,' etc.; names of metals for the separate races, — silver, First Race, gold, Second Race, etc.; another series for 'straight,' 'place,' or 'show'; and then a last set, identifying the bet, which needless to say was the most important from the con-man's standpoint — 'ramify' — bet $2500, 'quadroon' — bet $40,000, etc. With it were numerous admission cards used by the spieler in introducing himself and party at the exchange or race parlor. These were similar to Miller's cards, shown in Chapter XXXVI.

It is the clerk or bookmaker's job to furnish the exchange. The paraphernalia which first catches the sucker's eyes when he enters the center room is either an oil cloth blackboard for stock quotations or a series of race-charts, used when the horses are to be played. Just before the victim arrives the bookmaker hangs the proper set on the wall behind his desk. Then after the victim leaves they are taken down, carefully repacked in the suitcase, and returned to the Lookout.

The blackboard used by Blonger's men was about eight feet long by four feet wide. Across the top, in big letters, was the name 'Int. Brokerage Co.,' and under that 'Exchange No. 4.' The names of a few selected New York stocks were painted on the left side, and a similar set of curb stocks on the right. Then under the columns for the respective companies the clerk chalked up the quotations for the day.

The racing-sheets are called the entries for the fake races. Each entry card is put on the wall with thumb-tacks, and six races are run.

For the races, cards like those turned over by Harry Williamson, the Federal officer, are used, while in the stock market transactions, all kinds of buy and sell and call slips are available. Much of this literature is printed in English on one side and Spanish on the other, so that it can be used in Cuba or Mexico. A buy card appears in Chapter XXXVI.

When the spieler has the sucker sign a slip to make a trade, the last morning of the 'pay-off' game, a credit order is used. The one executed by Tang Nielsen of Tempe, Arizona, was seized at the Store. The arrests just saved Nielsen his five thousand dollars.

But best of all was the statement made out by Les Randle, while bookmaker on the Frank Norfleet deal, and found by Roy Samson in 'Tex' Cooper's room at the Melton Hotel. This sheet is used to record the play on which the sucker makes his big winning. It is on this paper, in the second half of the confidence-game, that the bookmaker, with a rubber stamp, places the words 'O.K., International Exchange,' so that it can be used for trading purposes. This statement is always prepared by the bookmaker in duplicate. He keeps one copy, the spieler the other.

Occasionally a victim is given a flier in the commodity market, then the con-men use a blank printed for that purpose.

Bank wrappers for 'boodle' packages formed an interesting array. They are kept on hand by the bookmaker, at the Lookout, and are in bundles, ready for use in any amount needed. When he gets ready to open the Store, he makes up some packages of boodle money, usually enough to look like about one hundred thousand dollars, and leaves it out in plain sight on the table. Then a few loose hundred-dollar bills are tossed on top. He then puts on an eye-shade, which gives him a busy appearance, and also helps as a disguise, as it partially covers his eyes.

Cheap fake money is sometimes used by a mob that is broke and does not have any real money for boodle. In such cases that gang has to 'play-to-the-wall' for the sucker, as it has no money to rent rooms for an exchange. So they put the fake

KEY
Dis.—Discount
Int.—Interest
Bal.—Balance
Lst.—Total List

WEEKLY STATEMENT

Branch No. 4 City Denver

**International Investment Exchange**

Statement of your Account to L. A. Mulligan and R. C. Davis

| Old Balance | Date | Stocks in Detail | Bought | Sold | Date | New Balance |
|---|---|---|---|---|---|---|
| | | Balance Brought Forward | | | | |
| | | National Lead | $100000.00 | | | $100000.00 |
| | | 102 @ 104 1/8 | | | | |
| | | | Profit | Loss | | $200000.00 |
| | | | $200000.00 | | | |
| | | | | | | $3000.00 |
| $3000.00 | | BALANCE | | | | $303000.00 |

Please examine this statement upon receipt and report at once if you find any difference, so that the International Investment Co., above branch, may know if their books agree with your own. If no error is reported in ten days, account will be considered correct. All items credited subject to final payment.

$10000 Date Aug 7-22

INTERNATIONAL EXCHANGE

CUSTOMER'S CREDIT ORDER

Gentlemen:

I Buy Ten thousand shares of Mex Petr at the market 172 on a 2 1/8 point Margin and charge to the account of

Tempe Natl. Bank
Tempe Ariz

Tang Nielsen

BOOKMAKER'S STATEMENT AND CUSTOMER'S CREDIT ORDER

money on the outside of the boodle which they made up from newspaper clippings cut the same size as the fake bills. The sucker never has a chance to handle the fake boodle as he does the real boodle in the regular play. He gets only a flash of this or sees it in the hands of the steerer or spieler.

Some samples of this money were obtained from one of the men's luggage.

Found in Randle's japanned-tin suitcase at the Lookout, as well as in the pockets of many of the men, were many memoranda of loans obtained by members of the gang from their fellows to pay for bail bonds or attorney fees in former arrests. The following typical list contained the names of sixteen con-men, all but one of whom had been active in the Denver gang:

| | |
|---|---|
| J. H. FRENCH | $250. |
| ROY FARRELL | $250. |
| JOE RUSH | $250. |
| A. B. COOPER | $100. |
| MC'BRIDE | $50. |
| FUTILO JOE | $200. |
| SOX [WALTER BYLAND] | $50. |
| F. SMITHY | $50. |
| TOM WILSON | $250. |
| POTTS | $25. |
| CAMBBELL | $20. |
| J. S. SIMMONS | $100. |
| J. HOGAN | $100. |
| SCHULTZ | $10. |
| FELEX [LEON FELIX] | $50. |
| JIM WATKINS | $50. |
| TOTAL | $1805. |

The amounts opposite the names gave a clear picture of the financial status of the donors, and were a good indication of how recently each had made a 'sale.' But all the lists were searched in vain for the names of either Blonger or Duff. They were not making loans to con-men! Their money went into real estate and bonds where it was available when needed.

An illuminating letter from Emory S. King, found in Tex Cooper's room, indicated, in the plainest of con-parlance, that the 'firm' in Salt Lake City had a privileged 'store' and that a 'salesman' had to make application for the privilege of working in a protected domain such as Denver. Salt Lake City itself had long been recognized by the underworld as one of the leading Western 'fixed' cities, with direct alliance between police and con-men. The letter:

June 18 22

FRIEND COOPER

I was in your City a few days ago but was so busy with Deal I Did not get to see you but Did not sell but Peg is still there trying to sell there is quite a few salesman with the Firm here and I want to ask you if I can get Job there or in Colo Springs Territory Will you writ me and Let me Know

Your Friend

E. S. KING
Gen Del
Salt Lake

By themselves, these captured documents were almost enough to prove the entire conspiracy case. The thirty-four defendants were all tied together by their individual memoranda, while the phoney stock exchange and race-horse paraphernalia showed that their transactions were the rawest kind of swindles.

The scene now changes to the court-room, where airtight cases often evaporate. Would clever lawyers and tricky gangsters defeat the Law in its own domain?

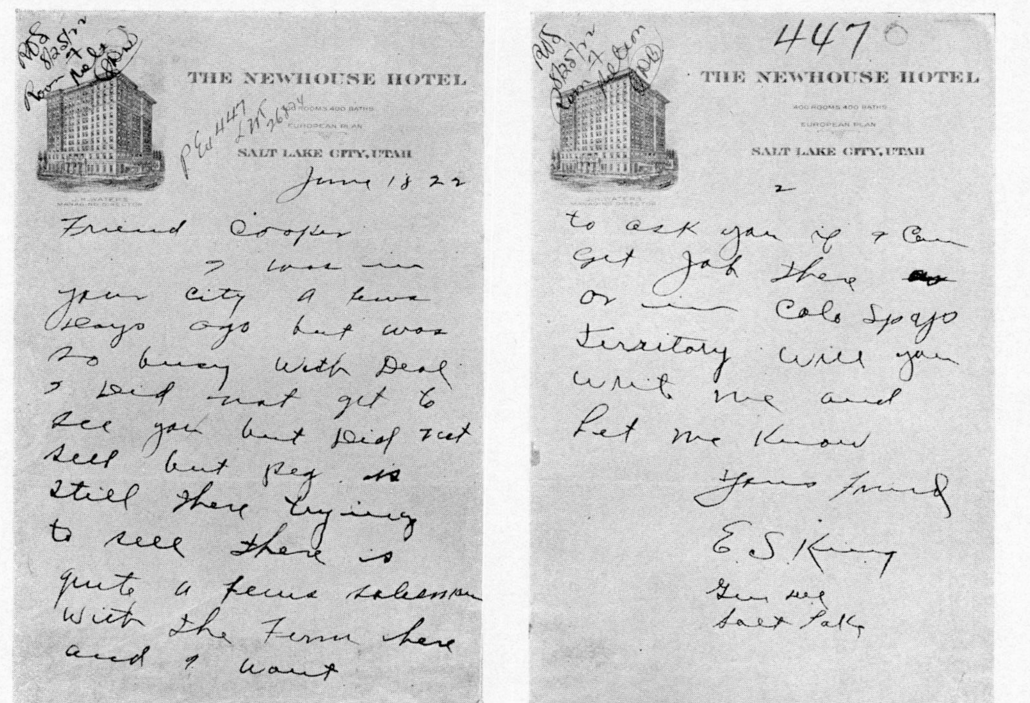

THE NEWHOUSE HOTEL
400 ROOMS 400 BATHS
EUROPEAN PLAN
SALT LAKE CITY, UTAH

June 18 22

Friend Cooper
I was in your city a few days ago but was so busy with Deal I did not get to see you but Did not sell but Reg. is still there trying to sell there is quite a few salesmen with the Firm here and I want

THE NEWHOUSE HOTEL
400 ROOMS 400 BATHS
EUROPEAN PLAN
SALT LAKE CITY, UTAH

447

2

to ask you if I can get Job there or in Colo Spgs territory Will you write me and let me know

Yours Friend

E. S. King

Gen Del
Salt Lake

A LETTER FROM 'STEERER' KING TO 'SPIELER' COOPER, ASKING FOR PERMISSION TO WORK IN DENVER OR COLORADO SPRINGS

# XXXI

## *Skirmishes*

The arrest of Blonger's gangsters created a furor in Colorado. The press entered the fight and stated that con-men never could have operated in such numbers as they had in Denver without absolute gilt-edged police protection. The 'Blonger Cherry Club,' as those who had received cherries from his orchard were beginning to be called, was apprehensive, fearful that any day would bring publication of the names on the list. 'Respectable' business men no longer thought it smart to know the Boss.

The people were indignant, but the City Hall officials were defiant. The Mayor issued a bombastic and amazing statement that the stock-brokers of Denver were behind the movement to clean up a few petty crooks who were operating fake stock exchanges so that the big fellows could win their millions.

Then Blonger's political friends and the underworld went into action to prevent the conviction of the mob. The county jailer, John Drake, was particularly bitter. He favored the con-men in every possible way, and did all he could to obstruct the District Attorney in taking victims into the jail to see the grafters in order to make more identifications. Hal Crane, of the sheriff's office, hobnobbed daily with Lou Blonger and Adolph Duff, and went back and forth to the jail with messages to the con-men who did not get out on bond.

The police, many of whom were fearful of landing in jail themselves, did not know what to do, but helped the mob wherever they could. With the exception of the two deputy sheriffs, 'Doc' Dawson and Jim Marshall, no official help or co-operation of any kind could be expected by the District Attorney. In his own office the latter still harbored Oliver Smith, the hoodwinked spy, who might still secure information for the enemy.

Hoping to repay the subscribers to the bunk fund, the Colonel asked the City Council to appropriate $15,000 for that purpose. However, these politicians were afraid to vote on it in the open, so held a secret session, in which they refused the request by a vote of 7 to 2. They gave as their reason that the contributors had not asked for reimbursement, and that the police department was not used in making the arrests!

The prosecutor countered with a statement showing that the city administration, since taking office in 1919, had received at least eleven complaints of con-game operations totaling $174,000, and that arrests had been made in only one case — and that under the personal order of the late Chief Hamilton Armstrong, three years before. He also said that nine detectives had been assigned — but in vain — on these charges!

In addition to that he called attention to the fact that, in this period, the total swindles of which he then had a record amounted to $648,720, and that his arrests prevented $222,000 more from being perpetrated in 1922!

And there the matter rested for months.

While Kenneth Robinson was in Los Angeles, District Attorney Thomas Lee Woolwine had told him that he was particularly anxious to get J. Roy Farrell, who was one of the slickest con-men in the country; that he had many cases against him, and if he was arrested in Denver to hold him for California. Robinson had agreed to do so.

J. Roy Farrell was one of the men captured during the raid, and was both a clever and a pleasant crook. You liked him as soon as you met him.

A few days after the raid Robinson wired Woolwine that Farrell had been arrested; that Denver had a good case on him, but would turn him over to California if it still desired him, and Woolwine replied that he wanted him badly, and was sending his star detective, Charles Riemer, with proper papers to get him.

Woolwine's emissary arrived in Denver a few days later, and Farrell declared that he would waive extradition and go at once. The District Attorney walked from the jail to the automobile with the two men, and Farrell said: 'Colonel, I think it is going to go pretty hard with all of the boys here in Denver. You don't know how much I appreciate your sending me to California, and you can be assured I won't give Mr. Riemer any trouble.'

He didn't. Riemer took his prisoner to jail. Forthwith Farrell furnished a $20,000 bond, and was released the day after he reached Los Angeles. The bond turned out to be 'straw,' with the bondsman a dummy. Farrell promptly left California, and has never been arrested since that time.

District Attorney Woolwine was highly embarrassed and apologized profusely for the way in which the clerk who handled the matter in the Criminal Court had allowed Farrell's bond to be made without consulting his office. The crooks had been arrested, now the far-flung power of the underworld was working to get them out.

About that time Duff started to talk. He just couldn't keep his mouth shut. Shortly after the arrests, as he was coming out of the court-room, he encountered Frank Norfleet.

Norfleet said 'Good morning, Mr. Duff. How are you feeling this morning?'

And Duff said, 'Fine, fine, under the circumstances.'

Norfleet had two Texas friends with him, J. R. Barnhill and

B. C. Paxton, and introduced them to Duff, who asked them if they lived in Denver.

Barnhill said: 'No, we are from Texas. We heard that Norfleet was into some kind of a jackpot or trouble, and we just came up to see if he needed anything.'

Duff sized them up, and then called Norfleet aside and said, 'Say, Norfleet, can't we fix up this matter?'

And Norfleet answered, 'Well, Duff, if you had a little more sense and would turn in my man, Spencer, for me, I'd go home.'

Duff answered, 'If you had come to me before this happened, I would have had your man and your money, too.'

'Where is my man?' said Norfleet.

Duff answered: 'I don't know where he is now, but I know where he was before I went to jail. I saw one of the boys from City Hall this morning, and he told me that Spencer's suitcase was down at the Empire Hotel. Spencer registered under the name of Harris.' Duff then gave his office number to Norfleet, and told him to come and see him.

Norfleet and his friends went to the Empire Hotel and found Spencer's suitcase. Norfleet opened it and there was his old gun! Spencer had stolen it from him in his hotel in Fort Worth on the night of December 2, 1919.

Later Duff ran into Roy Samson in the courthouse, and complained that the District Attorney had 'set him out on the street,' meaning that he could not make any money while the case was going on. 'Why, Roy, you know I was in the bunk business up to five or six years ago, but no one's had anything on me recently, and it is a hundred-to-one shot that you could ever put me in "stir."'

Samson answered: 'Quit your kidding, Duff. You have been trimming them in Denver, Kansas City, and Florida. Any time you see a chance to beat a sucker, you rap to it.'

And Duff said: 'The answer to that, Roy, is, show me a chance to make some money, and I will do it. I will put up five or six thousand any time to make money.

'Say, Roy, here's a funny stunt. You know, when I got back to Denver in April, I looked around for an apartment, and among others I looked at one belonging to the District Attorney's mother up on Gaylord Street. Wouldn't it have been funny if I had been living there when arrested?

'And say, Mead made Blonger get him out on bond, and do you know, that s— of a b—— Mead threatened to kill me five minutes after he got out of jail? Why, the poor bastard, if I didn't have a wife and two boys, he would never have walked down the sidewalk. I would have shot him where he stood.

'Say, Roy, what did you take Jack Hardaway [one of the steerers arrested in the raid] for, anyway? Take a good look at that poor old man. You fellows certainly played a bum lead when you picked him up. He couldn't beat a sucker under any circumstances.'

Samson: 'What's he doing, then, running around with you fellows? From our observation of him he was one of the busiest bunk men in the crowd.'

Duff: 'Oh, he might have been busy, but he couldn't have beaten anybody. He was just begging and borrowing a dollar off the boys, getting along as well as he could.'

Roy: 'Well, if he had ever landed his sucker, you would certainly have played him.'

And Duff replied, 'Oh, sure, but he never landed anybody.'

Just then Blonger came out of the courtroom, and, seeing Duff with Roy Samson, went straight for him, and said, 'You G—— d——ed fool, if you don't keep your mouth shut, I am going to put a trap on it.'

Following the arrests, Pete Land telephoned the District Attorney and stated that he would like to see him at his house. The prosecutor told him to come up, and soon the fat detective appeared, a much-perturbed man.

Pete Land wasted no time in coming to the point, because no sooner had the two men entered the den than Land started to cry like a baby, and said, 'Colonel, I have a wife and a fine boy, and I don't want that boy to have his father in the penitentiary.' And then he sank upon his knees and stated what a fine church member and good Catholic he was. He swore by all the Saints that he had not had anything to do in protecting the con-men. It appeared that Cooper's report of Ed Ginney's statement was going to be true when he said that 'Land did not have any guts, and would holler if the District Attorney ever hemmed him up.'

'Honest to God, Colonel, I don't know any of them except Blonger and Duff, and everybody in town knows Blonger. Why, even you knew him yourself before you were elected, and that's not any crime. I didn't know what Duff was doing. If you only promise not to send me to the pen, I will tell you anything I know.'

The District Attorney answered: 'Land, you are such a damned liar that nobody would believe you on oath if you did tell the truth. When you were down to the Springs you got my list from Bruce, and took it right to Blonger. What do you say about that?'

'Well, now, Colonel, that list was posted on the bulletin board down there, and given to all of us, and we didn't know what it meant. Bruce told us to look out for those fellows, but we hadn't heard any of their names, and I got sick and had to come back to Denver, and went in to see the doctor who had the office next door to Blonger.

'After I came out of there, Blonger's door was open, and he said, "Hello, Pete," and I went in and he asked me where I had been. I told him down to the Springs, and he asked me what I had been doing, and I said looking for pickpockets.

'Then I added: "By the way, Lou, something funny happened down there. Bruce had a list of a lot of fellows that he said were con-men; gave us each a copy of it, and it's got A's and B's and X's, "Short Blacky's" and that sort of thing written all over it. Look here, I have it with me." And then Blonger said it looked curious to him, and asked me to leave it with him, and that is all there was to it.'

The District Attorney replied: 'Yes, that was all there was to it! That is not what you said to Blonger. You told him you had my list. Then Duff came in and you talked it over with both of them. You're one of the gang and you are going to the pen along with the rest of them.'

'Oh, my God, Colonel!' said Pete, and boo-hooed as hard as any school-girl.

Pete was just on the verge of confessing to try to save his hide, when the District Attorney made a slip and said, 'How did Blonger pay you fellows, Pete?'

Instantly Land concluded that the prosecutor didn't have enough evidence on the police. Jumping to his feet he said, 'Well, I must be going. I just dropped around to let you know I didn't do anything out of the way about Bruce's list,' and putting on his hat he beat a quick retreat from the house.

Moral: When a crook wants to talk, keep quiet and let him.

# XXXII

## *Defense Tactics*

At the opening of court Friday morning, the day after the con-men were turned over to the police, the attorneys for the mob went into court. They demanded either that the District Attorney be compelled to file his charges forthwith or that writs of *habeas corpus* be issued, and the amount of the bond be fixed so that the prisoners could make bail and be released.

The Clerk of the District Court telephoned the District Attorney's office, and located Kenneth Robinson, who was busy preparing the information. The latter agreed to file a case during the afternoon, but from two to four the telephone buzzed with heated demands from the Judge that the cases be filed instantly, and the cool rejoinder by Robinson that he would file them as soon as they could be prepared, and before closing time.

Colorado is not hampered by the archaic constitutional requirements of the Federal courts and of those of many of the eastern and southern States where felony charges can only be preferred against defendants by the slow and tedious method of an indictment by a grand jury. As far back as 1891 its legislature provided, as an alternative to the indictment, that the District Attorney, at his option and upon leave of court, might use direct informations. As a consequence nearly all criminal cases in that State are instituted by filing written charges supported only by the affidavit of the complaining witness. This eliminates the expense of a grand jury, saves the time of witnesses before it, and expedites trial.

The Denver criminal procedure called for the appearance of the defendants in court on the first Saturday after their arrest. This is the time for arraignment, when the defendants either plead to the charge or secure time in which to file motions attacking the information. Blonger and Duff, being out on bond, came through the front door, the others were herded over from the jail. The prisoners filled all available space inside the rail.

As their names were called each defendant was given a copy of the information. Two weeks time was then granted in which to file motions and secure additional attorneys. The court battle was on.

At that session the lie was passed between a defense attorney and the Colonel. Instantly the latter punched the lawyer on the jaw, and a wild scramble ensued, which was quickly broken up by court officials.

There was a peculiar coincidence about that little altercation. By that time the District Attorneys of three large cities in the United States had attacked the con-men in their respective towns of Los Angeles, Atlanta and Denver. And each had now had a fist fight with the opposing counsel the first day that the gangsters appeared in the courtroom! Thomas Lee Woolwine in Los Angeles, and John A. Boykin in Atlanta, were not as lucky as the Denver prosecutor, as both they and their opponents were fined.

Now came the tactical moves so common in all criminal trials. The con-men assembled an imposing array of counsel well versed in criminal law, headed by Horace N. Hawkins, one of the strongest advocates who ever practiced at the Colorado Bar, and ably seconded by Mike Waldron, a shrewd warrior of many battles. Neither had ever represented the gangsters before.

It was later learned that dissension soon arose in the legal camp of the defendants. All but Mike Waldron insisted on every possible legal delay. Waldron, however, declared that even though the District Attorney had been working for fifteen months, he was not ready, and could not be ready for several weeks, and that they should demand an immediate trial. Waldron was right in his analysis of the case, but was overruled by his associates, who delayed the case from August until February, when a jury was finally empaneled to try the defendants.

The regular Judge of the Criminal Division, Charles C. Butler, then returned from his vacation and for the first time entered the case. He is now Chief Justice of the Colorado Supreme Court, and has always been noted for his integrity, impartiality, and freedom from any political bias. But at the outset he was very skeptical that the prosecutor had the evidence to justify his arrests, and felt that the District Attorney had allowed his enthusiasm to run away with his judgment.

Here was a case where the police were set aside and the District Attorney performed their functions, where a jail was the information center for the underworld and a church furnished refuge to the Law. So Judge Butler listened with utmost attention to every proposition advanced by the defendants and gave them as much time as they wanted on motions which would ordinarily have been overruled in a few minutes. Though the prosecution chafed the defense rejoiced in these delays. But in the long run the State was the gainer, as it thus secured the much needed time thoroughly to prepare its case.

The information charged the defendants with conspiracy to defraud the public in general, by means and by use of the confidence-game. Under the statutes of Colorado an information must be sworn to someone who has knowledge of the facts charged, and it was, therefore, signed by Andrew Koehn, the star detective. Koehn personally knew more about the actual operations of the grafters in Denver than all the rest of the prosecutor's force put together.

As their first attack, the defense filed a motion to vacate the orders given by the court granting leave to file the information. These were upon two grounds, first, that Andrew Koehn was not a real person but a fictitious one, and second, that if he existed, that he knew nothing whatsoever about the charges to which he had sworn against the con-men. The main purpose of the motion, of course, was to force the District Attorney to produce Koehn in open court so that he could be identified by the defendants. If that were done his use as an undercover man was at an end.

The prosecution opposed the move with all its strength. In the argument the State told the court that Koehn was a real individual, a man of good reputation, had been working for the District Attorney for eight months, knew what he was swearing to, and that his production would hamper the prosecution. But the court was adamant, and ordered that Koehn be placed upon the witness stand for examination by the defense.

Andrew Koehn entered the room, took the witness stand, and soon satisfied the Judge that he was a reputable person and had real knowledge of the operations of the con-men. The Court held the interrogations of the defendants within reasonable limits, and then refused to withdraw its orders for leave to file the information. The State had won the motion, but the defendants were the gainers, as they had now seen Koehn.

The next assault was a motion to reduce the bail of all but Duff and Blonger. This had been fixed originally at $50,000 for each man. When such a motion is made, for the purpose of that motion only the defendant is presumed to be guilty of the offense charged, but the prosecution must show the reputation of each defendant and some of its evidence against them as a basis for fixing the amount. The State contended that the bonds of known criminals should be placed high enough to insure their presence at the trial, and that nothing less than $50,000 for each of the con-men would do so. It then presented the criminal records of the defendants and some of the facts about them.

A typical instance was John J. Grady. He had a record of twenty-three arrests in nine years, on charges ranging from gambling to murder, but no convictions. But the Judge was still skeptical of the prosecution, did not believe it had presented enough facts to justify high bonds, so cut the amounts radically. The highest was left at $25,000, while he placed Grady's at $3500 and two others as low as $2000 on each. As a result Grady and five others, who had the low bonds, promptly made bail and jumped town at once. However, the security on those bonds had been carefully checked, and $25,500 was collected on them; this sum was a material aid to the county in the expense of the trial.

Having succeeded in smoking out Andrew Koehn, and having been successful in cutting the bonds of all defendants who applied, the defense now turned its guns upon the District Attorney in person, in an effort to show that he was personally interested in the outcome of the criminal cases, and should, therefore, be disqualified from further connection with the prosecution.

This attack arose out of the efforts of the District Attorney to assist victims to recover their losses from the con-men.

Immediately after the raid, as a result of a special request to Postmaster General Hubert L. Work, a Colorado man, Inspector H. N. Graham, of New York, had been sent to Denver to assist in the preparation of the case for trial.

He went to the jail, looked over the prisoners, came back and studied the evidence, and then found that the District Attorney had the names of only a dozen victims.

'Say, look here,' he said, 'you haven't nearly enough suckers. You haven't ten per cent of the victims of the last three years. You've got to get some more!'

'What's the idea?' said the District Attorney. 'We don't want to tire the jury out with the same story repeated over and over. And by what magic will we produce more witnesses?'

'Well, the reason you need a lot more victims is that they are going to bribe these fellows to stay home. They all live out of Colorado, and you can't make them come if they don't want to. And if this gang is at all smart, they will start somebody out on the road with a little money, go to each victim, and offer him part of his cash if he just does nothing. They will put it up in escrow with a stakeholder to be delivered to him when the trial is over.

'Don't you think these victims are human? They need that money badly, and they're going to get as much as they can, and you can't blame them. So your entire case may pass out from under you unless you get so many victims they won't have enough money to go around.'

'How are you going to get more victims?' queried the prosecutor.

'That's easy, too,' replied the expert. 'These victims are hit in their pocketbook. You give them a chance to get something back, and they will all come flocking in and help you out. On the other hand, if all they get out of it is advertising to the world that they were played for suckers, the greater bulk of them will keep their mouths shut, and not only say nothing, but if approached, will absolutely deny that they ever heard of such a transaction.

'Besides that, many of them never have discovered that they were trimmed, the con-men played their parts so perfectly; and you would be surprised at the number of people who have read the full details of the operations of the con-men, and then who turn around, get picked up themselves, go through the play, march up with their money, and lose it all on the identical transaction which they saw in the paper.

'The thing for you to do is to try to locate any property which the con-men may have, get some victims to bring a civil suit and attach that property. Then have the papers play up to the world that suckers are getting the con-men's cash and you'll be swamped with victims.'

'Too bad we didn't think of this earlier,' said the Colonel.

'Blonger and Duff have probably transferred all of their property by now. If we had only had a sucker file suit the day after the arrests and garnish every bank in town, we would have reached the securities of those two and possibly have put the defense out of business. Well, we didn't do it in time, but we'll do the best we can now.'

'The thing to remember in fighting the underworld,' said Graham, 'is to hit crooks hard and in as many places as possible at the same time. They can't get lawyers, fix witnesses, and bribe jurors without cash.'

Two victims were in Denver, eager to recover their money by civil suits. So John Peck, of Kentucky, who had lost $19,000, went to Attorney Henry E. May, and Frank Donovan of New Orleans, an old man of eighty, who had lost $65,000, employed Harold Webster. The latter was one of the headquarters force, which had helped at the church on the day of the raid. Webster was in the law office of Clyde C. Barker, who had occupied the same suite with the prosecutor just prior to the latter's election. Barker and the Colonel had formed a nominal partnership when the latter went over to the District Attorney's office, but had never participated in any cases nor shared in any fees.

Frank Donovan was one of over sixty witnesses whose names were endorsed upon the information against the defendants. However, he had not sworn to any of the charges as the prosecuting witness against them. He was also, through his attorney, Harold Webster, suing the con-men in a civil action to recover his $65,000. Then, without the knowledge of the Colonel, and in an entirely different civil suit of which he had never heard, the name Barker, Van Cise & Webster was signed to the complaint filed in the latter case. Some of the defendant's attorneys now took the position that the Colonel was attorney for Donovan in his civil case against the con-men, and therefore a party in interest in the criminal case, and for that reason ineligible longer to act as prosecutor. Clyde Barker and Harold Webster were fine fellows and good lawyers, but the mistake in their office was now the ground upon which the defense was to move to disqualify the District Attorney.

It was later learned that once again there was dissension among the defense attorneys. Mike Waldron said: 'The last thing we want to do is to disqualify the Colonel. I want him in the courtroom as much as we can get him there, so he won't have time to mass his facts. The worst thing we can do is to turn him loose. If he is left free of court worries we're sunk.' But again Waldron was overruled.

The evidence consisted in the presentation of the complaint filed in court, and the testimony of the Colonel, Barker and Webster that there was no partnership between the three of them, that the District Attorney had nothing to do with the civil suit to which his name was signed, and had never heard of it before. There was no contradictory testimony of any kind. Nevertheless, the Judge entered an order disqualifying the District Attorney. He then ruled that he would appoint special prosecutors.

Judge Butler leaned over backward so much that he called the attorneys for the defendants, but not the District Attorney, into conference to talk over with them prospective special prosecutors. This was done to make sure that there would be no further delays because of any legal objections to his final selections. He then appointed S. Harrison White, former Chief Justice of the Supreme Court of Colorado, a Democrat, and Harry C. Riddle, former Judge of the District Court, a Republican, and the court proceedings were thereafter handled by them. Their selection was fatal to the defense.

Though Frank Donovan started his suit, he died a short time afterwards, largely from worry over his losses. But Henry E. May vigorously pushed Peck's case against both Blonger and Duff and recovered quite a substantial sum. Peck, however, was the only victim who went through with a suit.

The defense had ousted the District Attorney. Was Waldron right or wrong?

# XXXIII

## *The Con-Men Make Two Assaults*

MIKE WALDRON was right, the disqualification of the prosecutor turned out to be a boomerang to the defendants, as it left the District Attorney absolutely free to direct the attack from his office. A general does not fight battles in the front line, but at his Command Post, and the Colonel, relieved from the trial, could gather evidence and assemble the facts while Kenneth Robinson briefed the law. Thus the prosecutor's force could spend its full time in preparation of the case, while Judges White and Riddle centered their entire attention on the events in the courtroom, confident that the facts and the law would be on hand as needed.

Chief defense counsel Horace N. Hawkins later stated that the District Attorney's removal was a tremendous advantage to the State, and the grave error of the defense.

Then came a very serious and clever move by Hawkins. He petitioned the Court that it order the return of all of the documentary evidence taken from the defendants, on the ground that the District Attorney, as such, had no powers of arrest other than those of a private citizen; that the arrests were illegal, and that the seizure of property was in violation of both the Federal and State Constitutions.

This was a battle royal, in which the defendants were bound

to gain something, no matter what the outcome. They were now going to make the State show them all of the captured documents, and there was a possibility that they might secure an order that all the documents be returned, that the arrests be held illegal, and that the information be quashed.

Twenty days of court time were consumed in this hearing, the District Attorney alone being on the witness stand seven days, and Kenneth Robinson three. The District Attorney was now required to prove everything necessary to establish an arrest by a private citizen: first, that a felony had actually been committed; second, that he had reasonable grounds for believing that the defendants had committed it; and third, that he had arrested the gang because of that crime and because of his belief that the defendants were guilty.

The prosecutor's staff planned their case so as to give as few facts as possible to the other side and to hold back their best information. The defendants' play was to drag out every bit of evidence, so that they might learn the State's case in advance of the trial.

The victims all resided out of the State, and were scattered throughout the United States, with one in England. Their business would not permit them to come to Colorado more than once, but one witness, at least, to prove an actual felony, had to be produced. Hence the prosecution had to select the witness whom it could most afford to lose. One victim, William E. Griffith, of Iowa, was a sick man, who would probably not live for the trial, so it was decided to use him. He testified to having been swindled out of $20,000.

The hearing then developed both the dramatic and the comic. One day Frank Norfleet, minus his guns, was on the stand. Examining him was Sam Crump, a powerful, belligerent lawyer, famed for his powers of cross-examination.

Crump: Didn't your wife, with your knowledge and consent, go to Mr. Blonger's office about a month ago and make a demand for

$30,000, with a promise from him that if this money was paid, you would quit this prosecution?

Frank's eyes lit up. 'No, sir,' he said, 'who says she did?'

Crump pointed his finger at the Texan. 'Do you say that your wife did not come up here and endeavor to make that deal?'

Frank's right hand flew to his hip, and his left hand shot towards the lawyer. Leaning forward in his chair, he answered, but in a cold, fierce voice: 'I do say it. Do you say she did?'

Crump jumped from the lawyer's stand, took refuge behind the table, and in a faltering tone asked, 'Have you got a gun on you now?' and sat down!

The comedy came when Lewis D. Mowry, deputy District Attorney, who had made some arrests in the raid and had later gone to Brighton with the prisoners, was being examined by Mr. Hawkins. The latter was trying to show that all of Mowry's actions were illegal; that it was against the statutes for an attorney to be a deputy sheriff; and that Mowry was a defendant in a false arrest suit started by the con-men.

Mr. Hawkins: You are a defendant in a suit which has been brought for damages on account of the raid?

Mowry: I was not aware of that fact until a moment ago when someone told me that I had been flattered by having been sued for $25,000.

Hawkins' questions of Mowry then took a different tack.

*Q.* The Ranger was there to back you up, wasn't he?

*A.* I hoped that he would. He stood about six feet six and I was hoping if there was any trouble he would back me up.

*Q.* He did not say at any time, 'I, a Ranger of the State of Colorado, arrest you'?

*A.* No, he was not a talkative man.

*Q.* Had you anything to do with selecting him to accompany you?

*A.* I certainly did. I picked out the biggest man in the crowd!

*Q.* When you get through with the lawsuit, you will not think it was lucky you did any arresting.

*A.* They will be lucky if they collect very much money from me.

Then the queries veered to happenings in the Golden jail.

*Q.* You were a lawyer and slept in a cell that night?
*A.* I was a deputy sheriff that night.
*Q.* Where did you go the next day?
*A.* I went to bed.
*Q.* You did not try to make any more arrests?
*A.* No, I was a district attorney then!

Judge Butler, usually the most solemn judge on the bench, whirled his chair toward the wall, and shook in silent mirth while the courtroom roared.

The only witnesses called on this motion for the return of the seized property were those presented by the State, and none of the defendants took the stand. The entire matter was a skillful fishing expedition on the part of the defendants, and their attorneys in this manner saw a large portion of the documentary evidence of the State.

The prosecution thoughtlessly returned the typewriter taken from Cooper's room. It overlooked entirely the evidentiary value of this machine and of the one taken from the Lookout. The writings on these two would have corresponded with many of the documents taken from the defendants and further tied them in.

By this time Judge Butler was finally convinced that the State had the evidence to prove its case, and that the arrests were legal. At the close of the hearing, he ordered only those documents returned which were taken from the apartments of some of the gang in their absence, but ruled that all evidence seized on the persons of the defendants or in their rooms when they were there arrested should be kept by the District Attorney. The Court then set the case for trial in February, when another judge would preside.

While the State had sustained a major victory, the defense had seen all of the captured documents. But it had not heard the daily reports of the detectives, nor other important evidence which the prosecutor withheld. The defense, however, by its initial victories and its tactics in the fight for the documents, had made the prosecution furious. Knowing this, some of the defense lawyers now hoped so to worry the Colonel that he would have to cool down on the case and turn his attention to his personal matters.

When criminal lawyers have no defense, they attack the law-enforcement officers, in an attempt so to prejudice the jurors against the State that the latter will forget the evidence against the defendants. And with their backs to the wall, the majority of the defense counsel decided to make now a second assault upon the District Attorney.

Mike Waldron, again cast in the rôle of Cassandra, and Horace N. Hawkins joined forces this time and opposed the new move of their fellow-counsel. When overruled, however, they told the other attorneys they could plunge into disaster if they wanted to, but to leave them out.

So seven civil suits were filed, naming as defendants the twenty-eight main participants in the August attack, the District Attorney, his deputies, the headquarters force at the church, and the car drivers. And all the mob asked for damages was a paltry $192,000 for alleged false arrests and seizure of baggage!

The cases didn't bother the Colonel, who regarded them as a bluff. But they badly worried some of the other men sued, who feared that they faced expensive litigation. However, the con-men's counsel had overplayed their hand, and at once the District Attorney turned the tables upon his adversaries. Attorneys Henry E. May and Charles Irwin, the former one of the prosecutor's opponents in the primary election, and both able trial lawyers, volunteered to defend the cases.

In civil actions in Colorado it is quite customary to compel a party to an action to give his testimony in advance of trial. This is called 'taking a deposition.' A notice and subpoena to appear are served upon the other side, and the evidence is taken either before a court or a notary public. Such party must then be present and answer all questions relative to the facts in the case.

So notices were forthwith served on the gang plaintiffs that their depositions would be taken and they were subpoenaed to appear and testify. Then they knew they were up against it, just as Hawkins and Waldron had advised before they sued. The mob could now be questioned in court as to their criminal records and activities. If they refused to answer on the ground of incrimination, their false arrest cases would blow up, while if they talked, they faced perjury charges or admissions against themselves in the conspiracy cases.

Under the filing system then in use in the Denver District Courts, cases as docketed were rotated among the five civil divisions. Two of the cases fell before a judge who was strongly opposed to the District Attorney. The remaining cases were assigned to the judges in the four other divisions, who promptly ordered the plaintiffs to appear and give their testimony. Finding these judges would not allow any delays the con-men quickly got out from under and dismissed those actions.

The remaining judge, however, was a bosom friend of the attorney who had advocated the filing of the cases. And that lawyer was not going to retract until his friendship had been pushed to the limit. So George Leo Kelley and Eddie Straub, the plaintiffs in the remaining actions, appeared in answer to their subpoenas, and were sworn to tell the truth. Having done so, they refused to answer any questions at all on the ground of incrimination, and attempted to make a farce of the proceedings. A citation was then secured requiring them to show cause why they should not be compelled to answer questions, and this was set down for argument.

On the date set, the Judge and his friend were closeted in the court chambers for half an hour. When they emerged, Henry E. May winked at the District Attorney, and said, 'We are going to get it in the neck this morning.' The Judge very solemnly waited until the citation was read. Then he refused to hear any oral arguments at all and stated that he preferred to have briefs submitted. Twelve days were given for that purpose, but no decision was ever rendered. Later, after the verdict was rendered in the criminal case, the civil suits were dismissed.

A peculiar aftermath of these damage cases was that they had a marvelous effect upon the District Attorney's credit. As soon as the merchants of Denver found out that he was being sued for $192,000, they thought he must be wealthy. A piano salesman tried to sell his wife an Aeolian piano for $4500. The Cadillac and Packard car dealers thought that nothing less than their best cars were fit for a person who could defend so large a suit, and storekeepers vied with each other in trying to sell him their best wares. But a salary of $4600 a year does not allow such luxuries, and the District Attorney was lucky to own a Ford.

The prediction about William E. Griffith turned out to be true, and he died in January, 1923.

The attempts to blot out the documentary evidence and to divert the time of the prosecutor had both failed. Could later attacks as successfully be turned aside?

# XXXIV

## *Wives*

WIVES are of all kinds and dispositions, as the women know and a few men sometimes realize. Lawyers who have had many domestic complaints see more of wives in their true light than do most people. Some wives talk, others keep their mouths shut, but the women of con-men are in a class by themselves.

Duff and Blonger were actually married, but many of the others were not. Most of the men had their girls with them, and these women were devotedly attached, either to their men or to their men's money, and stuck with them to the bitter end.

The day of the arrest it was the wives and sweethearts who first sensed that something was wrong, and sent the word along the underground grapevine to all the con-men whom they could reach, that trouble was brewing and to get out of town. They were directly responsible for the getaway of most of those who escaped capture.

These women, the 'molls' of the underworld, are always an important adjunct of every gang. They know what their men are doing, plot with them, scheme with them, fight with and for them. When prosecuted themselves, they usually escape the toils of the law because of their sex, as jurors seldom believe that the female of the species can be as criminal as the male. Those who have had experience with the underworld watch the sweethearts of the gangs, because they are dangerous, vindictive, and particularly adept at the tip-off. The French are right, *Cherchez la femme!*

Two con-men's wives now figure actively in the rapidly unfolding drama. One of them, 'California Kate,' the wife of William Elmer Mead, the 'Christ Kid,' was a woman of striking appearance. Tall, stately, well-dressed, and good-looking, with fine complexion and white hair, she would have been picked for a woman of society in any company as long as she said nothing. When she started to talk, however, her language revealed her true character. She was a pickpocket and 'store-booster,' or shoplifter, and worked in close association with her husband.

William Elmer Mead, one of the men wanted by Albert Backus in 1919, had a surly disposition, and was not very well liked by his own crowd. While playing cards in Los Angeles he got into a fight with a fellow con-man, and was shot through the right side of the mouth. In consequence he lost some teeth and had a little droop to his lip. His bond was reduced from $50,000 to $25,000, even though the day of his arrest he was preparing to swindle C. H. Hubbell out of $50,000!

Mead couldn't, or wouldn't, raise the bond, because he was afraid that if he put up his own money it might be attached by some of his victims, so 'California Kate' went on the rampage. She first talked to Jack French, but he refused to help her, so the latter part of September, Kate went down to see Blonger, and while she was talking to him Mrs. Steno's dictaphone buzzed.

Walking into his office Kate said, 'Are you going on Elmer's bond?'

'Why, no,' said Blonger. 'I can't go on his bond. If I did that, they would all say I am in on this thing, and you ought to know better than to come up here to see me, anyway.'

Kate said: 'Don't you tell me what I should do. You either get Elmer out tonight, or I am going to the District Attorney and tell him every damn thing I know, and I know plenty, and Elmer is going to add to it.'

Blonger said, 'Go on and see him, and see where you land.'

Then Kate started in. 'You dirty son-of-a-bitch, you God-damned, lousy liar. You're running this show, and my Elmer's in jail... Now,... I got you,' and Blonger let out a whoop.

'You let go of my nose, God damn you! Get out of here!' And a chair was upset in the scuffle, but Kate held on.

She said: 'I'll not only twist your nose; I'll chew your ear. Does Elmer get out on bond or doesn't he?'

Blonger said, 'You let go and I will fix it up.' Kate gave his nose a final twist, then flung him into his chair, where he fell back, a thoroughly exhausted and utterly cowed fixer.

Before night a bond was made for Mead, and he went out of jail.

But the joke was on Kate, after all. The Federal authorities had a warrant for Mead which he had not been able to square, and while he was perfectly willing to forfeit Blonger's $25,000 bond, he was not going down to Florida and put up any of his own money on a bond which he intended to jump. So the 'Christ Kid' surrendered himself back to the State authorities the next day, and went to jail, where he remained throughout the trial.

The other women pursued a different tack. They soon became convinced that Blonger, to cover himself up, would not furnish the security to the bonding companies for any of the defendants. So an interesting but highly secret game developed on the part of the wives to see which one could first obtain the ear of the District Attorney, and induce him to accept their man as a witness for the State and against the gang. So messages came in daily, and sometimes hourly, some legitimate, some fraught with danger to the senders, some hopeful of making appointments to plead for their lovers, others attempting to entice the Colonel to their rooms and there frame him. The woman-racket is an old one, and many public officials have been fooled by it, but it was one game against which the District Attorney was thoroughly forewarned, and one into which the wives had no chance whatsoever of inveigling him.

He was asked to meet the women on vacant lots, in hotels, rooming-houses, and homes on Capitol Hill. He informed all of them that, if they had anything to tell him, he would send his own wife and Kenneth Robinson to get them and bring them where the District Attorney would talk to them.

In this connection the latter's wife was of very material assistance from the time he started the investigation until the case was over. She knew all the ins and outs of the entire transaction, handled confidential telephone calls at the house, and mail that came under assumed names; transmitted information to the District Attorney over his secret line or sent orders to the detectives on various matters; and she and Kenneth Robinson went out at night for many a woman who wanted to talk to the District Attorney about securing leniency for her man.

But a District Attorney should get something of real value before he allows a defendant to turn State's evidence. There is no use taking one of the small fry who knows nothing. It must be one of the big fellows on the inside, who knows the facts, can prove them by statements other than his own, and whose story will dovetail in with that of other witnesses, so that it cannot be discredited by the defense.

One day a woman with a nice voice telephoned. She said that she was the wife of one of the higher-ups, and that she wanted to meet the Colonel that night under the trees by the Perrenoud Apartment at Seventeenth and Emerson. She told such a convincing story that the District Attorney agreed to have somebody meet her, and Kenneth Robinson and the Colonel's wife picked her up and took her to the District Attorney's house. There the visitor introduced herself as Mrs. Les Randle. Her husband was the 1922 bookmaker! He had not made bail so was still in the county jail.

Mrs. Randle was a brunette, above medium height, and good-looking. She was interesting to talk to, and possessed real ability. Her background was one of early poverty and adult crime. Devoted to her husband, she wanted him to get out of his trouble so both could turn over a new leaf and go straight. And she knew if Randle turned State's evidence he could never again be a con-man.

'Colonel,' she said, 'if Les testifies for you, can you turn him loose so we can go away together?'

'If the judge first agrees that he will give Randle immunity for testifying, if Les can give evidence of real value, if his statements can be corroborated and if he tells the absolute truth at all times, and nothing else, I can use him and then release him from all charges,' answered the District Attorney. 'But that's a large order. Just because a defendant wants to talk about the others of his gang is no reason why I should turn him loose. So give me the high-spots on both of you.'

For over two hours she told her life history as the wife of a confidence-man. It developed that Randle had for five years been a member of the Denver gang, and was one of the two crooks whom Fred Tate had seen with Blonger and Duff at the Arlington Hotel in Hot Springs, Arkansas, the spring of 1922. He stood fourth in rank in Blonger's crowd, with only Jackie French between him and the fixer and manager. And he dealt directly with them! This was the inside man whose testimony was needed to tie the gang together. Could Randle deliver the goods?

Before the conference broke up Mrs. Randle was given a list of questions to submit to her husband at her next visit to the jail. Owing to the antagonism of the warden, it was impossible for the District Attorney or any of his assistants to talk to her husband without the con-men knowing that he was planning to testify. If any of the gang found it out threats would be made against Randle, and he might be killed in the bastille, as he was in the same cell block with the gang.

Hence Mrs. Randle had to make numerous trips back and forth to the jail to get Les's story on different incidents, so that the District Attorney could find out if he actually knew the inside as he claimed to, and if he could corroborate it with details which would match facts which the prosecutor possessed. These trips were followed by night reports at the District Attorney's house. In two weeks Mrs. Randle proved that her husband could testify to the needed facts.

Then her getaway had to be arranged. She feared for her own life if she remained in Denver, once it was known that Randle would testify. So it was decided that she should have a twenty-four hour start before her husband was taken from the jail to the District Attorney's office for the first interview. All future communications between the two were to be through the District Attorney until Randle's final release.

She left town the night after her final report to the District Attorney. Then other wives, to the number of about ten, likewise sought leniency for their husbands, but, having nothing to offer, were not successful.

During the trial the wives of the gang had the front seats on the jury side of the courtroom, while the District Attorney's wife and her friends had theirs directly behind the con-men. But the clothes of the defendants' wives far outclassed those of the other women.

Throughout the trial the con-men's wives were in daily attendance, and in addition to them a large bevy of females who were infatuated with French. Among the latter was a woman who had been giving lectures for one of the local newspapers on the proper raising of children, and so much did she fall for Jackie that after his incarceration in the penitentiary she went to Cañon City and gave a large sum to the warden to be expended for French's use and benefit.

Why so many rattle-brained women make a hero out of a contemptible crook is one of the problems which alienists have not yet been able to solve. His female admirers starred Jackie throughout the trial, and showered him with gifts. The fact that he had been in jail only a short time before he got out on bond probably helped him to acquire the bevy of women who were at his constant beck and call when the trial got under way.

JOHN H. 'JACKIE' FRENCH
(Bookmaker)

BUDA GODMAN, ALIAS HELEN STRONG, BADGER GAME ARTIST

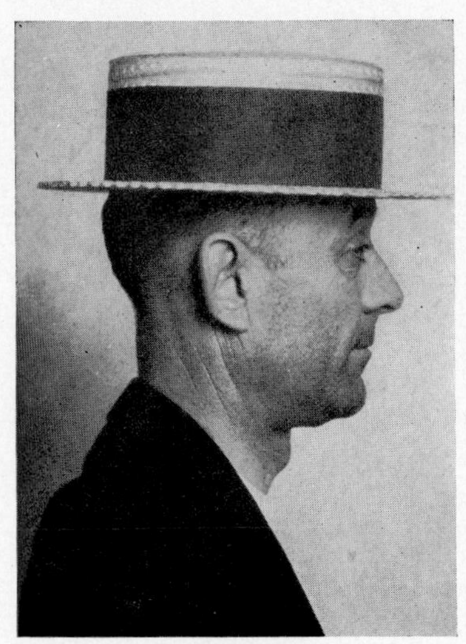

GEORGE KELLEY
(Spieler)

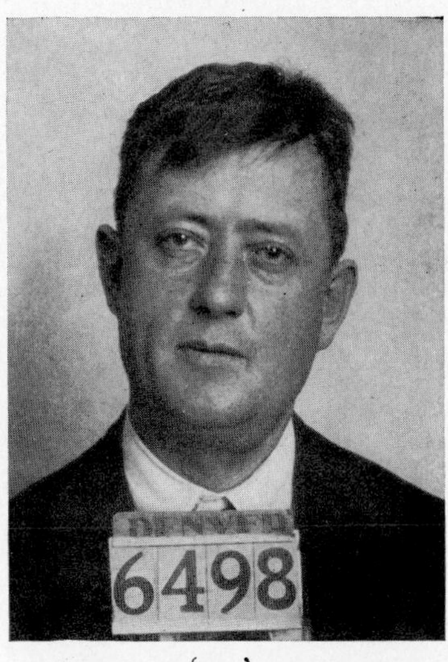


GEORGE 'TIP' BELCHER
'THE TAILOR'

Blonger's wife never appeared at his office, nor did she attend the trial. But all during the case Berna Rames daily drove Lou Blonger to the courthouse, and when adjournment came her fine limousine was waiting at the curb to carry him back to 601 Williams Street.

# XXXV

## *The Stool Pigeon*

LET us consider for a moment Les Randle, the man who turned against his former associates, the man who took his life in his hands to testify for the State, not for the enforcement of the law, but to save his own hide from incarceration in the penitentiary; the man who was bound to be described by the defendant's attorneys and by the underworld as a rat, a skunk, a crook, a liar, and by every name in the category; who would be distrusted by police and criminals for the rest of his life. What manner of man was he?

Of course he had a record; of course he had aliases, such as 'Leroy' or 'Leonard Rogers' and 'George Leroy Rhoden,' and of course he was not the highest type of man. He had been a waiter, a tout, a pickpocket, was a hop-smoker, but had never served time in the penitentiary. He had been picked up many times as a confidence-man, but had never been prosecuted. He was a little fellow with a receding chin, about thirty-five years of age, and weighed one hundred and fourteen pounds. He was arrested in the Lookout, but, until confronted by Norfleet, none of the prosecution knew the high place he occupied among the con-men.

He had probably smoked opium the night before he was arrested, because he was a nervous wreck when arraigned on

Saturday. Sunday morning he saw the District Attorney in the jail, begged to talk to him, was brought over to the prosecutor's office, and wanted to break down then and tell his story. He agreed to do so without any promise of any kind, so much so that C. P. Gehman, Judge Butler's court reporter, was called in to take down his statement, while Randle paced the floor like a caged lion, shaking like a leaf, wanting to talk and then catching himself. With his face twisting and his teeth chattering, he would tell a little, then shut up like a clam. He was wild for dope, promised to do anything if they would get him some, but finally controlled himself, refused to talk further, and was taken back to the jail.

The underworld reviles the man who turns against it. The attorneys for the defendants liken him to Judas Iscariot, Benedict Arnold, and all the traitors of history. The jury is inclined to discredit everything that he says, and frequently adds to its verdict a recommendation that he likewise be convicted, because of the impression made upon them by the assaults of the attorneys for the defendants. Society in general, as it were, pulls its skirts close so that by no possibility can it be contaminated by association with such a person.

And yet Society is wrong. The greatest protection to government from organized criminals comes from the fact that gangsters all know that at any minute some one of their number may squeal, and it is the fear of the possible squealer which keeps gangs from becoming so large that they will overpower the government in this modern age. Therefore, Society should support the gangster who takes his life in his hands, and, whether it be for a price or not, takes the witness stand and tells the unvarnished and actual truth about all the operations of himself and associates.

Out in the world, this man, who turned State's evidence, uses his own name. For that reason, in this book, 'Les Randle' is used as a pseudonym.

Early one evening, with Randle's wife a good twenty-four

hours on her way, Les was brought to the District Attorney's office by faithful Doc Dawson, and there all night long he told his story, giving the intricate facts of the inside picture of the gangsters and their activities in Denver. The next morning he was taken before Judge Butler, and a formal order entered that if he testified and told the truth the criminal cases against him would be dismissed.

Then the Court ordered that Randle be put in a separate cell in the county jail, in a different wing from all of the con-men. The only one that filled the bill was the condemned cell, where men convicted of murder and awaiting hanging in the penitentiary were kept until taken to the gray walls of the 'Big House.' So Randle, condemned to die by the code of the underworld, was properly housed in that cell's doomed walls until his testimony could be completed and the trial finished.

Here is the amazing story told that night by Randle to the District Attorney, Robinson, Samson and Koehn.

'I was in Hot Springs, Arkansas, this last spring, with Lou Blonger, and "Kid" Duff, and "Tip" Belcher,' said Randle. 'Lou said we might not make as much money as we did last year, but that we would do the best we could on account of conditions.'

'"The District Attorney is not with us," he said. "He will not take money at all, and it is hard to work without him, but we will do the best we can to get by."'

When asked what he had heard about a dictaphone, he stated: 'Duff said he and Lou had searched their office for a dictaphone and had failed to find one. According to his story, one of the detectives told him there was a dictaphone in the office. Duff said after searching for it they thought the dick was trying to get a few dollars out of them for bum information, but that he and Lou were going to try to protect themselves from a dictaphone, if there was one in the room, by not talking too loud, but at the same time they felt sure there was not any there.'

Les was then asked what happened when Byland was arrested,

and said: 'We did not believe the District Attorney's office was after us because, in the first place, when Sox Byland was arrested by the Federal authorities, Duff knew that if you wanted anybody you wanted Sox. Yet you did nothing to interfere and paid no attention to him. Next, when Sammy Abrams's place was raided and you and your deputies caught Painter and Potts and let them go after a few questions, and later got them on the running-board of your car and again let them go, Duff was convinced that you weren't after them. However, we were on the lookout for Samson, as we were told he was doing nothing else but bunk work in your office. We had a bum description of him, and none of us knew him even when he arrested us.

'You nearly lost us a few days before the raid. Duff came tearing into the Lookout and said to get the whole gang down there that night, and the room was jammed with con-men. Duff stood up and said, "What do you think I have? Pete Land got a list down to Colorado Springs which was sent to the police down there by the District Attorney, and I am going to read it to you."

'And he proceeded to call off the names of many of us, and a lot of letters and funny descriptions. Roy Farrell, a spieler whose name was called, and Bill Loftus, then a steerer, said it did not look good to them, and they were going to get out of town right then.

'We had one hell of a discussion for about a couple of hours, and we cussed the District Attorney up and down the place. Finally, however, Duff wanted to know how many boys we had "tied up," and when he found we had about a dozen, for a total of $350,000, with others in sight, he said: "To hell with that fellow. He can't get to first base without calling in the police, and as soon as he pinches the first one of us guys, we will get the word and he will never get another. We will either spring our man with a straw bond or bail him out with real cash, so nobody's going to get into trouble. Besides," he said, "Pete Land is going to have a talk with him."

'And we all agreed with Duff to stick it out, though Cooper said it was against his best judgment, and he was only staying because the rest of the crowd wanted to. But from then on we were a skittish bunch of con-men.

'One thing that helped about that list was that Filger's name was on it, and he had been dead over a year. Two others were named who had not been here this summer, so some of the grafters thought it was an old list. But we were all told to look out for the District Attorney's snoopers.

'When Duff brought the list to the Lookout, he and I searched all over for a dictaphone or loose wires, but found none.'

'By the way, Randle,' said the District Attorney, 'did you ever run into Spencer, Norfleet's man?'

'Yes,' answered Les, 'but that's not his name. His real moniker is "Whitey" Harris.

'Early in August, Whitey showed up and registered at the Brown Palace Hotel. He was pretty flush, as he had just made a score. Duff told me he was here, so we went up to the hotel to see him.

'Harris said, "Hello, Duff, how about going to work this summer?"

'Duff answered, "Whitey, you can't do it. Norfleet is on your trail and will never let up until he gets you. It's an even bet that he will come to Denver this summer looking for you, and if you get pinched, the publicity will be bad. The papers will spread it all over the front page."

'Duff said he didn't care if Harris stayed a few days, but that he would have to move to a cheap hotel, and get off the main streets, so Whitey went to the Empire and registered as Mitchell.

'Then a couple of dicks ran into him over there and Duff had to front for him. Duff told me what he said to him after he got him out of that. "Whitey," he said, "I'm dead right about you. You only mean trouble for the gang. So vamoose, and do it now. I'll give you two hours to clear town, or I'll turn you over to Norfleet myself."

'Whitey left in a rush.

'Now tell us something about yourself, and the "cut" and the inside stuff,' said the District Attorney.

'I joined the "pay-off" game in Denver in 1908,' continued Randle. 'I had played it some, but not very much. "Pretty" [George Leo] Kelley, a spieler, took me to the Lookout. Duff asked me where I had worked, and if I had ever made any money. I told him some, and he asked the details.

'Kelley vouched for me, and Duff said, "All right. You can go to work as a steerer at forty-five per cent if you steer a man." I made no scores that year, but Duff told me to come back the next season — that he thought they would be open. Duff always told us when the season was over.

'His system of employing men was, if they were old-timers and their work had been satisfactory, to give them a job. If they were greenhorns, or unknown, unless their criminal records were "good," or they were properly vouched for, they were told to get out of town.

'For each deal which we pulled, the steerer got forty-five per cent, the spieler ten per cent, the bookmaker five per cent, the tailer two and one half per cent, the crooked teller in the bank, when we had one, five per cent, and Duff and Blonger the balance, after paying higher-ups and police as little as they could. They netted about ten per cent apiece.

'The tailer and bookmaker were in on all cases. In 1922 there were five spielers, or betting commissioners, and sixty-five steerers on the job.

'Blonger's office was the headquarters. His job was to stay in his room, keep in touch with the police and higher-ups, and do the fixing.

'Duff's work was to run the Lookout and the stores, hire and fire the boys, manage them, get the money and divide it. In a few cases, where the steerers were in bad with Duff, Blonger hired them, as he did the "Christ Kid" this year.

'The "Big Store" is the town that is wide-open and protected for the bunco-man. Denver is the Big Store of America. The "store" is the fake stock exchange or pool-room, and there may be more than one of these in the same town. We had two here. The Lookout is upstairs, to see better. It is the active office, and is exactly what the name implies, because the tailer or some other con-man is always sitting in the window where he can look out on the street to get signals from the steerers. He has a typewriter as a stall.

'Steerers are only supposed to go to the Lookout when they first come to town, to see about going to work. Duff would then give them their orders and they were to 'phone in only when they had a sucker to play for. In that way, no one but Duff, Belcher, the spielers, and bookmakers would be hanging around.

'In 1921 I saw a good deal of Blonger at the Grafters' Club. This was run by Belcher, and we played for pretty high stakes. In 1922 I was with Blonger at Hot Springs, Arkansas, but had only two dealings with him in Denver.

'One time this year Duff sent me down to Lou's office for the "boodle," and I drove down and blew my horn and he came out. He handed me a newspaper package, and said:

'"It looks like you will have to try to get along with as small a bank-roll as you can this year." The package contained $3500, twenty one hundred dollar bills, and the balance in ones, with a few twos.

'Aside from that, he 'phoned me only once to see how I was coming with a sucker whom we had tied for $25,000.

'I put the boodle in a safe-deposit box every afternoon and got it out the next day.

'I participated in about sixteen sales, totaling about $400,000 since 1918, and rented the 1922 Lookout, on Seventeenth Street, in the name of A. L. Long.

'Duff was always at the Lookout between ten and eleven in the morning, and the bookmakers, spielers, and Belcher, the tailer, had to be there at that time. The Lookout was moved from the Shirley Hotel, where we first had it, because we found we couldn't use the 'phone through the hotel switchboard and insure the necessary secrecy.

'When possible we had three connecting rooms for the stock exchange, although we could use two if we had an adjacent hall. In nearly all cases there are only three men who are ever seen by the victim, though sometimes it was a double steer, with two steerers picking up the sucker, and sometimes it was necessary to have a few men hanging around the store. Occasionally, like when Norfleet was there, two suckers will be taken through at the same time, one from each room. That way they see more action, but we have to be more careful.

Randle detailed the operations of each member of the gang since 1918. He stated that about one hundred and fifty con-men had been in Denver during this four years, and that their annual winnings were over $1,000,000, but only Blonger, Duff, and the bookmakers knew the exact figures.

Les had also been in the pay-off game in Salt Lake and Florida. In the winter of 1920 he had worked for Duff, Joe Rush, and Mark Tillery who owned the Miami store, while Duff, French, and Joe Rush, with Belcher as the tailer, were the proprietors of that Florida emporium in 1921.

'We were never allowed to pick up a Colorado man in this State. Sometimes one of the gang was in bad and would take a sucker out of the State and trim him elsewhere. But if he did, he was never allowed to work in Denver again.

'The reason was that these suckers would be likely to find their men in Denver and would stir up the papers. We can't stand publicity, no matter what the protection.

'Our boys have a lot of clothes — some have fifteen or twenty suits. And nearly all play golf, because the golf course is a good place to take a sucker. We try to change our clothes often to confuse the victim on later identification.

'We used to hang out a lot at the Albany Hotel on Seventeenth Street. This was because there was a newspaper stand outside where tourists bought out-of-town papers, and a stoop where we could sit around while watching for suckers. Also, we would give the Albany Hotel as the address for suckers to send telegrams to, and these telegrams would be posted up by name on a little bulletin board there. The steerers would go in and see if their names were listed, and if so ask for the message.

'The steerer's telegrams would be phoney, made out on the Lookout typewriter. The messages to the sucker were actually sent. At the proper time the spieler would suggest to the steerer that he go see if he had a message, and after a short interval the latter would come back with a phoney telegram. Most of the boys had cars, which they would bring to a steerer whenever he raised his hat as a signal for a ride. This made it easier to get the sucker where we could talk to him.

'We lived all around town, wherever we wanted to. Neither Blonger nor Duff placed any restrictions on our residence, except that we were not to make many acquaintances. Our bosses didn't want people speaking to us.'

And now Randle gives the inside picture on the police!

'Blonger owns Denver. By that I mean that no con-man and no gangster can operate here unless approved by him. If any grafter comes to Denver whom Blonger doesn't like, he has the police run him out of town.

'He does this by 'phoning the Captain of Detectives, who has the man arrested. Then he is taken before the police judge, and fined, or given hours to leave town, and he gets out. If crooks don't do business with Blonger, they don't work in this man's town.

'Denver is one of the best places in the United States for bunco-men to come in the summer, and they then make more money than in any other place. Conditions here are right.

'Duff has told me that the protection is ironclad, and that none of us would be bothered by the police. The detectives are on the pay-roll by the week, and they get that, no matter how much the store wins. It costs ten to fifteen per cent of all scores for protection.

'If a man loses his money and kicks, the police walk him around a few days, and then we give up a certain proportion to them for getting him out of town without arrests. But in those cases the cops find out how much we win, and hold us up plenty. In the Unzner case in 1921 we made $19,300 and the dicks took all but the ten grand!

'Only a few of the big con-men were ever allowed to go to Blonger's office. We 'phoned there when we arrived to find out where the Lookout was, or to see Duff about going to work, and got our first mail there, but that was all. This was because some of the detectives or officers of the police department might be at Blonger's office, and would get to know us. This the police didn't want. They were not supposed to have any personal dealings with us, or to be able to recognize us on the street.

'You see all professions have ethics. The cops were not supposed to know us, and were never to pinch us unless put up against it where they had to in order to save their faces. In such case we had no kick coming.

'I never saw any cops paid off, but some received pay envelopes in the doctor's office next door, and on one occasion this summer Duff said:

'"I am going up to that big Trinity Church and give some dicks their bit behind the pillars."

'We had two good cases where the cops saved our hides. One was last year after we trimmed old man Donovan of New Orleans for $65,000. We had put him on the train and blown him off. But he came back to Denver, made a complaint to police headquarters, and the Captain gave him a couple of wise detectives to go out and find us, then he 'phoned Blonger.

'"Say, Lou, did you trim a fellow named Donovan for $65,000 a few days back?"

'"What about it?" says Lou.

'"Well, he is here putting up an awful squawk, and I have

sent Land and Lusk along with him. When they get through with him, he won't have the remotest idea what building he went to or who he saw, but you had better check up and keep the boys off the street who played with him until he gets out of town."

'I had acted as a steerer in that play, French as the bookmaker, and Cooper as the spieler. Duff didn't know where to reach us. We were in the Quincy Bar on Seventeenth Street having lunch when in came Donovan with the two dicks, who brought him in there as the last place they expected to see any of us.

'They spotted French at once, and those boys were certainly quick on the trigger. There was a player-piano near the door. One of them grabbed a nickel, said, "Donovan, let's see how this works," and crowded the old man over to the wall, the two of them getting close in to him, while we slipped out the door behind the detectives' backs. Those dicks got a few hundred dollars apiece, and say, boy, they earned it. They kept the papers away from him, too.

'The other was a case in which Steve Olson had taken a tourist through the stock exchange on the first play. However, he was a wise guy, and after they left the store he claimed that he had a bad toothache and had to see a dentist at once. So he made an appointment to meet Olson in the Civic Center at four o'clock.

'As soon as he got loose, he 'phoned the Captain of Detectives, told him that he had been picked up as a sucker by some con-men who had made an appointment with him, and he would like to have some detectives arrest them. The Captain thanked him very cordially for the information, told him he would have the detectives on the job, and as soon as the stranger hung up, again 'phoned Blonger.

'"That you, Lou? Well, some of your boys picked up a hot sucker who is wise to your little tricks, and he is waiting for them in the Civic Center at four o'clock. I am going to send a man over to pick them up."

'"Thanks, Captain," chuckled Lou; "this sucker isn't going to find anybody."

'Lou 'phoned Duff, and the latter called four or five of the boys, and told them to surround the two blocks, and stop Olson from going in to the man. When Duff's group arrived, the squealer and a dick were standing by the theater.

'Duff pointed the bum sucker out to me, and said, "There he is with the detective, and if the steerer gets by us the dick will give him the 'office' not to get in to the sucker!" The cop was keeping the boob in earnest conversation when Steve got through our lines and started for them. But the dick gave him the high sign, and Olson lit out. Only fifty dollars extra this time, because Olson hadn't made a score.'

# XXXVI

## *The Tie-Up*

'In order to be a successful con-man,' Randle went on, 'each one of us had to know our parts by heart. During odd hours Duff ran a school for the newer spielers and steerers. The latter part of 1921 French taught me how to book, that is, to act as manager or clerk in the stock exchange and race-parlor. I worked with French for nothing on all jobs the last six weeks of that season, while learning the game. We all had the same story, except for our names, which we usually changed for each sucker.

'Early in the 1922 season Duff gave the steerers orders they were not to work below Curtis Street because the pawnbrokers and curio-dealers around the depot might complain about them picking up their customers. Later, however, because of the railroad strike, business was bad, and we were allowed to work anywhere.

'The steerers worked the principal streets of the town, the hotels, depot, Capitol grounds, Civic Center, and looked around the parks and museums, seeking out any place where tourists would be apt to go. The news-stands on the principal streets and automobile tourist agencies were favored places. If a man were seen walking down the street with a guidebook in his hand, or buying an out-of-town newspaper, or inquiring about an automobile excursion, a steerer promptly accosted him with some question, as the name of some street or building, or about one of the parks; if the sucker says he can't tell him, the steerer then knows that he is a perfect stranger, and we play for him. He is then asked what State he is from; if the sucker tells him where he is from, then the steerer tells him his State.

'He is then asked if he is acquainted with anyone here in the city. If the man says he doesn't know anyone in Denver, the steerer tells the sucker he is in the same fix, that he doesn't know anyone. Then the steerer asks the man what his line of business is. If the steerer finds that the man is well fixed, he is ready to play him. If he has nothing, or won't talk, we drop him. We never take them unless they have at least $5000.

'Having finally worked out a good prospect, the steerer commences with the game. He suggests that he and the sucker take in the sights together, as they are both strangers. If the sucker falls for it, off they go to see the city. In the meantime the steerer is trying to find out all he can about what the man is worth, so he will know how much to tell the spieler to tie him up for.

'We had two games, the stock market and the horses. If the sucker is a sport, or a fellow who looks like he would want a good gamble, we put him into the races; otherwise we use stocks. But except for names of horses instead of stocks, the scheme is exactly the same.

'As soon as the steerer finds out that the sucker is all O.K., he is ready to play him into the store. So he walks his man on the opposite side of the street from the Lookout. When they get across from it, the steerer raises his hat; that means he wants the spieler to come down and play for the ripe sucker. There is always someone looking out of the window at the Lookout from 10 A.M. until 4 P.M. Usually this is the tailer.

'The watcher in the Lookout calls for the spieler who is next for duty, and that one goes down and gets on a corner or in a doorway and waits for the sucker and steerer to come by. The spieler stands there counting a roll of money or looking at a telegram or some papers. When the steerer passes the spieler, he says to the sucker: "See that man right there. I saw that man in Kansas City about a month ago. He is the man they called the plunger. They say he cleaned up several hundred thousand dollars in Kansas City trading in the stock exchanges; they say he knew what he was doing. In fact, they say he had a sure thing. They even had his picture in the paper. I wonder what he is doing out here."

'Then the steerer raises his hat for the spieler to come nearer. The spieler walks towards them and the steerer says, "I am going to speak to him."

'So the steerer steps over to the spieler and says, "Beg your pardon, but didn't I see you in Kansas City?" The spieler says, "I never met either one of you in my life."

'The steerer says, "I never met you, but I am sure you are the man I mean for two reasons, one is I saw your picture in the paper and the other I saw you talking to the Judge. I was in the lobby of the Majestic Hotel, and the guests were pointing you out as the plunger, the man who had cleaned up several hundred thousand dollars on the stock market. And just about that time in came Judge Brady. He went over and shook hands with you. The Judge and you talked a few minutes and then the Judge went out. I followed him out and said, 'Judge, who is that man you were just talking to in the lobby?' The Judge said, 'He is a good man and not a bad man to know. Not giving you a short answer,' the Judge said, 'but you buy the paper and you can see for yourself,' so I bought the paper and right on the front page was your picture." '

So much for the spieler's usual method of approach. Then Randle described an alternative introduction.

'Sometimes we play the spieler to the sucker by the pocket-book trick. The spieler follows the steerer and boob to the park, or a fairly quiet spot, gets ahead of them, and, while the sucker's attention is diverted the other way, drops a pocketbook and goes on.

'Enclosed in this pocketbook is the fake bond, sometimes with the spieler's picture printed on it, but usually not, and the fake newspaper clipping. If the fake horse-race is to be used, it also has horse-racing literature, a code letter from the American Turfmen's Association, and race-cards. If the fake stock exchange is to be pulled the spieler places in it a letter from the broker's office, letters of credit, and drafts for large amounts of money showing that the spieler is a man of real responsibility.

'The steerer and victim then find the book and examine it. The steerer sees that the sucker reads each piece of literature carefully, and they comment on it together. In that way the sucker is properly impressed with the financial standing of the owner of the pocketbook. When they have finished the steerer gives a signal and the spieler comes up. He then secures his introduction by claiming the wallet and identifying its contents.

'In August, just before the arrest, we picked up a sucker named Ray Peterson. I was bookmaker as A. B. Zachery, A. B. Cooper was spieler under the name of P. J. Miller, and William H. Loftus, was the steerer, as Sam Bradford.

'After the talk about the Judge the spieler says to Peterson and Bradford, "You men are not newspaper men, are you?" Bradford answers, "No, no, we are from Dallas and Chicago; Mr. Peterson is a banker and I am a grocer." Miller, "Do you mean to say you are a friend of Judge Brady?" Bradford, "I have known the Judge all my life. He and my father were great friends." Miller, "Well, men, I will have to admit that I am the man you mean, but I want you to give me your word that you won't mention it to anyone about my being here in Denver."

'Bradford says, "Don't worry about me. We don't know anyone here in Denver, we are going back home in a few days." Then he adds, "Are you doing the same thing here?" Miller answers, "Yes; in fact, I am on my way to the exchange now to make a trade for my company. You see, men, this is not my money. I am merely a salaried man working for a big company back East. But I am in a big hurry now, so I will say good-bye. If you will come up to the Metropole Hotel tonight and have dinner with me I will be glad to talk more to you."

'As Miller turns to go, Bradford speaks up, "Just a minute, can't you give us a little something?" Miller answers, "Why, sure, are you men broke?" And he pulls off a fifty- or a hundred-dollar bill and offers it to them. To which Bradford replies, "No, no, we are not broke; you didn't understand me. I meant can't you give us a tip on the market, just to win a few dollars, just a little cigar money?"

'So Miller says, "Why, yes, I guess I can do that." And Bradford asks, "How long will it take?" Miller, "Just a few minutes." Bradford, "Well, take this ten dollars and make a trade for me." Miller takes the ten and tells the sucker and the steerer to wait on the corner for him, as he will be back in about ten or twenty minutes.

'When the spieler comes back, he gives both Bradford and Peterson tickets on a certain stock. The stock has to go up one point to win. As soon as it goes up, the ticket will call for twenty dollars. The spieler then shows them a $5000 ticket, on a trade he is supposed to have made for his company.

'Then Miller states that this stock is sure to go up, as the people he works for know exactly what they are doing. To make a long story short, it is a sure thing.

'Miller then produces his phoney newspaper clipping which is supposed to be the same as the steerer read in the paper in Kansas City. He waits while the sucker reads it through. Miller then tells them that he is under a heavy bond, and shows his phoney bond (page 42) which the sucker now examines. Miller next states that he has an auditor who travels with him; that he (the spieler) has to be very careful not to give out any of the company's information, as he is under bond, and that he is not allowed to invest any of his own money. The slip reads:

**Int. Brokerage Co.**

**RECORD SLIP**

Stock Int Paper

Buy One 1/8 Points

Quotations 56 6/—

Close 57 7/—

Amount $5000

Name P. J. Miller

Date 8-20-22

Ticket No. 2023

'He continues, "My company wires my auditor what stock to buy and when to buy. The auditor gives me the wire and I do the trading. The messages must always come in code form. So he shows his code telegram:

NEW YORK, N.Y.
8/1/22

MR P J MILLER
DENVER COLORADO
24–23–16–25 — 10–23–19–11– STOCK GOOD TEN GROSS AMBER 26–16–20–19–5 — 26–23–18–21–2– KENTUCKY THIRTY GROSS ITS A BOY

J O STONE

'This telegram is read by the sucker and explained in detail by the spieler, who hands the victim his code so that he can interpret its meaning.

'Going over these papers takes some time. Then Miller says, "It is time that stock has acted, so give me your ticket and I will cash it. Wait here for me and I will bring you the money." Bradford and Peterson wait about fifteen or twenty minutes and the spieler comes back and tells them the stock has gone up and hands them twenty dollars.

'Miller bids them good-bye, again telling them that he is very busy, as he has more trades to make. Bradford then asks for another chance to make a few dollars. The spieler says, "I have been thinking if I give you men a chance to make some money without the use of one dollar of your own, will you give me your hands as men that you will never tell anyone about it." Bradford and Peterson agree to that and shake hands on it. If the sucker doesn't agree, the steerer does, and then tells the sucker just to come along and watch. Nearly always we get him in the play, sooner or later.

'Miller explains that he will furnish the money out of his own pocket. All he wants to do is to use their names and for them to do the trading. For this the spieler agrees to give the steerer and sucker twenty-five per cent of the profits.

'The victim is now set to go to the store, so the spieler gets away on some excuse, and 'phones me at the Lookout, as I am the bookmaker. He tells me how soon he will be ready, and we fix the time when I shall open the exchange for Peterson's play. I pick up my suitcase, go to the office, install the phoney telephone, hang up the oilcloth blackboard, and equip the joint. Then a few minutes before the sucker is due, I unlock the outside door, and all is set for the killing.

'The spieler then takes the sucker and steerer to the phoney exchange. They first enter one of the side rooms, and Miller slips the night-latch behind him, so that no stranger can get in. He then knocks on the door of the center room where I am waiting for them. I open it and Miller hands me his card, and then introduces himself and his associates. He says, "These men are established and want to do a little trading."

'"Tex" Cooper used the same card again in the Norfleet case, and the District Attorney seized it in Cooper's room in the raid. This is it:

**The holder of this ticket is not permitted to transact business on exchange.**

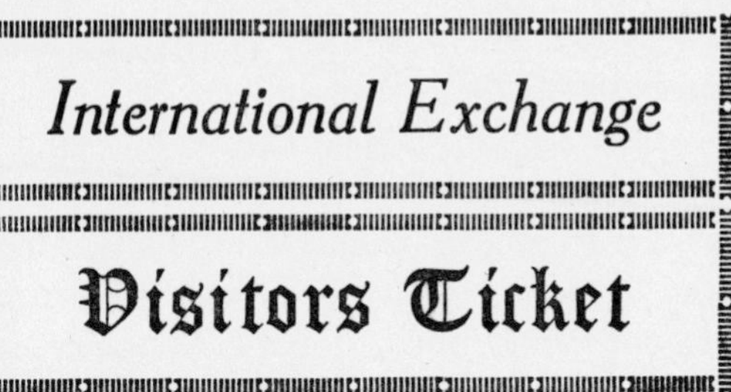

*International Exchange*

**Visitors Ticket**

**Admit Mr.** P. J. Miller

**Introduced by Mr.** A Cort

Good for 6 admissions
Within 30 days from date.

**1 2 3 4 5 6**

*John O. Ballard,*
PRESIDENT
*Eugene Smith,*
SECRETARY

'Miller then asks, can we have a private room? I tell them to "use that room you just left; you may close the door if you like." Before going, the spieler shows them the blackboard on the wall, points out to them the different stocks and the prices; then all three go into the private room.

'Miller then says: "I will go in first and make a buy for my company." So he comes into my room and shuts the door, and tells me more about the sucker. When he goes back he shows them a ticket on some stock for five or ten thousand dollars. He then gives the steerer and sucker five hundred dollars each, tells them to buy General Motors stock on a one-point margin, open at 100 and close at 102. They come in, give me the money, buy the stock, and I give each a buy ticket on General Motors stock.

NO. 582 BRANCH 4

**International Exchange**

DATE 8-20-22 **BOUGHT** TIME 2.35 p.m.

STOCK General Motors

POINT MARGIN One AMOUNT $ 500.00

RECEIPT FOR ORDER EXECUTED

CASHIER Zachery

'They go back and show the spieler their tickets and he says, "Fine, we won't have to wait but a few minutes for the stock to act." After about five minutes he sends Peterson in to ask me if that stock has acted.

'While Peterson is in talking to me, Miller asks Bradford how much he wants to tie Peterson up for. In other words, how much does he want to beat him out of? In this Peterson case the steerer said "Let's take him for $20,000."

Peterson goes back into the room and tells them something to the effect that "The clerk says our stock has acted, it's gone up one point or more."

'Miller: "Good; I will go in first and cash my company's ticket and then you men can cash yours." After again entering my room and closing the door for a few minutes, Miller goes back and tells the sucker and steerer to go in and cash their tickets. They come in and give them to me. So I take the phoney telephone and pretend to call the main exchange.

'I say over the phone, "General Motors one-point margin, open at 100, close at 102, five hundred cash, names Peterson and Bradford, one thousand dollars. O.K. Pay off." Then I count out one thousand dollars to Bradford and the same amount to Peterson. In that way each man gets back his five hundred plus a winning of another five hundred dollars. They take this money back to the private room and give it to Miller. He shakes hands and says everything is fine.

'The spieler then tells them he has only one more trade to make today, and it may be several days before he has any more business, as his company doesn't have him operate every day; if they did, the exchange people would soon get next to him trading every day and never losing, and he says, "So, I am going to give you men a chance to make some real money. With the two thousand dollars cash we have here, we can take an option on twenty thousand shares of Mexican Petroleum stock on a two-point margin, making us a forty-thousand-dollar profit. Are you willing?"

'The steerer always waits for the sucker to agree. If the victim doesn't, the steerer speaks up, "Yes, if you think it is safe."

'Miller answers, "It is as sure as the hat on your head."

'So Bradford replies, "Good. We are game if you are, for I am sure you know your business."

'The spieler then says, "Wait until I go in and make my trade for my company." Upon his return he shows them a big ticket for his company, then he gives them orders to take the two thousand cash and tell the bookmaker they want to take a two-thousand-dollar cash option on twenty thousand shares of Mexican Petroleum stock on a two-point margin, open at 174 and close at 176 1/8, and to give him their names, just their last names, *and not their initials*.

'Miller says, "I am sure all he will ask for is your last name. Tell the bookmaker you want to buy the stock jointly, that is, in both names."

'The steerer and sucker enter my room, lay down the two thousand dollars, and tell me what the spieler has told them to say. I take the two thousand dollars, make out a ticket, two thousand cash option on twenty thousand shares of Mexican Petroleum stock on a two-point margin, open at 174, close at 176 1/8, names Bradford and Peterson.

'When I give them the ticket I say, "You men are established, are you?" Bradford answers, "Oh, yes, we are established," and takes the ticket into the private room to the spieler. Miller jumps up, smiles excitedly, shakes hands, slaps them on the back and says, "Men, our fortune is made; all we have to do now is wait for the stock to act, which will only be a few minutes." The steerer joins in the enthusiasm and even the sucker gets mighty excited.

'Then the spieler figures up their per cent, also his. "We will make forty thousand dollars," he says, "ten thousand apiece for you and twenty thousand for me." Then he tells them never to tell this to anyone as long as they live. They agree never to tell it even to their wives or any of their people, not even their banker at home. You'd be surprised how many suckers keep their promise and never tell anyone.

'Then Miller comes to my door and asks me if that Mexican Petroleum stock has acted. I tell him that it has gone up two or more points. The spieler then tells them that he will go in and get his company's money first, then they can go in and get theirs. So again Miller and I close the door and visit.

'The spieler then returns to his friends, tells them that on account of this being an option buy he will have to make out two credit orders, just as a matter of form. He adds, "I will make out one for myself also." So he takes two of the credit orders that are lying on the table, makes each out for twenty thousand dollars, one for Bradford and one for Peterson. He then asks the sucker and steerer their initials. Then Miller puts down their *right last names* but deliberately uses *wrong initials*.'

Sometimes the sucker notices these wrong initials, but if he does not the steerer calls the spieler's attention to them. Then the spieler looks at his watch, and says he has not time to rewrite it, as the market will close shortly.

The Ray Peterson order looked like this:

# Customers Credit Order.

J. Peterson

bot Mexican Petroleum

$20,000

174 @ 176 1/8

'Then he tells them to take the credit orders to the bookmaker and get a statement. They enter my office and Bradford says, "We want the statement on this purchase." Then I write it out and give it to them.'

And here Randle picked up the one used on Norfleet (page 224). 'I wrote that out,' he said. 'In the Norfleet case it shows they made a profit of $200,000 and also got back their $3000 in loose cash which the spieler gave them to make the play.

'As soon as he gets the statement the steerer takes it back to the private room and gives it to the spieler. The latter examines it and hands it to the sucker, telling him to take it in, and get the cash money.

'"Ask for large bills, but *don't ask for the credit order back.* The bookmaker will likely pay you the full amount of the cash instead of giving you back your credit orders; so you bring all the money back in here and then we will take the cash and go in and take up the credit orders. In that way we will be sure to have them. Be very particular to get this straight. He will pay us sixty-two thousand dollars, and we will owe him twenty thousand dollars. Then all we have to do is to divide the profit on the forty thousand dollars."

'Peterson and Bradford go in to cash their statement. The

sucker hands it to me, and tells me he wants the cash, and says, "Give us large bills if you can."

'I take the phoney telephone and pretend I am calling the main exchange, "Hello, main exchange, Branch Four, Zachery speaking. Mexican Petroleum open at 174, close 176 1/8, two-point margin, two thousand cash option on twenty thousand shares, names Bradford and Peterson. O.K. Pay off."

'Then I turn to them and say, "Gentlemen, you have made a tremendous winning. Luckily I have the cash on hand this morning to pay you off."

'I then pick up several already prepared boodle packages, each with its hundred-dollar bill on top and bottom. This Bradford-Peterson deal calls for sixty thousand dollars, plus the two thousand initially put up. So I have two packages with twenty thousand dollar wrappers, two with five thousand dollars each, and four of twenty-five hundred dollars each. And I now do my best acting and pull the play which determines the success of the whole game. The sucker must be impressed by actual money.

'I flourish each package separately, and as I call each figure I drop the boodle on the table in front of the steerer and the sucker. "Twenty thousand dollars, another twenty, that makes forty thousand; now five and then another five, that's fifty thousand dollars; I wish I was getting that money; now twenty-five hundred, and two, three, four for the same amount — sixty thousand dollars. Oh! Yes, you had a deposit of two thousand dollars on that deal. Here it is." I take up a pile of loose hundred dollar bills, and count them out, one at a time until I come to twenty. Then I grab up the whole bunch, and put them in the delighted sucker's hands. I sure put on some act, ably seconded by apt remarks from the steerer as I count out the dough.

'Peterson thought he had $62,000 in his hands — all in real money, and the actual feel of that sixty-two thousand dollars ties any sucker up for good. As a matter of fact he had only about $4500 in cash in the package.

'Did a sucker ever open the boodle package, Randle?' queried the District Attorney.

'Gosh, no,' answered Randle, 'we never gave one a chance. If he had, we'd have knocked him out right there or the joint would have blown up.'

# XXXVII

## *The Boob Bites*

Now comes the play to start the sucker toward bringing in his money. He has his hands full of currency, apparently hundred-dollar bills, and, highly elated, starts toward the door with it. But Randle shows how it is taken away.

'As soon as I hand the sucker the money, the steerer speaks up and tells me the exact opposite of what the spieler had told him to say; "We would like to get our credit orders back. Can't you deduct the amount of the credit orders and then give us the profit and the credit orders?"

'I answer, "You men have an account at our main exchange here in the city, haven't you? I am paying you in full and will deduct the amount of the credit orders from your account at the main exchange."

'The steerer speaks up and says, "We are not established here in the city, but we are established at home."

'Then I reply, "Why, I understood Mr. Miller to say you men were established with us here in the city. Of course, I am duty bound to pay you, but before I pay this profit, I would like to know if you men are responsible and reliable men; in the event the market had gone the other way, could we have been paid?"

'The steerer says, "Oh, yes, we are worth the money many

times over." "I don't doubt that in the least," I answer, "but let's call Mr. Miller." The steerer steps to the door and calls him. Miller comes in. I tell him, "Why, Mr. Miller, I understood you to say these men were established here in the city."

'The spieler, "No, no, you misunderstood me. I meant they were established at home."

'I answer, "Why, Mr. Miller, we couldn't afford to allow a total stranger to trade with us and they be established in banks hundreds of miles away. If we did business in such a manner we would have street car conductors, janitors, street-sweepers, and all sorts of people in here trading with us, and at the end of the month we would have paid out all our good money, and all we would have left would be a roomfull of worthless paper. So before I pay this profit I must know that these men are responsible and reliable men; in the event the market had gone the other way, could they have each paid us twenty thousand dollars?"

'The spieler replies, "Why, these men are worth the money, many times over, aren't you, Mr. Bradford and Mr. Peterson?" If the sucker does not answer, the steerer says, "Oh, yes, we are worth that many times over." In the pay-off game the sucker is always given the chance to answer, but if he does not answer, or does not answer correctly, the steerer speaks for him.

'I say, "That may be true, but how do I know they are worth it for sure?" The spieler, "I will vouch for these men myself. I have an account at your main exchange." To which I say, "Would you vouch for them to the extent of endorsing their credit orders?" The spieler says, "Sure, I will endorse their credit orders."

'I hand the spieler the credit orders, tell him to endorse them on the back, and say that I will then pay them the full sixty-two thousand dollars, and will have the amount of the credit orders deducted from Miller's account at the main exchange. The spieler, "Well, just a minute. I don't mind endorsing the credit orders, but I had rather not have you deduct it from my account, for my account is a joint account. Isn't there some other way you could suggest?"

'I reply, "In what way would you men have gone about paying us in the event the market had gone the other way?"

'The spieler, "Why, they would have given you their checks for the money."

'Then I state, "Well, in that case I would suggest that each of the men tender us his check for twenty thousand dollars; we will send it through our bank to your bank, not for collection, but for verification, and as soon as your bank wires us that your check is good, then I will notify you men and you can come up and I will gladly pay you your profit."

'The spieler appears puzzled and says to me, "Would you excuse me for just a minute? We would like to go into the private room and talk it over."

'"Very well," I answer. I hand Peterson the statement and then I take back the money which the sucker has held all that time. You should see the expression on his face when he releases all that "real" money! The three return to the private room, and the spieler asks, "What is the trouble?" The sucker usually says something to this effect: "The clerk [or bookmaker] paid me all the money. I had it in my hands when Mr. Bradford asked for the credit orders."

'The spieler cries out, "My God, why did you ask for the credit orders? I told you we would go in later and take up the credit orders with the cash; to let the bookmaker or clerk pay you in full. It is just too bad you couldn't keep still long enough to get the money."

'The steerer, in an apologetic tone, says, "I understood you to say we would get our credit orders back, so I asked for them." Miller answers hotly, "From now on do as I say. We will get the money all right, but we will have to wait a day or so. You see, all the exchange wants to know is that you men are each worth twenty thousand dollars. As soon as we leave here, I will wire my uncle to wire me forty thousand dollars, and he will wire it to me at once. I am sure I will have the money tomorrow morning. I will give each of you men twenty thousand dollars apiece so you can come up and show them you are worth the money; then they have got to pay us. Now, we will go in and see the bookmaker, and let me do all the talking this time."

'The spieler then asks me to permit them to make a personal representation with cash, giving them a few days in which to do so. I ask, "Is the idea that you had rather we would not send your checks to your home town for verification, but want to make a personal representation with the cash? I will call the manager at the main exchange and get you an answer."

'I take the phoney telephone and pretend I am calling the manager. "Mr. Manager, this is Branch Four speaking. In regard to that Mexican Petroleum trade in the name of Bradford and Peterson that I was just talking of to you, these men tell me they had rather we would not send their checks to their home-town banks, for banking reasons; they want to know if it would not be just the same if they wired home for twenty thousand dollars and as soon as it comes bring up the cash and make a personal representation with it... I see, so that won't be necessary.... Well, I will explain it to them."

'I turn to them, "Gentlemen," I say, "the manager says it won't be necessary to bring up that amount of cash money. Just leave it in the bank, or deposit it in any local bank in the city and let me know when you have done so and I will take the 'phone and call the bank here, and as soon as they tell me you have a credit of twenty thousand each, then you can come up and I will gladly pay you your profit."

' "Well, that's fine," the spieler says. "We expect to have the money tomorrow." To which I respond, "Well, you know according to law you have thirty days [or such time as it may take the sucker to get his cash] as this is a thirty-day option; but at the same time we would like for you to straighten it up as soon as possible."

'Miller says, "Very well, we will be up to see you as soon as we can. We want to thank you very much. Good-bye." I answer, "Come up at any time, gentlemen, we will be glad to have your trade." And Miller, Bradford and Peterson leave.'

'Randle,' said Robinson, 'You now have this sucker crazy to get that money, haven't you?' 'Yes,' answered Randle, 'And he is absolutely sold on the proposition that the spieler will have it for him in a few days. He's so sure of it that he's already planning how to spend his share.'

Going on with his interrupted story, Randle said: 'There is one other way used in the pay-off game where the mob does not have an office building or hotel, and that is to "play-to-the-wall" for a sucker. In that scheme they keep the sucker in his hotel room. Then the spieler sends the steerer to an alleged broker's office to make the buys or bets, whichever it is, stocks or races. Each time the steerer comes back, he tells the sucker all about the exchange, all the people he saw in there trading or betting. "Why," he says, "I never saw so much money in my life. There are great piles of it, that place must be for millionaires, for they sure look the part. To tell you the truth, I felt out of place in there with all those swells."

'Then when the spieler offers to let the sucker go to the exchange to make a trade or bet, the sucker usually remembers what the steerer said about feeling out of place in there and asks to be excused and to let the steerer go. If the sucker should act like he is willing to go, which he seldom does, the spieler speaks up and says, "Maybe it is best for Mr. Bradford to go, as he has been there and made himself known."

'Before the play is finished, the sucker is shown a building and told that it is the exchange. All he sees, of course, is the outside walls, hence the play is called "play-to-the-wall."

'The spieler and steerer use the same general talk in playing-to-the-wall as they would if they were using the fake exchange except that the clerk comes to the victim.

'The spieler tells the sucker and steerer that he will ask the exchange to have one of their men bring over the money they have won. He adds, "They often deposit money to one's credit at the banks or deliver it to a customer's private office, so we can have them bring it here to us. You see, our business is strictly private and for that reason they have these private exchanges."

'So the spieler pretends to 'phone the exchange and asks them to have one of their clerks bring the money they have won to Peterson's room.

'When the fake clerk arrives at the hotel room he brings with him a large tin money box filled with boodle and starts to pay off. Then the steerer asks for the credit slips back; then the spiel of the bookmaker and spieler is the same as in the other system.

'Let us now go back to the point where Miller left the exchange with Bradford and Peterson. As they go out, the spieler says he wants to speak to the sucker privately, and so calls him to one side. The steerer goes down the street a way, and the spieler says, "How long have you known this fellow Bradford you are with?"

'The sucker tells him the particulars of meeting him, and that he has only known him for a short time, and the spieler then says, "He does not strike me as being a very careful sort of fellow. I think he is too talkative, and in this business discretion is essential. Now, you impress me as a man who can keep his mouth shut, and so I will tell you what I want you to do. I am going to tell this to the two of you together, but I want to tell it to you first. Get a room together at some hotel — get one, of course, with two beds. Then I want you to take charge of your friend. Keep him with you, and don't let him out of your sight, or give him a chance to talk to anyone until I see you both tomorrow morning. In that way there won't be any more mistakes made, and we can get our money quickly."'

[If there ever was a clever play, it is this one of making the victim think that he is in charge of the crook. Hence the steerer has no chance whatsoever of losing the victim, who believes he is sure to get his money if he keeps the steerer under his vigilant eye.]

'The sucker and spieler then overtake the steerer, and Miller gives them the directions about the hotel. He says, "I am going to wire for the money as soon as I leave you, and will have it here the first thing tomorrow morning. Now, I want you men to be in your room tomorrow morning at ten o'clock. I will have the money by that time sure, so don't worry. I want you men to promise me that you won't tell anybody about this deal, for if it gets out that we have a sure thing, we never will get the money and it would ruin me, for you know I am under a heavy bond; so keep your business to yourself. Good-bye; will see you at ten in the morning." The steerer and sucker go and get a room at the same hotel, and the sucker moves in and "takes charge" of the steerer.

'The next morning at ten the sucker and steerer are in their room. The spieler comes up almost crying and says, "Well, men, we are out of luck," and shows them a phoney telegram written on the Lookout's typewriter, stating, "Uncle is down in Old Mexico on business; will not be back for thirty or sixty days."

'The spieler, mournfully, "Well, it is too bad. I am afraid we will lose all that money. And to think it is already won. All we have got to do is to show them that we are worth the money. Well, men, there is no way for me to raise the money now, as my uncle is down in Old Mexico and won't be back for thirty or sixty days, and by the time he gets back our time limit with the exchange will be up. We have only thirty days [here the spieler fixes the time in which he believes that the sucker can raise his share of the money] to show them we are worth forty thousand dollars [or whatever may be the amount involved in the particular play]. The only thing left for me to do is to make a confession to my company; tell them just what I have done and let them take it up. Of course, they will keep all the profits and we won't get a cent." There are tears in the eyes of the spieler while he speaks that line.

'The steerer speaks up, "Well, it sure is a shame to lose all that money, and to think it is already won. We surely can raise the money some way." Then the steerer adds, "Will you excuse me just a moment? I want to speak to Mr. Peterson."

'So Bradford takes Peterson off to one side and says, "I can raise the money. I have twenty thousand dollars in the bank at home in cash and my brother has the same amount. I can wire for my money; also wire for my brother to come out here and we can explain the deal to him, and I am sure he will furnish your share for a small amount of your percentage. But if we furnish the money, don't you think we should get more than twenty-five per cent of the profits? You know when we started with Mr. Miller yesterday, he said he would furnish all the money, but now he has fallen down and it is up to us. I want a better cut. I am going to tell him that."

'Bradford calls the spieler over and says to him, "I can raise the money for Mr. Peterson and myself." The spieler's face brightens, and he says, "You can! Well, my God, we are saved. I had no idea you men were worth that kind of money." The steerer continues, "But if we furnish the money, don't you think we are entitled to more than twenty-five per cent of the profits?" The spieler says, "Sure, I am willing. How would it be to cut the profits three ways; each one of us taking one equal amount? Then we will each have one-third of forty thousand dollars."

'The steerer agrees and says, "Now, I will tell you, I have twenty thousand dollars in the bank at home in cash, and my brother has the same amount. I can wire for my money, also wire my brother to come out and we can explain everything to him about the deal. I am sure he will furnish the twenty thousand dollars for Mr. Peterson for a small per cent of his profits."

'The spieler says, "You know, I told you men yesterday that we could not tell our business to anyone, as I am under a heavy bond and can't afford to bring any outsiders in on this deal. I know you men are all O.K., but I can't take a chance with anyone else. If you men could raise the money among yourselves, that would be fine, but no outsider."

'The steerer waits for the sucker to speak first, so that he will know just what to say, and the sucker usually says one of two things, either that he has money in the bank and can draw a check on it [which practically never happens] or that he will have to go home and sell some securities and make arrangements to get the money. In the first case, the steerer says that he can likewise write a check; in the second case, that he will also have to go home and get his money.

'The victim is again cautioned that he must tell no one about his business, not even his banker, because if he does the spieler will lose his job. He is told to get his money in the form of a cashier's or certified check so that it will be easily credited to his account in a Denver bank. The victim is likewise told to wire the spieler, at the Albany Hotel, when he gets his money, but to word his wire as follows: "Business arrangements successful, arrive in Denver at" — here inserting the date and hour. "Do not even state our business in the telegram to me," says the spieler. The latter does not stay at the Albany, but it posts on a bulletin board a list of all telegrams received, and we con-men look there daily for messages.

'Then the steerer and spieler accompany the sucker to the train, give him a box of cigars and magazines, and wish him good luck.

'The sucker is so well hooked that he nearly always returns to Denver, and very, very seldom does the sucker tell his banker or anyone else anything about the transaction, but gets his money and comes prepared to go on with the play.

'Meanwhile the steerer stays in Denver. Unless his man will be gone for over two weeks he does not dare look up another prospect, because his first sucker may come back before he is through with the second. In rare cases, like Herbert J. Gray, where the latter went to England, the steerer went to New York City, met him at the boat, and accompanied him to Denver.

'The spieler and steerer meet the sucker at the train and again the steerer rooms with him. At the hotel the spieler says, "You men had better go and put your checks in a bank here for collection. It will take about a week for your checks to go home and come back. [And this is where the Federal offense comes in of using the mails to defraud.] Maybe you men had better put your checks in different banks; one go to one bank and the other to another. Mr. Bradford, you go to the Colorado National Bank, and I will go with Mr. Peterson to the Hibernia Bank. After you finish meet again in this room."

'The spieler takes the sucker to the door of the Hibernia Bank [or whatever bank Miller selects for him], and tells him to go in and put his check in for collection. On the other hand, the steerer doesn't go to any bank, but simply walks around the corner, waits about twenty or thirty minutes, returns to the hotel and says, "I put my check in for collection." The sucker says, "I did the same."

'The spieler says, "Now, men, all we have got to do is wait about a week for your checks to clear. During the next few days I want you men to stay together all of the time. Don't worry, for we are sure to get the money from the exchange. I want to see you men every day, so I will meet you at the Civic Center each morning at ten A.M. Remember, don't mention this deal to anyone. Good-bye, will see you tomorrow."

'So the spieler meets the sucker and steerer from day to day. And every day he sends them to the bank to see if their money has come. The steerer always gives the sucker time to go to the bank and get back to the spieler first. Finally some morning the sucker comes back and says his money is here. Then, when the steerer gets in sight, the spieler raises his hat, the signal that the sucker's money is here and for the steerer to say that his money is here also.

'We now have the boob where he is all ready to be beaten. His money will be ours before night!

# XXXVIII

## *The Blow-Off*

'Now comes the play to take the money away from the sucker. The steerer makes an excuse that he has an errand, but will meet Miller and Peterson in the room at the hotel in about fifteen minutes, and then goes to the 'phone and calls the Lookout to make sure that the bookmaker or one of the gang will be at the exchange to answer the 'phone. Then he rejoins the other two at the hotel.

'Miller then says, "I am going to 'phone the stock exchange and tell them that we have the money in the bank and are ready to make a declaration so we can get what is coming to us." So he picks up the telephone and this conversation occurs:

'"This is Miller talking. Is Mr. Zachery there? Mr. Sam Bradford and Mr. Ray Peterson are here with me, and we want to get that $62,000 that we have coming on the Mexican Petroleum deal of August 22.... What's that? You haven't any account with Sam Bradford and Ray Peterson? You have an account with J. Bradford and J. Peterson? Oh, hell, wait a minute."

'Miller then turns around and tells the other two, "Isn't this a nice mess? You remember the day we made the trade, I got the wrong initials on the credit orders, and though you called my attention to it, I did not have time to change it, and so instead of having your names on the books of the International Exchange as Sam Bradford and Ray Peterson, they appear as J. Bradford and J. Peterson, and Zachery, the clerk, says that a statement from the bank that Sam Bradford and Ray Peterson have twenty thousand dollars apiece on deposit won't agree with his books and will not satisfy his auditors; and they therefore can't make the payment under those circumstances. — Wait a minute. I'll see what I can do."

'So the spieler picks up the 'phone again, "Hello, Mr. Zachery, I remember now, it was all my fault. I was in such a hurry to place the order that I got the wrong initials on the blanks. If we bring the money up in cash, won't that take care of it?... You say it will?... All right, I will let you know in a few minutes."

'The spieler then hangs up the 'phone and turns to the others, and says, "Zachery says if we take up the money in cash, all we have to do is to show it to him, and he will pay us right away. So the thing to do is for us to get our money as soon as possible. Now that is quite a lot of money to carry around, so I suggest that you boys wrap your money up in newspapers, and you'd better get it in hundred-dollar bills. I have some business to tend to while you are at the bank, so I will meet you on the corner of Seventeenth and Champa Streets, by the Colorado National Bank."

'At this point the sucker has lost sight of the original assurance, that sent him home for his money. This was that all he would have to do to get his third of the forty thousand dollars would be to place his money in a bank to prove his worth. But Big Money is so near that he plunges ahead!

'The store has been informed by the spieler in what bank the sucker has his money, and I send the "tailer" over to the bank to "tail," or cover, the sucker. The spieler walks down with the sucker to the bank, so that the "tailer" can identify his man. Then the spieler leaves and the sucker enters the bank to get his money. But, unknown to him, he is followed by the "tailer," who, heavily armed, covers him from that time on and thus makes sure that no other gangsters get away with the money.

'The sucker gets his money in cash, as instructed. The steerer goes to the Lookout and makes up his own boodle in three or four packages to represent his twenty thousand dollars. The sucker returns to the hotel and tells the spieler that he has his money, and Bradford shows his.

'The spieler looks to see that each money package is properly wrapped, then says: "While you men were gone to the bank, I stepped over to my hotel and to my surprise I got a telegram from my company transferring me to San Francisco. I am to leave this afternoon. I have also got two trades to make for my company today, so we will go right over to the exchange and get our money."

'All three go to the phoney exchange. Again the "tailer" is on the job and follows the three money seekers to the exchange and enters the elevator with them. Although he gets out at the same floor, he goes down the hall. However, as soon as they enter the exchange, he goes to the third room, taps lightly on the door, and is admitted by Duff, who has been waiting there ever since word was sent to the store that the sucker had his money in the bank.

'Meanwhile the spieler has handed me the statement and says they are ready to close the deal and have brought the cash money. Bradford hands me his bundle of money, supposed to be twenty thousand dollars. The sucker also hands me his twenty thousand. I give the sucker and steerer their credit orders and place their money on the table in front of them.

'I tell them, "I wish you men had notified me you were coming up today, as I have got to 'phone the main exchange and have them send over the record sheet of that day's business before I can close the deal, as I have to compare the statement you have with our record sheet."

'Then I take the phoney telephone and pretend I am calling the main exchange. "Hello, main exchange, give me the bookkeeper. Hello, bookkeeper, this is Branch Four speaking. Will

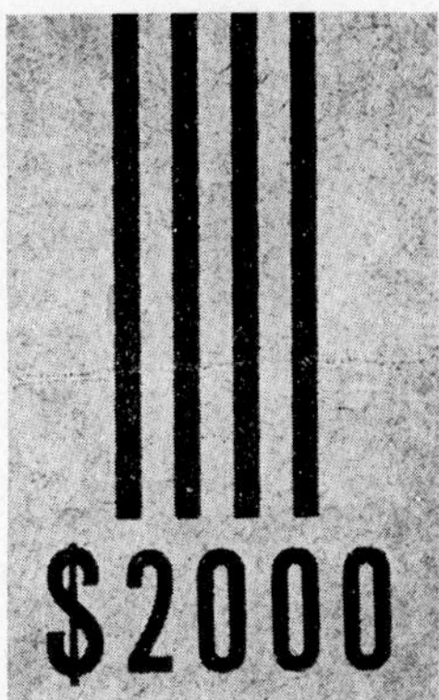


$2,500

BANK FORM

*Check by*______________

$50,000

BANK FORM

*Check by*______________

FAKE MONEY AND BANK WRAPPERS

you send over the record sheet of August 22d. I want to close that Bradford-Peterson deal.... He is. How soon do you expect him back?... Well, if he comes in before that time tell him to bring the record sheet right over."

'Hanging up the 'phone, I say, "Gentlemen, the auditor is out on his collection tour at the present time and has the record sheet of that day's business with him. They expect him back in about an hour, maybe sooner, so I will have to ask you to wait. We waited several days on you. Surely, you don't mind waiting an hour on us."

'The spieler, "May we wait in this private room?" I answer, "Yes, just make yourself at home." The spieler says, "I want to make some trades and I expect to use some of the money we have coming to trade with." "Very well," I reply, "just hand me your statement. I will stamp it O.K. Now it is just the same as the cash; you may trade with any part of it."

'The spieler suggests to the sucker and steerer that they go down and get a cold drink. All three go downstairs, leaving the money with the bookmaker.

'But in the meantime the back-room gang get busy. As soon as the three men leave the exchange, I lock the door behind them, and Duff and Belcher the "tailer" come in from their side room and get the sucker's money, and take it back into their room. Then, as soon as they are sure the spieler, steerer, and sucker have gone down in the elevator, to get their drink, they leave the building. Duff takes the money down to the safety-deposit boxes of the Union Deposit Company at Sixteenth and Arapahoe, where Duff and French and I had a safety-deposit box under the names of A. W. Duff, J. H. Francis, and A. B. Leonard. There the money is kept in the box until any squawk is over, at which time it is divided.

'On this walk to the box Duff is tailed by Belcher, who, armed to the teeth, is ready to shoot anyone who attempts to hijack the money. In the meantime I make up a new boodle package to replace Peterson's currency, and put it on the table.

'After getting a drink, the three men return to the exchange. The center-room door is open, and there on the table are Bradford and Peterson's money, apparently just as they left them.

'Miller comes to my room to make the trade for his company, and then returns and tells the sucker, "You go in and tell the bookmaker you want to trade one thousand dollars out of your statement. Tell him you want to sell Standard Oil stock open at 60, close 58, one thousand dollars. You see, Mr. Peterson, 'sell' means that, in order to make a profit, the stock must go down, and 'buy' means the stock must go up." Peterson goes in and makes the trade as Miller tells him to, and returns to Miller with a "sell" ticket for one thousand dollars.

'The spieler waits a few minutes for the stock to act, then says he will step in and see if it has done so. He returns to his room and says, "Yes, the stock has acted, gone down one point." Miller says to Peterson, "You go in and cash your ticket." The sucker goes in and hands me the ticket. I take the phoney telephone, and for the last time pretend that I am calling the main exchange, "Hello, main exchange, sell Standard Oil stock one-point margin, open at 60, close at 58, one thousand dollars, name Peterson.... O.K. Pay off." I hang up the 'phone, pick up some money and pay the sucker one thousand dollars in hundred-dollar bills.

'The sucker again goes back to the private room with the money. The spieler says, "I will go in now and make my last trade for the day for my company." He comes back, shows the steerer and sucker a big ticket and says, "This trade is also a 'sell.' You see, my ticket is a 'sell' ticket." The spieler says to Bradford, "I am going to send you in to make this next trade. I want you to trade five thousand out of the statement, and this one thousand in cash that we just made on the last deal. Go in and tell the bookmaker you want to sell Studebaker stock open at 84, close at 80, six thousand dollars, five thousand out of the statement and one thousand in cash." The steerer comes to me, but he doesn't follow instructions. Instead of "sell" he "buys," and I give him a "buy" ticket.

'The steerer returns all smiles and says to Miller and Peterson, "I have made us all rich. I bet all of our profit, Mr. Peterson's twenty thousand and my twenty thousand." The spieler exclaims, "You did! I only told you to bet six thousand dollars. You had no right to bet all of our profit and Mr. Peterson's twenty thousand. You should not have done this. Of course, we won't lose it, for the stock will go down sure, but you should do as I say. Let me see the ticket."

'Bradford hands Miller the ticket. The spieler looks at the ticket, jumps up and cries out in anger, "My God, man, this is a 'buy' ticket. I told you to 'sell.' You have made a terrible mistake. Come, we must go in and change it."

'They all three rush into my room to change the ticket. Miller yells at me, "Change this ticket. This is a 'buy' ticket; we want to 'sell.' This man made a mistake." I answer, as coldly as possible, "That stock has already acted. It has gone down ten points. Too late to change it now."

'The spieler then strikes at the steerer, and pretends he is trying to beat him up. The steerer may be knocked down. They tussle for a few seconds, and the sucker thinks it is a real fight. I then come out from behind my desk and separate them, telling them I will call the police. The spieler says, "I am very sorry. This man made a terrible mistake."

'I reply, "That's no fault of mine. He told me he wanted to buy the stock and I gave him a 'buy' ticket. I will ask you men to take a seat in the private room. I am going to call the manager at the main exchange and have him come over and investigate you men."

'All three step into the private room. The spieler says, "We must get out of here right away before they come." The spieler steps to my door and tells me, "We are going to step downstairs for a minute to get a cold drink."

'All three rush downstairs. The spieler is still mad, the steerer appears dazed, and the victim is up in the air. The spieler and sucker walk together down the street. Bradford trails along behind them. Miller tells the sucker, "Mr. Peterson, I have got to get out of town on the first train. I will take you to San Francisco, where my company has wired me to go and I have about five thousand dollars we can use to trade with. We will only have to make two or three trades and you will have your twenty thousand back, but I won't have anything more to do with Mr. Bradford but I will get your twenty thousand dollars back sure."

'Bradford now calls Peterson and tells him he wants to speak to him. Miller says to the sucker, "Go see what he wants." Bradford tells the sucker to tell Miller that he is sorry he made that mistake and to ask Miller to give him another chance, that he can go home and get some money to help replace their losses.

'Peterson goes and tells Miller what Bradford said; then the spieler calls the steerer and asks him how much money he can get. The steerer tells him he can get five or ten thousand, but he will have to go home to get it.

'Miller says, "Well, I will give you one more chance. You go home and get all the money you can and meet Mr. Peterson and me in San Francisco." The spieler then says, "Now you men go to your hotel and pack your grips. I have got to go to my hotel and meet my auditor. I will meet you at your hotel at four P.M."

'At that time Miller returns to the hotel, and tells Bradford, "Your train leaves for your home in one hour, so you will have to hurry. Meet Mr. Peterson and me in San Francisco at the Saint Francis Hotel. Good-bye." The spieler then says to Peterson, "Our train leaves at five P.M., but I think it best that you and I don't go on the same train, as my auditor will be with me, and I don't want him to see you." So Miller takes Peterson to his train, buys him a ticket, gives him a hundred dollars for expenses, and tells him to go to San Francisco, and stop at the Saint Francis Hotel. "I will leave here on the next train. Good-bye and don't worry." That is the last Peterson sees of P. J. Miller or Sam Bradford.

'The spieler, of course, stays in Denver. He goes at once to the Lookout, and writes a letter to a con-man friend in Chicago, or some other middle-western city. He also makes out a telegram, addressed to the sucker at the Saint Francis Hotel in San Francisco. He tells his friend in Chicago to send the telegram at once; and puts a ten dollar bill in the letter to pay for the trouble and the telegram. When the spieler's friend in Chicago receives the letter he sends the telegram from Chicago to the sucker. When the sucker gets the telegram it reads,

'"Got a telegram after you left calling me to Chicago. You go to Houston, Texas, and stop at the Rice Hotel. Will meet you there. I wired Mr. Bradford."

'When Peterson gets to Houston [or to whatever city he is sent], he receives another telegram at his hotel.

'"I am called into headquarters, New York City. Go home and wait until you hear from me."

'At this point the sucker either goes home and keeps his mouth shut, or comes back to Denver to make a squawk. If he does, he goes to the police department. He is sent to the detective department, and the Captain calls in two of the payroll boys to take him in tow and walk him around. Their job is to confuse him so he will be unable to locate the stock exchange, and, as he is a stranger in town, the chances are pretty good, anyway, that he will have no recollection of where it is.

'In the meantime the Captain of Detectives has 'phoned to Blonger, telling him the name of the sucker who is making the complaint. That is so Blonger can get in touch with Duff and locate the boys who handled the deal. Then they will stay off the streets until the sucker goes home.

'The detectives earn their money by telling the victim that the men probably just blew in town for a few days and skipped out as soon as they got his money, and that it is almost impossible to hope to find them, but that they will do their best and keep him informed, and they soon get rid of him.

'The spieler, either through his telegrams, or with the help of the police, has now "blown-off" his sucker, and is ready to work on the next victim entrapped by the steerers.'

The long tale was finished. It was absorbing in the quiet seclusion of the District Attorney's office. How would it sound on the witness stand?

# XXXIX

## *The Underworld Fights the 'Rap'*

The underworld is engaged in business — the business of fighting the Law. To survive, it buys protection, and usually gets a lot for its money. But eventually the Law sweeps in, some of the 'big shots' are caught, and a trial must be faced. Then the underworld swings into action to 'beat the rap'; that is, win the criminal case, by any possible means.

And so the usual category of criminal tricks was to be expected from the con-men — disguise of the defendants, bribery of witnesses and jurors, intimidation, and the old, old game of framing the prosecution with a woman. Where and when would they commence?

Disguise was the first to be tried.

About twenty of the con-men were unable to make bond, so remained in jail. Even Jackie French was slow in getting the securities for his bail. Meanwhile, the widespread publicity of the arrests and telegrams from the District Attorney brought victims from all over the country to attempt to identify the men who had swindled them.

When the mob had been engaged in the pay-off game, they had been well-dressed, clean-shaven, and looked like gentlemen. Now, however, they grew beards, mussed up their hair, soiled their hands and faces, and appeared in overalls, undershirts, and broken shoes. They looked and acted like common hoboes.

The disguises worked well and many of the suckers were unable to recognize them.

In all well-regulated jails prisoners are required to shave and wash. And when suspects are put through the 'show-up' — appearing for observation with other persons — they are made to put on their good clothes, walk around, and answer questions in order to assist in the identification. But that custom was not enforced in the Denver County jail, while its officials were hostile to the District Attorney.

All that the warden would permit when victims appeared was that the con-men be called into a corridor, and there stood in a long line while the witnesses passed in front of them. On one occasion Tilton and Cobbs, two Iowa farmers, entered the jail. Walter Byland, the steerer in their case, was on the right of the line, while Jackie French, the man who had acted as the bookmaker in the stock exchange when Tilton and Cobbs had been swindled, stood on the left. The farmers picked Byland at once, called him by the name he had used while with them, and had a short conversation with him.

Walter Byland was 'broke,' and was afraid the other grafters would not help him defend his case. Jackie French had plenty of money, but had not yet been identified by any sucker. So Byland decided to look out for himself. As soon as Tilton and Cobbs quit talking to him and started down the line, Byland dropped out of his place, sneaked behind the other con-men, ran over, and placed himself alongside of French. Tilton and Cobbs halted in front of the latter, but hesitated.

So Byland spoke up: 'If you are going to pick me, you had better pick this fellow too. Take a good look at him. If you put a green eye-shade on him, wouldn't he look like the clerk in the exchange?' That helped a lot, so the visitors promptly identified French.

Then along came George Kanavuts, the Greek from whom Kenneth Robinson had first heard of the con-men, but he couldn't recognize the hobo jailbird as Jack French the dandy.

However, the District Attorney had French brought over to the prosecutor's office, put Kanavuts in an adjoining room, and then started a conversation with French. Jackie had said only a few words when Kanavuts recognized French's voice, burst into the room, rushed at him with hands clenched, and said, 'I got you now, you Jackie French.'

For a few days French was sore at Byland, but Kanavuts's identification disconcerted him, and Walter Byland, mimicking the Greek, soon kidded him out of it. A few days later, when French made his own bond, he was so completely reconciled that he put up Byland's at the same time and helped finance the latter's defense.

Ever alert to squirm out of prosecution, the con-men tried to fix the witnesses, even while in jail. But the first one they tackled proved a tartar.

Morris Freeman, the Denverite mentioned by Arch Cooper in one of his early reports, was among the callers at the county bastille. Freeman at once identified Leon Felix, Norfleet's steerer, as one of the men who had swindled him out of six thousand dollars at Hot Springs, Arkansas, in April.

As soon as he was recognized, Felix called Freeman aside. 'If you keep your damn mouth shut and don't identify me, you will get your mazuma back.'

Freeman said, 'When will I get it?'

Felix answered, 'I will give you two thousand dollars down, and notes for the balance, provided you go to my lawyer and sign a paper stating you made a mistake in your identification.'

Freeman replied: 'Not for the world. You pay the six thousand dollars into court, and I will ask the Judge to be lenient with you.'

But Felix said: 'I would be a damn fool to do that. I had better spend the money in law.'

Felix then asked him who his lawyer was, and Freeman said he had no lawyer.

A few days after this conversation, Freeman was called to the office of Sol Larke, a notorious Denver criminal lawyer. Larke said: 'Freeman, Mrs. Felix has asked me to send for you. Here's some easy money. Just sign your name to this paper stating that you were mistaken in your identification of Felix, and I give you two thousand dollars.'

But Freeman turned Larke down cold, and the lawyer, for one of the few times in his career, failed to get a witness to take money.

About the middle of November, with Jackie French and Walter Byland out of jail, plans were made by the con-men to contact all the other victims who had made identifications and try to buy them off. The proposition could be made very alluring by telling the sucker that he would simply be settling his civil claim by getting back a portion of the stolen money. And the mob reasoned that a clever lawyer could rig it up so that the victim would not be involved in a criminal offense. Under present laws, there is no way by which a witness outside a State can be compelled to return and testify in a State court. State compacts for that purpose have been talked about, but none has yet been put into effect. Hence the witness is safe from subpoena or extradition.

So Walter Byland and his brilliant wife Gladys, and Jackie French's amorous partner in blackmail, Buda Godman, the lady who had been working on the Episcopalian minister in Estes Park at the time of French's arrest, set out on the underworld trail of fixing the witnesses.

The scheme, of course, was planned with a crooked Denver lawyer named Charles Rink, who through his gangster connections got in touch with similar shysters in the towns where the victims lived. Byland was to talk to the lawyers, but was not to meet the victims under any circumstances, though Gladys and Buda could and would, if necessary.

The first inkling the District Attorney had about the expedition was Blonger's statement over the dictaphone, 'Here's

Byland and he's got everything ready to fix those witnesses. He has got the dough in his pocket, and yet here he is in Denver.' But the prosecutor was unable to discover what witnesses were referred to. Then he found that Byland had left town, but the District Attorney was still in the dark as to his whereabouts. An honest witness soon enlightened him.

This victim wrote that he had been approached and offered $9000 of the $15,000 which he had lost if he would not come to Denver to testify. Other victims began to refuse to answer letters, and the prosecution was faced with the proposition that when the trial started there might be no victims to testify, just as Inspector H. N. Graham had predicted.

Kenneth Robinson went into action to smash this dangerous attack of the gang. Going to Iowa, he tried to contact Cobbs, the man for whom Byland identified French. But Cobbs could not be found, and Mrs. Cobbs was very guarded in her answers. She said that a lawyer had telephoned her husband and asked him to go to his office, but she claimed she did not know who he was, or why the lawyer wanted to see him. Robinson then looked up Tilton, Cobbs's brother-in-law, but he likewise was away on business with some strange attorney. Finally Tilton's mother said that a settlement was in process, and that Mrs. Cobbs knew all about it; that Tilton had been first approached by a lawyer in Burlington, Iowa, who had offered him $3000, but that he had turned that down. Then, just a few days before, Mr. and Mrs. Cobbs and Tilton had spent two or three days in Burlington with the mysterious attorney, a Mrs. Byland, and a 'Miss' French!!

Robinson went back to Cobbs's home at Davenport, where he again saw Mrs. Cobbs. This time she told him that Tilton and her husband had secured an attorney of their own to protect their rights and that the two lawyers, whose names she furnished, had drawn up a contract. The original offer had been raised from $3000 to $8000, of which $500 apiece was to be paid in advance. The agreement was simple, that Tilton and Cobbs would stay out of Colorado until July 1, 1923, and that if they did so the remaining $7000, which was to be placed in escrow, would then be turned over to them.

Robinson again sought the renegades, but they tried to avoid him. Finally he got Tilton on the telephone, but the latter refused to see him except in the presence of his lawyer. They met at the attorney's office and Robinson did his best, but they were getting back $8000 out of their $10,800 loss, and they refused to talk at all. All he could do was to tell them he would have them called before the Federal grand jury in Denver to testify against French and Byland on the use of the mails as a Federal offense. But their attorney laughed at that.

The United States District Attorney at Denver, Judge Granby Hillyer, tried to help out and subpoenaed them. But Tilton and Cobbs had been well coached, and refused to answer any questions whatever on the ground that they might incriminate themselves!

Walter Byland's jail strategy had worked, and French's $8000 had cleared the two gangsters from the identification by Tilton and Cobbs. At least two witnesses were now lost to the State. And Buda Godman, Walter, and Gladys Byland were still after more.

Letters were sent to all victims warning them that the crooks were trying to reach witnesses, and asking them to wire in if approached about their testimony.

Then Robinson pushed on to Walnut, Iowa, where he first talked with a banker who was a close friend of William E. Griffith. Griffith was the sick man who lost $20,000 in 1921, and who had already testified for the State at the hearing of the motion to return the captured documents. The banker was the one who had corresponded with the District Attorney about Griffith's loss, so paved Robinson's way for a favorable talk with his friend. Griffith at once stated that he had already been offered several thousand dollars by a local attorney, so Robinson and Griffith went to see the lawyer.

When they went in, Robinson said he came with Mr. Griffith about his Denver matter, and the attorney winked one eye at him, and said, 'Are you acquainted with Charles Rink?' Rink was the Denver lawyer who had planned the expedition with Byland.

Robinson said, 'Yes.' Then Robinson asked the lawyer if he had had any better offer from Rink than the $5000 he had first offered Griffith.

But the Iowa shyster was smart and said, 'You ought to know better than I, since you are just coming from him.'

Robinson saw that the attorney had caught on, and so told him who he was, and that, when he was offering Griffith money not to testify, he was acting not only unprofessionally, but criminally; that the Federal Government was working on this case as well as the State Government, and that he did not propose to have the witnesses bribed, even though it was Iowa. He ended by stating, 'If there is any attempt of this kind made again, we will take every measure to stop it, and we won't overlook your part either.'

The lawyer was not as smart as the one Cobbs had, so backed down and agreed that Griffith should not settle under any circumstances. And Griffith didn't. In his case it is unfortunate that he refused the con-men's money, because, as already stated, he died about a month later, and the con-men would have spent their money in vain.

The witness fixers were next reported in Oklahoma, so Robinson went there to see C. E. Henson, of Haskell, the man who had written the District Attorney early in 1921 about his $14,000 loss in September of 1920. Robinson found that Henson had been approached and offered $2500 to stay out of Colorado. Lawyers again were involved — a former county judge and also a legal member of the legislature even tried to put political pressure upon Henson to make him take the money. But Henson refused to do so unless the three men who had defrauded him appeared in person. This was because only two of the men who had defrauded him — French and Byland — had been apprehended, and he desired to have all three behind the bars.

Robinson wound up at Sapulpa. There lived George Kanavuts the Greek. Kanavuts was a $25,000 victim, and he was fighting mad and ready to clean house. He told Robinson, 'Some s— of a b—— come in here and offered me $20,000 if I no go to Denver and testify against them. I ran them out of my movie. I tell them I cut their throats first. I would not want that $20,000 as bad as I would them men go to jail. You betcha I come to Denver and help you out.'

There was a real man, a foreigner, an ignorant Greek, offered $20,000 cash of his hard-earned money simply to stay out of Colorado, and yet insistent that the crooks be sent to jail. He gave up $20,000 simply for the enforcement of the Law.

Kanavuts won a warm spot in the hearts of the prosecution by that act, and his driving of the bribers out of his theater, coupled with the fact that Robinson was hard on their trail, stopped Byland and his party from further efforts. Three other victims besides Tilton and Cobbs were bought off, but the other witnesses were untouched.

Thousands of dollars had been expended in bribing witnesses, but preparations for the trial went on relentlessly. The sucker witness list had been dented but not badly hurt, but there were still two moves which might be profitable, so the underworld turned to them.

The most dangerous witness against the con-men was Les Randle, who was to testify for the State. Money was to be offered to him, and if that did not succeed, the gangland threat of a ride!

So, late on the night of December 13, shortly after the arrangements for Randle's immunity had been published, Jackie French and George Leo Kelley, one of the spielers, were admitted to the jail and taken to Randle's cell by an accommodating jailer.

French said: 'Les, are you going through with what the paper says you are?'

Randle: 'I have not seen the paper.'

French: 'Looks like you were going to send everybody to the pen. Will you go out on bond?'

Randle: 'When I wanted bond you wouldn't give it to me. Now I won't go out if the back door is open.'

Kelley: 'Les, if you take bond nobody can stop you going out, and we will give you all the money you want to leave the country.'

Randle: 'Absolutely not. I will not consider it under any circumstances.'

French: 'You may not land in the pen in Colorado under your arrangement with the District Attorney, but you know Duff can frame up a sucker and get you brought back to Omaha, and the fixers can bury you there. If he can't do it in Omaha, Joe Rush [a con-man] and I can do it in Chicago.'

Les: 'Go ahead and do anything you like.'

Kelley: 'Les, we want you to talk to us.'

Randle: 'Get out, I am going to bed now. I am tired.'

French: 'You will never live to testify, Les, so look out.'

Randle was lost to the con-men, but the ace in the hole — the woman game — was still to come. It broke with a bang.

Early one morning, into the prosecutor's office burst two of the con-men who were out on bond.

'We have a good one on Jackie French,' they said, 'and we will spill it if you will keep quiet until after the trial.'

'Shoot,' the District Attorney answered.

And here is what they told him between chuckles:

'We have been having a lot of meetings about how to beat this rap, and finally Jackie said he could do it. "Frame that fellow with a woman," French said. "It's a cinch. I've got a dame who would get the President himself, and this District Attorney is a former A.E.F. officer, and they all fall for the skirts."

'Jack got enthusiastic about it — he served time at Atlanta, you know, for a badger game in which he impersonated a United States Marshal. In fact, he got so worked up over the idea that he made us a proposition. He agreed to bring the girl to Denver, pay all her expenses, and foot the bill if she failed to land you, provided we would pay if she succeeded.

'The scheme looked good. Most men fall for Jackie's "frails" and if you did not, we were not out anything, while if it succeeded, we would have you where you would have to quit. So we agreed to this proposition, and Jack went to work.

'He brought her from New York, a swell, dark-haired beauty about five feet six inches tall and built like a Howard watch. She had clothes by the trunk-full, and did she wear them? We'll say she did! French put her up at the Brown Palace Hotel — a suite of three or four rooms and a maid. The mob had orders to keep away from the hotel so that the District Attorney would not get wise, but we managed to get a peep at her, and how we envied you that first party!

'She got here two weeks ago, and as she is a fast worker she claims she met you in a few days, and that you visited her in her rooms Monday night of this week. Tuesday she told Jack she had you hooked, and that you were due to show up at ten o'clock last [Wednesday] night. Jack got some of the City Hall crowd lined up and the raid was planned for midnight, when pajamas were supposed to be in order.

'We were all waiting at French's room when about nine-thirty, she 'phoned and wanted to see him right away, stating that the party was off for the night.

'Jack went out immediately and came back about an hour later. "The damn District Attorney is getting cagey," he said, "and fell down on the appointment, and she is going to need more dough, so I slipped her a couple of extra grand and she is going after him another way."

'But at breakfast we learned that she took the midnight Santa

Fe for Kansas City with Jack's cash and all. She sure played him for a sap.

'You know,' they said, 'Jack thinks he is so damned smart that his getting hooked is almost as good as if we got you. Now tell us your side.'

'Mine is simple,' the District Attorney said. 'She pulled Jack's leg from the first, because I never heard of her until your story this morning.'

Disguise, cash settlements with witnesses, intimidation of Randle and the badger game all had failed. The 'rap' was too hard. But jury bribery was still possible. That sinister shadow was creeping towards the case as the trial date drew near.

# XL

## *Dictaphone Gems*

BLONGER: 'All these damn lawyers want is your money.'

Duff: 'I don't believe there is any God-damned lawyer or any law in the world that is going to get us out of this.'

Visitor: 'Well, Lou, I guess it is going to cost you a lot of money.'

Blonger: 'Yes, and that's not the worst of it. That fellow, the District Attorney, will be in there two more years. That makes it bad.'

Blonger: 'Hawkins is a mighty nice man. There is just as much difference between him and the average lawyer as night and day.'

Blonger to visitor: 'After I found out about that fellow having detectives in the King Block across the street, I got pretty careful. One day Crane, the deputy sheriff, came up, and I told him not to get near the window. I also told the same thing to Land when he was here.'

Visitor to Blonger: 'How do you make it out? There has never been a word against Land in the papers all this time until just now.'

Blonger: 'Maybe that fellow [District Attorney] isn't telling all he knows.'

Kelley and Blonger talking.

Kelley: 'Is Duff in Denver now?'

Blonger: 'Yes, he is sore at me, but I don't give a damn. He has a lot to learn about yet. He talks too much. He always wants his own way, and he wants everybody else to do as he says. If they don't, he is sore. He is chow-chowing all over the town. He don't do anything but raise hell.'

Blonger to visitor: 'Duff is still hollering his head off. He hasn't brains enough, and he isn't man enough to take the rap. He can keep up this jealousy stuff just as long as he wants to. Damn these lawyers, anyhow. All they do is sit around and collect the money and ask you for more.'

Byland and Blonger.

Byland: 'The District Attorney can make those guys in jail tell all kinds of funny stories if he wants to.'

Blonger: 'Yes, a lot of the fellows are scared to death that somebody will start talking, and if one starts, the whole bunch may.'

Visitor and Blonger.

Visitor: 'Now if Duff is responsible for the steerers, he had ought to have his percentage.'

Blonger: 'Yes, he gets fifteen per cent.'

Visitor: 'That is what he got?'

Blonger: 'Yes, that is what he got. Now don't say anything about fifteen per cent, or anything else.'

Blonger: 'Say, isn't it awful, by Jesus Christ, to get mixed up this way? I am scared to death that son-of-a-bitch Duff will squeal on French, and once things start, it will be all off with all of us.'

Blonger to visitor in very low tone of voice: 'Go to work and spend ten thousand or fifty thousand dollars, just to keep one man on that grand jury. I will get hold of French this afternoon.'

'The District Attorney is now working for an indictment, but we have one man on that grand jury. He tells us everything.'

Blonger: 'Rink and Byland have no business in that case. Rink wants five hundred dollars to give some sucker. I told him I wasn't going to do it. That isn't Rink's business. That's up to Duff. Duff is taking care of that case altogether.'

'Just as sure as anything Roy Samson took the contents of that waste-basket out of here every night. How else could he ever get those letters they are talking about?'

Blonger and visitor.

Blonger: 'God damn it, somebody ought to slap that fellow's face, the way he is stirring things up. What possesses Duff? He hasn't any sense. He gave Belcher fifteen hundred dollars. I told Belcher to lay still, you can't get out. I am not going to give any damn lawyer a cent, and then Duff was bellering around what was I going to do. Was I going to leave those fellows in there, and I said, "You listen to me. You go over there and tell them we can't get them out."'

'How are things coming along, Lou?'

Blonger: 'Oh, all right. The only thing I am afraid of is that God-damned Randle. If he gets started, things are going to be bad.'

Kelley and Blonger: 'That fellow wants to try them all together. Hawkins wants to get a severance. Those damn lawyers are the damnedest robbers that ever lived. I have spent twenty thousand dollars already on one of them and have nothing to show for it. They are all alike. They take your dough and then put you in the pen to get rid of you.'

Byland and Blonger.

Byland: 'I wonder what that bastard Randle is going to say about me when he gets on the stand.'

Blonger: 'Well, what can he say?'

Byland: 'Plenty.'

Byland and Blonger.

Byland: 'How is Duff?'

Blonger: 'He was drunk last night and hollered his head off and cussed me out. I said to him, "You lousy son-of-a-bitch, go in the house and get that double-barreled shotgun you filled with buckshot and come back out here and I will show you something." He rang up Hawkins and told him I was carrying a loaded gun and wanted to know what he could do, and said he had better have me arrested.'

Byland: 'You know you'd get off a whole lot easier if you killed a son-of-a-bitch like that.'

Tom Ward, the attorney, and Blonger.

Ward: 'Don't worry, I will get your bank-book back. Fred Tate, who furnished this detective, said that you were the head of all the bunco-men in the country. Say, Lou, was Randle in Hot Springs with you?'

Blonger: 'Yes, he was down there with us.'

Blonger and Byland.

Blonger: 'French is the finest fellow I ever met, but Duff is the dirtiest, lousiest son-of-a-bitch that ever lived. That fellow [the District Attorney] still has all my stuff. I had in my book Bacon $1500 and $1000. Now he says this is where I gave Bacon $1500 and $1000.'

'You know, when the telephone company could not find anything on my 'phone, I afterwards found out it was tapped in the alley, so I sent Billy Aarons over there, and he found that they had a plug in the wall and whenever my 'phone rang it would buzz and they would listen.'

Blonger and James.

Blonger: 'We will get a decision from Judge Butler Monday morning. I think he will turn us down. He just sits and listens.'

'Hello, Walter, this is Blonger. I see they want to take my deposition in the civil case. The Court isn't going to allow that, is it? Jesus Christ, I can't have my deposition taken, or any of us.'

Blonger on the 'phone: 'What did you say? The Judge decided against us? He didn't give anything back? Ain't that hell?'

He hung up and turned to Kelley, who said, 'What are they going to do now?'

Blonger answered: 'Damned if I know. You know as much as I do. Christ, Hawkins don't know himself what to do.'

There was a long pause. Then Blonger said: 'We are going to trial on that conspiracy case.'

Blonger and James.

Blonger: 'They want to take my deposition. I never heard of anything like that before. They want to know what I know. Did you ever hear of anything like that? I have been in lots of lawsuits, but never heard of them taking depositions. The law shouldn't allow it.'

Blonger and one of the bunk wives.

Blonger: 'Cheer up, it will take a year to try those cases. They will have a hung jury in every one of them. They will never get a conviction any place.'

Blonger and woman visitor.

Blonger: 'I told Delaney when he was Chief of Police a good many years ago, "You are double-crossing us just as sure as anything," and a few days later I told him, "My God, I will show you we will do as we like here." So in about ten days I told him to send down and get a woman, and you bet they stepped out and threw her in jail.'

Visitor and Blonger.

Visitor: 'When are they going to get started now?'

Blonger: 'Oh, I think in about ten days on the evidence. If that fellow has a hung jury he will have a hell of a time getting another one.'

Comment by Blonger: 'If they had anybody the head of this thing here it would be different. Look at our Chief of Police. All they need is a big, broad-minded business man with a good education, but they put in an old gambler.'

Blonger: 'Well, I have got to admit Randle is pretty square. You know he came up here one day in his automobile and stopped across the street. I went down there and handed him five hundred one-dollar bills and said, "Randle, here is the money. Now you can go to work."'

James and Blonger.

James: 'Well, how is the bad man [Randle] getting along?'

Blonger: 'He is on the stand this morning.'

James: 'Has he said anything about you yet?'

Blonger: 'No, he is telling all about how he came to Colorado, how he went to Manitou with a fellow named Red Brew, and another named Kennedy; that he had a fellow named Griffith. After he got through he told how the money was divided; he got forty-five per cent, French got five per cent, Red Brew got fifteen per cent; then he told how Duff got the rest. He had to split with Red Brew.'

James: 'Any of the rest going to squeal?'

Blonger: 'Well, I hardly think they will come clean. I don't think so.'

James: 'I suppose you will be glad when it is over.'

Blonger: 'Oh, Jesus Christ, yes. That District Attorney will have to start in preaching after this.'

Byland to Blonger: 'You know I hire my lawyer by the year. He has instructions that any time I don't 'phone him by ten o'clock in the morning he is to call the jail, and if I'm there to get out a writ of *habeas corpus* at once. But I slipped on this arrest. Next time I hire a lawyer he's going to call the churches as well.'

# XLI

## *The Writer of the Anonymous Letters*

ALL through the months of investigation and the checking up after the arrests, the District Attorney had been trying to get the concrete evidence of corruption, so that he could add Blonger's men in the police department to the list of defendants. But protection is paid when no witnesses are present, and there was not sufficient legal evidence to justify the prosecution of any officer. As the trial drew near but one possible source remained, and that was the writer of the anonymous letters. So in January the District Attorney began to inquire in every imaginable place to see if any trace could be found. Finally he called in Jim Marshall, the Deputy Sheriff and showed him the letters, asking him if he could figure out the writer.

Jim had an extensive acquaintance in the underworld, and almost at once said: 'Why, sure, I know that bird. He is running a big gambling-house down in Kansas City. His name is Tom Brown. I will find his address and let you know where to get him."

So that very afternoon Jim came back with the information. The next day the District Attorney and Roy Samson took an Eastbound train, the former headed for Kansas City and the gambler, and the latter for an Eastern penitentiary, which housed a con-man who was talking.

The Colonel put up at the Muhlbach Hotel and telephoned the 'gentleman of the cloth,' and said: 'This is Van Cise from Denver. I want to see you. Can I come down there, or will you come up here?'

The other fellow seemed rather startled, and replied, 'Why, I don't know you.'

The prosecutor said, 'Well, that is quite possible, but I am the District Attorney out there, and I would appreciate it very much if you would come to see me.'

The man said he would be right up, and came.

Cards were placed on the table at once.

'Tom, you wrote me five letters. Here they are. For some reason or other you say you were double-crossed, and you've got it in for a lot of the officials, as well as Blonger. I want to get Blonger's police, and you are the only man I know that can help me. I came here to see if you would do it?'

Tom sat a long time in silence. Finally he said: 'Colonel, come down to my place of business tonight. I want you to stay awhile, and after you have been there we will talk it over further. But if after you get through you say it is up to me to go to Denver and testify, I will go. It will be entirely up to you.'

'Fine,' said the District Attorney, 'that is a bargain.'

'Be at my place at nine o'clock,' answered the visitor.

So the District Attorney went to one of the big buildings in downtown Kansas City, Missouri, and found almost an entire floor occupied by a large and flourishing gambling-club. The old peephole was there, and he was accosted by the lookout as soon as he got to the door. This time he got by easily. He handed in his card and said, 'Tom is expecting me.'

'Righto,' said the lookout. 'Come on in.' The door opened.

Nobody paid any attention to him. Scores of men, but no women, filled the place. The occupants of several rooms were busy with craps; others with blackjack, poker, rummy, bridge, or any gambling game the patrons desired to play. Like all modern, illegal, protected gambling-houses, no booze or drunken men were allowed in the place, because they might lead to trouble. Also, no guns were permitted, so that no shooting could be done by those who got trimmed. Tom ran a swell joint, and was making a lot of money.

He took the prosecutor from room to room, not introducing him, but telling him all about various lay-outs, how much the kitty got on each play, and whether the games were straight or crooked. Some of the tables had loaded dice; others did not. Finally, about twelve o'clock Tom led him into his private room to talk it over.

'Well,' said Tom, 'you have seen my joint. I pay the police five hundred dollars a week to operate. I am a business man. In order to do business, the first thing I have to do is fix the police, and any town I operate in would be the same way. You can't beat the Law without paying to do so. Even then you get caught at last.

'My only business is a crooked gambler or con-man, and I can't work without protection. I know just how crooked those —— — —— are up in Denver. They take your money and double-cross you; but if I go to Denver and testify against them, I can never do business again the rest of my life. Every place I would go no crooks would do business with me, and the police would run me in. I would be a squealer. Do I go to Denver and testify for you, or don't I? It is up to you.'

'No, Tom,' said the District Attorney. 'I guess you don't. You have answered your own question. You can't do it. I will have to go back to Denver and give up the prosecution of the police because I lack the direct evidence of their operations. However, public sentiment in the spring election is going to overturn the administration, and a new one may clean up the police department.'

# XLII

## *Bribery and Gun-Play*

Two hundred names comprised the jury panel. Many of them were the big men of Denver, citizens who had real stakes in the community and who were vitally concerned in its future. The enforcement of the Law was now up to them. But the case looked like a long two months' job. Would these men, who could not be reached by bribery, put their duties as citizens ahead of the inconvenience to themselves, or would they rush to the Court with the time-worn excuse that 'business reasons' made it impossible for them to serve? A newly elected judge, George F. Dunklee, was to preside at the trial.

The answer came as soon as the panel reported. The large number of the leading members of the bar who were present in the courtroom was significant of the desire of their clients to shirk the service. And as the names were called, cogent arguments, written and oral, for immediate and complete excuse, were made to the Judge. He was very lenient, and one hundred and eight men out of the two hundred on the panel were successful. The defense could not have hoped for better luck. The Law had been flouted by those who should have been its friends!

Speedily the defendants' challenges excluded from the remainder all the other jurors who had much business or property. The last twelve in the box, the jurors to try the 'million-dollar bunco ring,' as the papers were calling it, was composed of petty clerks, men of small means, laborers, and even a colored janitor! To make bad matters worse, the jury was not locked up, but was allowed to go home each night.

Twenty-one of the original thirty-four defendants appeared for trial, but one of them jumped his bond before the jury was finally sworn. The remaining twenty were defended by six lawyers, among whom was Tom Ward, the regular counsel for Lou Blonger. Ward had now represented the master fixer for over twenty years, but always before Ward was appearing for Blonger's minions in the courtroom and not for Blonger himself. But this time the big fellow in person was on trial. The defense group occupied almost all the space inside the rail, leaving scant room for Judges S. Harrison White and Harry C. Riddle, the special prosecutors, and for Roy Samson, who handled the facts and exhibits for them in the courtroom.

'Tex' Cooper and Thomas Beech still hoped to escape some identifications and retained the beards which they had grown in jail. All the defendants, however, discarded their hobo clothes and were well groomed and natty in appearance.

The jury was finally passed by both sides and sworn. And at once rumors spread through the city that bribery was going on.

Juror Number 1 was named Herman M. Okuly, and gave his occupation, when examined, as a roustabout mechanic for a lumber company. He was a tall, rawboned Irishman, with a heavy head of black hair, and a genial disposition. He was witty, musical, and a keen judge of human nature, but no one knew that he had these qualities when he was selected. He was the kind who ordinarily would have been picked as a defense juror, because mechanics as a rule are a type of men who do not look with too great favor on conviction.

On February 19, the morning after the taking of evidence had begun, the District Attorney's telephone rang, and a voice said, 'This is Will McPhee. One of the jurors is an employee of mine and wants to talk to you.'

William P. McPhee was one of the men who had subscribed one thousand dollars to the bunk fund. He was the president of the McPhee and McGinnity Lumber Company, one of the largest timber concerns in the entire West, and a leading citizen of Denver.

'Why, Will,' said the District Attorney, 'I can't talk to the juror. What's on his mind? Tell me his story.'

'Well, Phil,' he answered, 'somebody tried to bribe Okuly last night. He lives over in Barnum in a rather modest frame house with no electric light on the porch. Last night after he had gone to bed somebody rang the doorbell, and, when he opened the door, there was a man about five feet nine or ten inches tall, with a cap on his head, wearing dark clothes, with his coat collar turned up around his neck.

'The man said, "Your name is Okuly, isn't it?" and Okuly said, "Yes." He said, "You're on the jury, aren't you?" and Okuly said, "Yes." "Well," he said, "don't you want to make some money?" And Okuly said, "How do you mean, make some money?" "Well," he said, "on this case. I will give you five hundred dollars if you will agree to vote not guilty, and I will give it to you right now," and he put five one-hundred-dollar bills in Okuly's hands.

'Okuly said, "I never saw a hundred-dollar bill in my life, let alone five of them. I am going into the light and look at them. Come on in."

Okuly went inside, but the man stayed on the porch in the dark. Okuly examined them, came back, and said, "Look here, partner. I never had five hundred dollars at any one time in my life, nor any of my family. If I took your money and put it in the bank, that G—— d—— District Attorney would get on to it in no time, and if I put it in my wife's name, it would be just as bad, and I haven't any friend I would trust with five hundred dollars. I just can't handle your money."

'"Besides," said Okuly, "it ought to be worth more than five hundred dollars. I'll tell you what, you take that money and go back to Blonger, your boss. I've heard about him as a pretty square shooter. You tell him I want twenty-five hundred dollars. I will vote for acquittal, all right, and that will get me the five hundred dollars, and if I get the rest of the jury swung over to acquit, I want two thousand dollars more, and you tell Blonger when he comes in the courtroom tomorrow to scratch his right ear with his right hand and look at me, and then I will know he has agreed to it, and everything will be all right."

'Now, Phil,' said McPhee, 'what do you want Okuly to do?'

'Tell him to keep his mouth shut and his ears open,' said the District Attorney. 'Tell him he is sworn to try this case on the merits, and it is up to him to decide this case on the evidence and the law, and if anybody else approaches him to let you know; otherwise to keep quiet and attend to business as a juror.'

Blonger scratched his ear shortly after court opened, to the edification of Samson, who was in the courtroom and reported promptly that the juror was on the job, and that Blonger passed a very pleasant morning in court.

The special prosecutors reported the attempted bribe to the Judge, and the latter talked to Okuly, telling him to report any further offers to him.

That fellow Okuly was smart. From that time on all through the trial he apparently was the defendants' juror. When the defense attorneys pulled a wise crack, Okuly's haw-haw was heard all over the courtroom, while he apparently had very little use for the prosecution. Reports came to the District Attorney that Okuly as well as others on the jury was bribed, and that there never would be a conviction in the trial.

Shortly after the evidence began, through underworld channels, the prosecution heard rumors that a certain member of the jury was to be elected foreman. This is not done under Colorado procedure until the case goes to the jury at the conclusion of the trial. And the individual who was reported as the one to be the foreman was later so elected.

The jury situation was a dilemma. One juror had been approached, to the prosecutor's certain knowledge; others undoubtedly were being solicited by the gangsters, and the evidence pointed very strongly toward three of them as favorable to the defendants. What is a District Attorney going to do when he suspects that jurors have been bought, but has no proof? If the special prosecutors had gone into court with Okuly's statement, they could have forced a mistrial and lost an honest juror. If they started all over again, they would be unable to get back their out-of-State witnesses who could not spend weeks traveling back and forth and loafing around Denver just to help prosecute some gangsters.

How were the facts about the claimed jury bribery to be obtained? The man who shadows a juror may be guilty of contempt of court, as in the Sinclair oil case. If a juror finds he is being watched, it will make a crook fearful. An honest man, however, will resent the surveillance, and get mad at the side which suspects him.

Hence the jurors under suspicion were followed only generally, and at long distances, where there was no possible chance of any contact being made with the man who was watching them. Reports revealed that two of the jurors went quite frequently to one bootlegging joint, and another man spent some time at a soft-drink parlor in the Italian section. The rumors in those establishments were that the three men would acquit, but except for the dictaphone statements by Blonger and Duff, no facts were obtained.

The sinister shadow of jury bribery had become the black cloud of reality which could not be escaped, and the approaching testimony of Les Randle, the ex-con-man, threatened possible tragedy in the courtroom. French and Kelley had told him in the midnight session at the jail that he would never live to testify. The underworld grapevine buzzed with rumors that Randle would be shot down on the witness stand. Precautions must be taken, but if armed guards were requested by the prosecution, they would be accused by the defense of seeking cheap publicity.

Doc Dawson, the square deputy sheriff, stepped into the breach. Going to the District Attorney, he said: 'Colonel, I want you to let me handle the courtroom when Randle testifies. If you do, and any shooting is attempted, we will get their men before they get Randle. Just give me free rein. I don't want you to know a thing about it, or who my men are, and they won't cost you anything.'

The District Attorney said, 'Doc, I trust you to the end. Plant the room as you see fit,' and Dawson did.

He brought in a lot of his old gunmen friends from Cripple Creek, fellows who knew how to fire a single-action Colt. Under his guidance many strange-looking characters went upstairs in advance of the crowd the morning Randle was to take the stand. Roy Samson reported that Dawson's friends seemed to be pretty well distributed throughout the courtroom, and that two of them had seats of honor in the dock, directly across from the jury and behind the witness box.

Joe Blumel, a friend and former associate of Blonger, came down from Edgmont, South Dakota, to be present when Randle took the stand, and lumbered up the stairs with two of his associates. He was met by Dawson, searched, and his guns taken away from him. Dawson's gimlet eyes bored straight through those of Joe Blumel as Dawson looked him straight in the face and said, 'You God damned ——, you and your men don't go in that courtroom. You go back and tell Lou that I am going to shoot him as soon as any gun-play starts, and he knows I mean business.'

That was about all there was to it, though the atmosphere was tense throughout Randle's testimony. Dawson and Jim Marshall frisked the spectators as they entered the building, took down any guns, and excluded about a score of men. For the two days that Randle was on the witness stand, Doc bossed the situation. Lou Blonger sat nervously in his chair, while about fifteen feet away, Doc Dawson lolled in the sheriff's seat, every once in a while looking significantly at Lou and putting his hand on the butt-end of his gun.

Randle told his story and told it well. He fitted each defendant into his part in the pay-off game, told about being present when they were hired by Duff, about where they worked, and how they operated, and whom they had trimmed, and what they did. Randle's midnight tale in the prosecutor's office was equaled on the witness stand.

Although the District Attorney had told Randle to be on the alert for trouble, the ex-con-man was perfectly at ease and at no time showed fear. Randle had nerve. He had agreed to talk and he kept his word.

# XLIII

## *High Spots of the Trial*

Over against the skullduggery of the defendants now came another serious threat to the prosecution. And once again the press became the menace.

The spectacular raid, the police history of the defendants, the parade of the victims, and, most of all, the long and dilatory tactics of the defense, had given the papers the story of the year, and for months before the trial they had played the case all over the front pages. For the first time in years the four dailies were in accord, and blistered the city administration, the police, the con-men and their attorneys.

The newspapers finally reached such a point that sarcastic verses and caricatures were the order of the day, and a mistrial was imminent. Proper affidavits to the Court would probably have resulted in reversible error if the jury was not discharged and the case commenced anew. Luckily the defense took no action about the newspaper abuse, and allowed the assaults to continue with increasing violence.

Perhaps the God of Chance, who had played such a part throughout the fight, cast his die and decided that the corruption by the defense and the attacks by the press made the score even. And the trial pressed on.

In all big cases one of the main problems facing the attorneys is the selection of the first major witness. The chief victim of 1922, P. G. Schaible, a banker of Chelsea, Michigan, who had lost $25,000, just nine days before the raid, was selected for that rôle. The latter part of December his name and address had been discovered on some con-man's junk that was just about to be discarded.

So a special delivery letter was sent to him asking about his loss, and he received this letter on Christmas Day. Then for the first time he discovered that he had been swindled. Up to then he had believed that he had been the unfortunate victim of circumstances in a legitimate stock exchange transaction.

Schaible took the next train for Denver, and was soon enlightened by the prosecutor as to the true facts, which became very real when he found the men who had swindled him were in the Denver jail.

The grafters count, and rightly, that a very large proportion of the men whom they trim cannot afford to let it be known that they have been so gullible as to be victimized by confidence-men. Bankers, business men, lawyers, doctors, and preachers much prefer to swallow their pride than to make complaints, and Schaible was no exception to the rule. He did not want it to get back to his home town that he, the president of a bank, had lost $25,000 to Denver bunco-men.

So Schaible asked the District Attorney to help suppress his name and address. The latter, in turn, was more than anxious to secure the testimony of Schaible and of the other victims, who would likewise want no publicity.

The proprietors of the papers were therefore again appealed to by the Colonel, and all four agreed to help, and did. They misspelled Schaible's name and gave another town and State as his address.

The con-men and their lawyers fought back. The attorneys asked Schaible if he had made any arrangements to have his name misspelled. He answered, 'No.' All he could state was that he had asked the District Attorney to give him as little publicity as possible. The lawyers got nowhere, but their clients fared better. They had already enlisted one of the courthouse newspaper reporters as an ally. Under his guidance they now sent long wires to the newspapers in Chelsea that P. G. Schaible of their First National Bank had been played for a boob in Denver. From that source it went out on the Associated Press wires and was carried over the country to discourage sucker testimony.

Thus, aided by a venal representative of the press, the con-men completely checkmated the efforts of the prosecution to conceal the identity of the witnesses, and no further effort could be made in that direction.

George Kanavuts, the Greek fighter from Sapulpa, was a real witness, and a colorful actor while testifying. French was the only one of his three crooks who had been arrested. When Kanavuts went over to identify him, instead of putting his hand on his shoulder, he banged him on the back and said, 'Dis is dat crook,' while Jackie's attorney protested loudly to the Court against the improper conduct of the witness. Then Kanavuts returned to the witness stand, took the phoney telephone in his hand and mimicked the way French, as bookmaker, acted when talking to the 'main' exchange.

Two of the crooks, who had defrauded a witness, were among the defendants in the courtroom. The latter was asked by the prosecutor to pick out the men who had trimmed him. Readily enough he pointed at the first one, and called him by name, and then was asked to get the other. Here he blundered, ludicrously. He looked around the room and then unhesitatingly went over and put his hands on Horace Hawkins's shoulders and said, 'This is the man.' Hawkins, with a shout of glee, rose to his feet and asked that the record show that the witness had identified Horace N. Hawkins, of counsel for the defendants, as one of the men who had swindled him in the bunco-game! This, of course, seriously lessened the value of his identification of the first man.

Herbert J. Gray, the Englishman who had insisted on taking his money out of the First National Bank, came all the way from England to testify. He was accompanied by his wife and two daughters, British to the core. The girls were between eighteen and twenty-two. All three of the women were dressed in English walking clothes. They wore heavy woolen stockings and carried large canes, and when they walked down the street everybody looked at them, and a good many remarked about them. So, about the second evening after their arrival, Gray and his family went to the District Attorney's house, very much distressed, and quite panic-stricken.

'My dear sir,' said Gray, 'I cannot understand it. Why, you know, when we go down the street everybody looks at us. It is most outrageous the way they treat us, and they follow us, and I am afraid of our lives. I want some police to guard me, but I want special bobbies, not the crooked police that you have in this town.'

The prosecutor looked the family over and had all he could do to keep a straight face.

'Mr. Gray,' he said, 'did it ever occur to you that the reason people stare at you and follow you is that you are different from the rest of us? If you were in England, you would look like a lot of people over there, but how many ladies in Denver have you seen wearing woolen stockings? How many women in Denver have you seen on the streets carrying canes, high canes with gold heads? And have you seen three women at once looking like that?'

'Why, no, old chap, I hadn't thought of that,' said Gray.

'Well,' said the District Attorney, 'you let the women go shopping tomorrow morning, and tell them to buy a few American clothes, to leave the canes home, and to get silk stockings and shoes with a little higher heels, and nobody will pay any attention to them.'

That was the last complaint from Gray.

The case drew to a close. So far there had been no mention whatsoever of the dictaphone. It had been carefully planned that that testimony should be held back until the last.

The 'bug' had been a disappointment in many ways. Owing to Duff's and Blonger's suspicion that one might be planted in their office, they had frequently gone into a huddle and whispered about their important matters, and nothing could be heard at such times. Often the conversations were so disconnected and piecemeal, that if given by Mrs. Steno on the witness stand, the wheat would have been so buried under the chaff as to be useless. Besides, she would never have stood a test on the stand as to accuracy on dictation or in reading her notes. What she and Koehn heard over the wires was not to be used on the witness stand.

There was a psychological value to the dictaphone as evidence — that it would be like a clap of thunder out of a clear sky. It was to startle the defendants, their counsel, the suspected jurors, the crooked politicians, and the underworld, and make them all worry over what had actually been received over the wire. The strategic value of the testimony, that a dictaphone had been in Blonger's office, was that the defendants would probably be afraid to take the witness stand, fearful of the facts with which they might be confronted on cross-examination. Therefore, that evidence was withheld until the last witness.

'Call Andy Koehn,' sang out Samson, and Koehn, the star detective of the case, the man who was more responsible for identifying, accurately observing, and getting the positive evidence on the gang than any other man, entered the courtroom.

Andy, as usual, was neatly dressed, quiet and modest in appearance. He took the oath, produced his notebook, and proceeded to point out to the jurors defendant after defendant, and tell what he had seen them doing, and where they did it, and how they worked and all about them, and the grafters were amazed at the accuracy of his statements. He went over his work as a detective, detailing what he had done, until finally he was asked if he had installed a dictaphone in Blonger's office. Lou and Duff came to life in a hurry, and all the bunks started to whisper, while the crowd in the courtroom craned their necks to get this morsel.

The plan had been to give the preliminary data about the installation of the dictaphone, but not give a proper legal foundation for the introduction of the testimony. The Supreme Court of Colorado had held that dictaphone testimony was inadmissible where the man listening over the telephone did not know the voice of the party to whom he was listening, and where the occupants of the place where the dictaphone was located were not actually identified. The prosecution had no quarrel with this law, and knew that the other side was conversant with it and would use it to object to dictaphone testimony.

Of course, a proper foundation had been laid from the first for legal presentation of this evidence, so that it could be used if wanted. Koehn had been in Blonger's room, had talked to him personally, had listened over the dictaphone from the office across the street, and had watched Blonger while he talked. Maiden had been in the lookout and had seen Blonger talking in his office, and the stenographer had been in the listening-post and had likewise talked to Blonger. But this foundation was intended to be kept out of the case so that the testimony would not be admissible, and that there would only be the testimony that there was a dictaphone without stating what had been heard. So much for plans.

However, one of the special prosecutors started in on Koehn, got ambitious in presenting the testimony, and before he knew it had qualified him. Then he asked him to state what he heard over the dictaphone. Before Koehn answered, the other State's attorney suddenly realized that they had upset the plans. He asked for a recess, which was given, and they went into a conference with the District Attorney and his staff. The decision was to ask Koehn only a few more questions and rest.

The Court reconvened, and Andy was asked about the installation and operation of the dictaphones. He stated that they had installed them in March, 1922, almost a year before; that they had placed one in the cup of the chandelier in the ceiling and the other by the steam-pipe in the attic, and added, 'They are there right now!'

One of the prosecutors then stated: 'Your Honor, this case has lasted almost two months, the Court and jury are tired, Mr. Koehn is our last witness, and the dictaphone evidence might be questionable from a legal standpoint, and much of it would be repetition of what has already transpired, so we will ask no further questions.'

Hawkins, quick to capitalize all breaks in the case, was on his feet. 'They haven't any dictaphone evidence and don't dare show they haven't,' he stated.

Luckily the clock struck twelve, and the Court adjourned at once until two o'clock. Samson ran downstairs to the office and told the District Attorney that Koehn had mentioned the dictaphone. The prosecutor picked up the telephone and called Maiden, who was stationed in Zang's office in the American National Bank Building. 'Get the "bugs,"' he said.

The con-men who were out on bail rushed out of the courtroom, jumped into their cars, and raced for Blonger's office and the attic. They found nothing.

At two o'clock the Court came to order, and Mr. Hawkins, in his best professional manner, took the witness.

'Mr. Koehn,' he said, 'you were telling us a very interesting little story just before Court adjourned, and I want to see if I am correct in what you said. I believe you stated that you installed a dictaphone, two of them, in fact, in the ceiling of Mr. Blonger's office, one in the cup of the chandelier and the other where the steam-pipe went through the ceiling, and you told us at twelve o'clock that they were still there. Is that correct, Mr. Koehn?'

'Yes, sir,' replied Andy.

'Do you mean,' demanded Hawkins, pounding the desk, 'that those machines are still there?'

'Oh, no,' said Koehn, blandly. 'At twelve o'clock I said they were still there. We took them out right afterwards, and here they are, if you want to see them.' And Andy held them up before the delighted eyes of the audience.

# XLIV

## *The Case Goes to the Jury*

The evidence for the State was completed. Mr. Hawkins, chief counsel for the defense, rose to his feet and stated that the defendants would rest without introducing any testimony. The courtroom was still, the spectators sitting on the edges of their seats as drama unfolded before them. Six weeks of testimony, and not a single witness to be produced for twenty defendants!

'Furthermore,' said Mr. Hawkins, turning to the special prosecutors, 'this jury has been here altogether too long, and we now offer to submit this case without any argument whatsoever.'

This was a move almost unprecedented in criminal annals, the defense challenging the prosecution to turn the case over to the jury without either side analyzing the evidence for it. In a long jury trial it is usually of the utmost importance that the disconnected pieces of evidence be fitted together in the final argument so that the whole picture of the case will become clear. And here the defense wanted both sides to submit the case under the Court's instructions alone.

One of the special prosecutors started to get on his feet and object, but his colleague seized him by the coat-tail, whispered to him, and then one of them told the Court that he thought it would be advisable to settle the instructions and then advise counsel on the other side the next morning whether they would argue the case or not.

The District Attorney's staff and special prosecutors had a serious problem. Prominent lawyers of Denver were asked their opinions, and without exception every lawyer urged that the case be argued.

The District Attorney's men, however, had a different view. They knew that Hawkins had been baiting Judge White, the special prosecutor throughout the trial. They believed that Hawkins was convinced that White would scorn the defendants' offer, and they stated that in their opinion it was a bluff on the part of Hawkins; that he was so sure of his belief in White's insistence on talking that he did not believe White would accept.

The District Attorney said: 'Let's call the bluff. Let us go to the jury without a single word being presented to it on behalf of the con-men, either by evidence or argument as to their innocence, and then let's see how long the members of the jury who favor the defendants can stand out against public opinion. They can't stand the gaff and will all have to capitulate. It is the only possible way we can get a verdict. If the defense jurors have any argument of any kind on which to base their ballot of "not guilty" they will stick. If they have nothing whatsoever, they will have to capitulate.'

And the next morning, to the surprise of counsel for the defendants, Judge White rose to his feet and very suavely told the Court, 'Your Honor, the prosecution accepts the challenge of the defendants, and submits the case without argument,' and the defense attorneys' faces blanched.

The Judge droned out his instructions, finally turned the last page, and put down the lengthy sheets. It was eleven-thirty in the morning. The bailiffs were sworn, the jurors marched out. What would the verdict be? How long would the jurors take to reach one?

The jurors went to their room, walked to lunch, returned,

were in their room all afternoon, and then went to dinner in the evening. Joe Cook, courthouse reporter of the *Post*, examined the janitor's trash-bag after the janitor cleaned up, and reported that the jurors were voting nine to three for conviction. The underworld rumor was correct. Three were standing out for the defense.

It is the almost universal practice in criminal cases that when the jury retires, the defendants are locked up in jail until the verdict is rendered. Sometimes they are allowed out on bond, but otherwise it is the duty of the sheriff to keep them in safe custody.

Hal Crane, however, was not going to put his bosom friend, Lou Blonger, behind the bars if he could do anything to prevent it. Consequently, he put in jail the remaining seventeen defendants, but took Blonger and Duff and French to his office in the courthouse, and there, with several newspaper men and despite rigid prohibition laws, both State and Federal, Hal produced the booze, and staged a glorious and riotous party until late at night. For some strange reason, Dawson was kept on the job by Crane, and Doc was the only man in the room who refused to drink.

In the meantime, the District Attorney and his assistants were busy in their offices on the floor below. The merrymaking grew hilarious, shouting and laughter and rough-housing creating a chaos that echoed and reverberated through the empty building.

Finally at midnight Crane came to the conclusion that the jury would not report that night, and that he would have to lock his prisoners up. So with a good deal of help from Dawson, Blonger, Duff, and French were taken over the 'bridge of sighs,' and down the narrow stairs into the jail, where at once they were given cells in millionaires' row. It was Blonger's and Duff's first night in a Denver jail! Then Hal decided to act smart.

'I am going in and tell Van Cise where to get off at,' said Crane, 'and if he thinks he is going to give me any of his lip, I will put him over where I just put Blonger.'

'I always knew you were a damn fool,' said Doc, 'but that is no reason to be a blooming idiot. The Colonel has given you quite a break already tonight, but if you go in his room, he will call your bluff, and you will land in the hoosgow.'

'Well, here's where I show him who's running this place,' said Hal, and, followed by Dawson, he strode to the office of the District Attorney.

The door into the prosecutor's private office was closed. Hal was staggering a little, his speech was rather thick, but he was still able to navigate. He pulled open the door, went into the room, leaned over the District Attorney's desk, pounded on it, and said: 'God damn you! I understand you are looking for me. Well, the sooner you know who's running the sheriff's office, the better off you are going to be.'

The District Attorney looked at him and said, 'Hal, get out of here. You're drunk, and you better get going.'

'You can't give me orders. I am going to stay here as long as I want to, and Blonger and Duff are going to get out. It will take a whole lot bigger man than you to convict them.'

Again the District Attorney said, 'Now, Hal, I don't want to start anything, but if you don't get out of here, and get out now, you are going to have a case filed against you in the West Side Court.'

Hal answered, 'I would like to see you do anything to me.'

'All right,' said the prosecutor, 'I'll call your bluff.' And going around the desk he stuck his hand in Hal's back pocket and pulled out a pint of whiskey, and said: 'Now, Hal, I have been trying to keep away from this all night long, but you brought it on yourself, and here's the whiskey taken from you. I am going to file on you for possession of intoxicating liquor. You either get out and go home, or I will have Doc throw you in jail right now.'

And Crane, now halfway sober, went out the door.

The next day a case was filed against Crane for the possession of intoxicating liquor. His brother-in-law, Vaso L. Chucovich, a former big-time gambler, but a square shooter, interceded in his behalf. He went to the District Attorney and asked if it was not possible to let Hal off without an actual plea of guilty. The prosecutor did not want to be a witness in his own case, so agreed that if Crane would enter a plea of *nolo contendere*, a technical plea of guilty, which means one will not contend against the charge, that he would be satisfied to have him get off with the usual fine of one hundred dollars.

So Hal Crane, the chief deputy sheriff in charge at the West Side Courthouse, the boss of the negro underworld, the close friend of Lou Blonger, the man who had given orders to Chief of Police Hamilton Armstrong to leave the con-men alone, had to sign his *nolo contendere* in the courtroom where he ordinarily herded prisoners into the dock, and pay his fine to the clerk.

He should have been convicted of contempt of court and put in jail for a long term and had his deputy sheriff's license revoked, but the main thing was to break his power. And the little plea did just that.

The next day the jurors remained closeted in their room except when they went out to meals, and people began to glare at them as they marched along the streets.

The third day came, and still the jurors were unable to reach a verdict. The prosecution was confident if the Judge kept them out long enough the three would capitulate. But would he do so? Much to the prosecution's surprise, the defense attorneys insisted that the jury be held until it reached a verdict. Then in the afternoon, the 'third-degree' instruction, as it is called in Colorado, was given to the jury.

This instruction in effect simply states that the jurors who are in the minority are to give careful heed to the views of the majority, so that a verdict can be arrived at, but the third-degree instruction brought no results. There was a good deal of arguing going on in the jury room. One of the jurors had sent for his guitar, and once in a while he was heard strumming away and humming a little ditty. The jurors seemed pretty solemn when they went out to meals. The populace was beginning to be aroused, and talk was spreading around the town of 'lynch the jury if it cannot convict in that kind of a case.'

Came the fourth day. The twelve good men and true sat down around the table, the foreman called for a ballot, and Okuly ran a bluff and said, 'The difference between me and you three —— — —— is that I got my five hundred dollars, but turned it over to the Judge, and you've still got yours,' and consternation arose.

Many of the jurors were Swedes and Danes, who are always the best possible prosecution jurors. They are honest, unemotional, and stand for the enforcement of Law. Up to that time these men had been arguing a good deal with the three defense jurors, and Okuly had tried to keep peace among them. When he opened up this last morning, the Scandinavians came in with the heavy artillery, and said they now had the facts, and these fellows had better vote guilty in a hurry or they would get what was coming to them. A ballot was called for, and the jury for the first time stood ten to two for conviction. The internal warfare continued until noon, when a ballot showed eleven to one, one juror standing out.

This man had fortified himself with a good supply of booze before he was locked up, but had run out of his last drop the night before, and was in pretty shaky condition. By afternoon he was a good deal of a wreck, and at three-thirty he capitulated, and the jury stood twelve for conviction.

At last they rapped on the door, notified the bailiff, the Judge sent for the attorneys, and the courtroom speedily filled. The jury was coming in after one hundred hours of deliberation! This was a record for a jury in Colorado.

The jurors took their seats, the defendants were brought in from the jail, Deputy Sheriff Hal Crane looked serious, Deputy Sheriffs Doc Dawson and Jim Marshall, apprehensive, but alert for any break by their prisoners.

'Have you arrived at a verdict?' asked the Judge.

'We have,' replied the foreman.

'You may give it to the clerk.'

The clerk took the verdict and handed it to the Judge, who looked at it. A smile came over his face, and he handed it to the clerk, who read, 'We, the jury, find all the defendants guilty as charged in the information.'

Drama again was in the atmosphere, and oh, how close to destruction was that verdict of guilty.

A hush fell over the courtroom, and Hawkins pulled his last desperate play — one that came within an ace of success.

'We ask that the jury be polled,' he said, and the clerk started reading the roll.

'Herman M. Okuly, is this, and was this your verdict?' And Okuly said, 'Yes,' and so on it went until juror Number 10, A. B. Frank, the last man to vote not guilty, was reached.

> Clerk George McLachlan: 'Andrew B. Frank, was and is this your verdict?'
>
> Frank stammered, hesitated, then said: 'It was under the circumstances. I was sick and could not do anything else.'
>
> Attorney Hawkins: 'I ask that the juror's answer be entered in the record.'
>
> The Court: 'Ask the question again.'
>
> Clerk: 'Was and is this your verdict?'
>
> Frank: 'It was because of conditions.'

Interruptions by Attorney Hawkins cut short a further explanation.

> The Court: 'Put the statement to the juror again.'
>
> The Clerk: 'Was and is this your verdict?'
>
> Frank: 'It was under the conditions I have had. I have been sick since Saturday night.'

If this statement of the juror was to continue, then no legal verdict had been reached. But Judge Dunklee saved the day by three pointed questions:

> The Court: 'Is or is not this your verdict?'
>
> Frank: 'Yes.'
>
> The Court: 'Does the juror desire further time to deliberate?'
>
> Frank: 'No, I want to get out of this.'

The Court: 'Do you, on your oath and on your honor as a juryman, say this is your verdict?'

Frank: 'Yes, this is my verdict and I stand by it.'

Hawkins tried to say something. The Judge interrupted him. He said, 'The verdict will be received and the jury is discharged.' And the jurors left the box with their duty done and twenty crooks convicted.

At once defense counsel surrounded Frank, escorting him from the courtroom and into a waiting automobile. A vital affidavit for the motion for new trial was possible, and all might yet be lost.

# XLV

## *The Underworld Survives*

THE motions for new trial were promptly overruled. The last scene was at hand. The defendants lined up at the bar for sentence. Lou Blonger, visibly nervous, had lost forever the poker face of yore. But the others grinned and whispered while the Judge passed on their fates.

Twenty professional criminals up for sentence. Society wondering how long it would escape their future depredations. The maximum term was ten years, but all received light sentences. Lou Blonger, A. W. Duff, and nine others received seven years; the rest, including the notorious William Elmer Mead, the 'Christ Kid,' were given only three years. If made trusties a three-year-term could be served in about twenty-five months, a seven-year stretch in a little less than four years. The defendants started to appeal to the Supreme Court, then changed their minds and decided to serve their sentences.

A few days before going to the penitentiary, Blonger sent a message from the jail. 'Colonel, will you let me talk to you in your office for ten minutes?' The answer was the dispatch of the faithful deputy sheriff, Doc Dawson, to bring Blonger to the prosecutor.

What a contrast to all those other meetings! No longer alert, no longer confident, no longer powerful, but broken physically, shattered in nerves, a wretched old man, the former czar of the underworld was to beg a favor like a mendicant of the streets! His meandering trail was near its end.

Asthmatic, feeble, tottering, Blonger sank into a chair and gasped for breath. His clothes hung loosely on his shrunken frame, and his cheeks were haggard.

'Colonel,' he said, 'I am an old man. I am seventy-three. I am in terrible physical condition. I have a bad heart, bad stomach, bad lungs, bad kidneys, all my insides are gone. Seven years, three years, one year, is death. Surely you don't want me to die down there. I'll go there for two months. But then, for God's sake, get the Governor to pardon me.' He held out shaking hands, a fifty-year criminal, now fearful of his doom.

This time the younger man was silent, while Blonger waited as the minutes passed.

Finally the prosecutor said: 'Blonger, this is not an easy matter to pass upon, especially when the applicant, like yourself, is sick. But when a defendant has been convicted and asks for leniency, the reasons for its granting must be given. You seek a pardon because of your physical condition. You ask for a release because you do not want to die in the penitentiary!

'Neither your sickness nor your impending death should be considered. What are your deserts? What leniency have you shown to others? What God have you worshiped except the Almighty Dollar?

'When you stole Preacher Menaugh's trust funds, did you hesitate? When, overwhelmed with shame, he committed suicide, did you give any aid to his family? When you took the life earnings of old man Donovan of New Orleans, and reduced him from comfort to penury, what did you do to ease the last months of his life?

'You have been a criminal from the time of your youth. You have been the fixer of the town. You have prostituted justice. You have bribed judges and jurors, State, City and police officials. You have ruined hundreds of men. With that record, tell me why a death sentence is not your due?

William Dougherty — 'Dockerty' — 'Gen. Del.' 3 to 10 years

George H. Williams 'Bump' — 'Jim Campbell' 3 to 10 years

John Allison — 'Denver Ed Smith' 3 to 10 years

Steve Olsen — 'Red' 7 to 10 years

Roy Coyne — 'Slim Blackie' Jumped $2,000 and $10,000 bonds

Emory S. King — '36710' Jumped $2,000 bond. P.G. 3 to 10 years

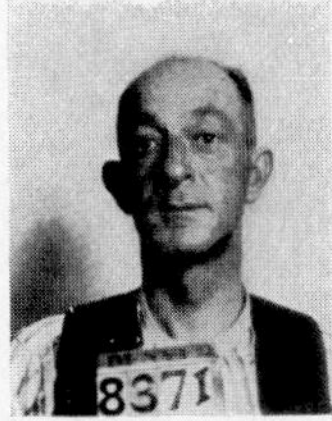


Grove Sullivan Convicted — Sent to insane asylum

T. J. Brady — 'Tom Hogan' Jumped $3,500 bond

John J. Grady — 'Mole' — 'The Perfume Kid' Jumped $2,500 bond

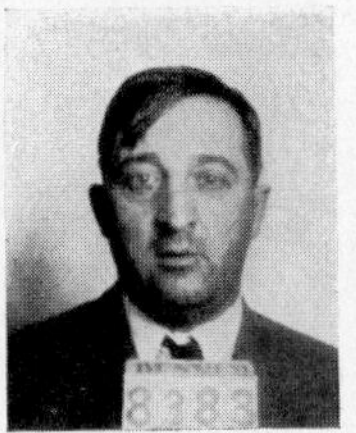


Robert Knowles — 'Nash' — 'Big Nose' Jumped $3,500 bond

J. R. Smith — 'Smithy the Bear' Jumped $2,000 bond

Harry V White Sent to Florida Fined $1,000

Ralph Sadler — 'Sissy' Sent to Florida

Ray Yeaman — 'The Blind Man'

Puss McCasky — 'J. D. Barry' Wanted in Atlanta

Jack Ryan — 'Fat'

SOME OF THE STEERERS

'As to your plea for parole, I say no, emphatically and for all time no. Before the king of the underworld is pardoned, the penitentiary doors should be torn from their hinges and all other occupants be first turned out. They would be less dangerous than you. You have met your day of judgment and the death sentence is your due. I will fight to the last any attempt to give you leniency of any kind or description.'

'I guess that's the end,' said Blonger, and the last conference was finished.

Five months later the death sentence took its toll. Lou Blonger died in the State penitentiary.

But he had one of the biggest funerals in the history of the State, and it was held in the largest church in Denver! His widow paid the bill!

'Kid' Duff made no plea for help. Like all con-men, who are the wisest of prisoners, Duff obeyed the prison rules and became a trusty a few days after his arrival in the 'Big House.' Always a money-maker, he took charge of the prison curio shop, where articles made by the inmates were sold to visitors, and he made it pay, and pay well. In addition, he made a contract with a large Denver curio company to supply it with 'genuine' Navajo rugs, and the prisoners were soon turning them out in near quantity production.

While in the penitentiary, Duff, French, and Beech were indicted in a Federal Court in Cleveland on the Albert Seurin case, as a result of Seurin's name in Duff's notebook. Duff personally gave bond and also put up five thousand dollars as the bond for Beech.

Before going to Cañon City, Duff had handed his wife about two hundred thousand dollars in securities. Upon his release from prison she returned these to him, and then divorced him. By the irony of fate Duff soon lost his all in the protected gambling-dens just out of Denver. Beech jumped his bond, then died, so Duff was out that money. Down and out, broke and discouraged, Duff took the easy way out. His body was discovered in a car, locked in a garage, a victim of carbon monoxide.

Jack Hardaway — 'Pappy,' as Koehn called him — 'that poor old man,' as described by Duff, died in the penitentiary, happy to be there. At the end of the first three weeks of the trial, he had sought out Kenneth Robinson.

'I guess I'll just withdraw from this case,' said Jack. 'No one seems to know me.'

Later, however, he wanted a little publicity for himself. Hardaway's ambition had been to be a big con-man, but he had never succeeded in being more than a small grafter. With the élite of the con-world on trial, Jack feared he would be the only one to be acquitted. And to be turned loose as innocent of crime while all the others were found to be big boys had been too much for him.

So before the case was finished, he asked to see the District Attorney.

'Colonel,' he said, 'for God's sake do me a favor. If all get off, that's O.K. by me. But I don't want to be the only one who doesn't see the "Big House" if the others go down. Can't you put on some other evidence about me? Anything you say I'll stand for.'

'No, Jack,' said the District Attorney, 'if you were on trial alone, you could make any statement of guilt you wanted to, but in a conspiracy case the only statement you can make is as a witness. I guess you'll have to take your chances.'

'Well, Colonel, that will be awful hard lines for me. Do what you can for me, won't you?'

Jackie French still liked the badger game, but Buda Godman had joined another mob, so after he got out French secured another girl. This time it was the daughter of Billy Aarons, Blonger's right-hand bower in the Department of Justice. But before French could do much damage, H. N. Graham of the Federal postal service convicted him on the Seurin case in Cleveland, and he received a five-year sentence, remaining behind the bars until January of 1935. As soon as he got out, he returned to the happy hunting grounds in Florida. His luck had ebbed and he died from pneumonia in Cincinnati in September of that year. Buda Godman helped a gang of thieves steal $300,000 worth of jewelry, then landed in the New York State Prison on a four-year sentence.

C. Frankie Dixon, the narcotic con-man arrested by Williamson in 1921, for many years has been the underworld boss of the protected store at San Antonio, Texas, and has found that area a profitable hunting ground for suckers.

The other con-men served their time, left the gray walls behind, and again plunged into the underworld, with Society as their prey.

But it remained for William Elmer Mead, the 'Christ Kid,' to make the record for the group. His Denver sentence served, he was met at the Cañon City, Colorado, penitentiary gate by a United States Marshal on a Florida charge, but gave bond and was released.

Jumping that, he trimmed his suckers throughout the United States and then left for England. His luck held there till he received a sentence at Bow Street Police Court and at its expiration was deported. Back in the United States, he organized a successful gang of his own, making a specialty of preying upon contractors. One such, from St. Paul, fell into his hands for $200,000. And to get enough money for that loss the contractor borrowed part of his money from Edward G. Bremmer, the banker, who a few weeks later was kidnaped.

Then Inspector H. N. Graham ran smack into Mead at the World's Fair in Chicago. Mead employed Louis P. Piquette, the lawyer who in April, 1935, was tried, and convicted, in a Chicago Federal Court, on a charge that he was one of the conspirators who had aided the 1934 public enemy Homer ('Baby Face') Nelson in his escapes. Piquette got Mead a $10,000 bond, which the 'Christ Kid' again jumped. And, now, once again Inspector H. N. Graham is seeking Mead, this time hopeful of a judge who will fix a bond high enough to hold Mead until trial, and then for conviction and the maximum sentence.

Mead again came into the toils for a minor traffic violation in Boston in July, 1935. His finger-prints were taken, but all had been horribly disfigured with acid. Despite that plain warning he was released on a $200 bond, which he hurdled as before.

Les Randle is the shining exception of the lot. Kicked out of the underworld by his stand in favor of Society, Randle has gone straight. Locating in a town far from Denver, he purchased a hotel, and, assisted by his ever-faithful wife, has made himself a respected and successful man.

The downfall of Blonger was followed by the overthrow of the city administration. Con-men were told to get out and stay out of Denver. But in 1934, with another loose police administration, they again appeared.

The con-men are still in the tourist towns, they are still in the cities where police protect and politicians wink, and the people do not care.

Fighting the underworld is like fighting a forest fire. Let a small or un-co-ordinated force attack a huge blaze, it stops it in one place only to have it break out on a score of fronts. Fighting the underworld is a local problem, a State problem, a national problem. It is a problem for trained and honest officers, for integrated police of city and State, for co-ordination of Federal agencies with State forces, for an aroused body politic.

Fighting the underworld — the problem of Society.

THE END

# ADDENDA

## District Attorney's Force

Kenneth W. Robinson, the Assistant District Attorney, Bernard A. Gates, Lewis D. Mowry, Andrew J. Reynolds, Roy Samson, Fred Sanborn, Deputy District Attorneys; Arch Cooper, Andrew Koehn, Robert Maiden, Fred Tate, Investigators; May Golin, stenographer.

## Headquarters Force

Cheney Bagby, Harold H. Healey, Lorenzo W. Linville, Harold M. Webster.

## Car Drivers

Robert G. Bosworth, George E. Cranmer, Christopher F. Cusack, William W. Grant, Jr., Fred W. Hart, Cass M. Herrington, Russell Jordan, Edwin S. Kassler, Jr., Paul Loughridge, William H. Loughridge, William D. Sanborn, Oliver Toll, J. Herbert Wilkins, Arthur D. Wilson, Earl Wright.

## Subscribers to Fund

Mrs. Verner Z. Reed, William N. W. Blayney, Claude K. Boettcher, Arthur H. Bosworth, Ernest H. Braukman, James H. Causey, George E. Cranmer, Alphonse E. de Ricqles, Tyson Dines, Sr., William D. Downs, John Evans, Edwin B. Hendrie, S. Nelson Hicks, William V. Hodges, William A. Hover, William S. Iliff, Charles A. Johnson, Edwin S. Kassler, Sr., Harold Kountze, Charles Loughridge, Henry McAllister, William P. McPhee, Hugh McWhirter, Harold W. Moore, John W. Morey, John K. Mullen, Thomas B. Stearns, William E. Sweet, James R. Thorpe, Jesse F. Welborn, Frank L. Woodward.

## State Rangers

Colonel Patrick J. Hamrock, Captain Orville L. Dennis, Elmer F. Arnbrecht, Edward T. Bell, James A. Chase, Myron Donald, Thomas Elkins, Claude G. Harrington, Claude F. Head, William

Q. Howell, Otis Mathis, Adolph Oster, Robert Perry, Charles E. Scarbrough, Lewis N. Scherf, Fred J. Soward, Fred Steffan, Robert E. Swingle.

### Names of Confidence-Men Arrested

| Real Name | District Attorney's Name |
|---|---|
| | *Fixer* |
| Lou H. Blonger | Lou Blonger |
| | *Manager* |
| Adolph W. Duff | Adolph W. Duff |
| | *Tailer* |
| George 'Tip' Belcher | George Dover |
| | *Bookmakers* |
| John H. French | Jackie French |
| Les Randle (in this book) | Les Randle (in this book) |
| | *Spielers* |
| J. Roy Farrell | McCune |
| George Leo Kelley | Long |
| Arthur B. Cooper | Arthur B. Cooper |
| | *Steerers* |
| Thomas Beech | Thomas Beech |
| Thomas Joseph Brady | 'Mohair' |
| Walter Byland | Walter Byland |
| Roy Coyne | 'Slim Blacky' |
| William Dougherty | 'Gen. Delivery' |
| Leon Felix | '8070,' then Leon Felix |
| John J. Grady | 'Mole' |
| Jack Hardaway | 'Pappy' |
| Emory S. King | '36–710' (auto license) |
| Robert Knowles | 'Big Nose' |
| William H. Loftus | Loftus |
| Puss McCaskey | Presence unknown until arrest |
| William Elmer Mead, the 'Christ Kid' | Presence unknown until arrest |
| Louis Mushnick | 'Thick Lips' |
| Stephen J. Olson | 'Red' |

*Steerers*

| | |
|---|---|
| Audley H. Potts | A. H. Potts |
| Jack Ryan | 'Fat' |
| Ralph S. Sadler | 'Sissy' |
| Edward P. Schultz | 'Z' |
| Chas. E. Smith | 'Uncle Ed' |
| James R. Smith | 'Sandy' |
| Grove Sullivan | 'V,' then Grove Sullivan |
| Harry D. White | 'Witting' |
| George H. Williams | 'Bump' |
| Charles V. Wilson | 'Red Hogan' |
| Frank Yeaman | 'Q' — blind man (The blind pose is entirely assumed) |

# *Glossary of Terms Used by the Underworld*

Accident — When crook is arrested.

Badger game — Entrapment of victim by woman and her alleged husband.
Ballyhoo — The come-on talk.
Big Store — A protected town.
Blow-off — Stealing a victim's money.
Blow-off wire — Last telegram from mob.
Blow-up — When victim gets wise.
Boodle — Crooked money package at exchange.
Bookmaker — Clerk in a fake exchange or race parlor.
Booster — Extra man in exchange.
Break-down — Fake telegram to start sucker into raising money.
Bunco-game — Con-game.

Con-man — Confidence-man.
Convincer — Initial winning.

Dick — Detective.
Dope — Narcotics; also information.

Entertain — To interest a sucker.

Firm — Fixer and his mob.
Fisherman — Con-man.
Fishing-season — When it is safe to pick up suckers.
Fixer — Man behind the scenes who handles police and public officials.
Frail — Woman.

Gang or mob — Con-men in a town.
Goods — Fake stock.
Grafters — Con-men's name for themselves.
Grand — One thousand dollars.

Honkey-tonk — Combination dance hall and saloon.
Hopped-up — Under influence of narcotic drug.

In the hospital — In jail.

Kick — Complaint to police.

Lay-out — Paraphernalia.
Lookout — The center of activity of a pay-off game gang, where one man watches for the steerer's signal.
Lookout, the — The watcher against the Law.

Manager — Active head of a gang.
Moll — Woman of underworld.
Mug — To take the picture of a criminal.

Nut — Expense in running the game, including protection.

Office — Underworld sign for an officer.

Pay-off game — Swindle in which the victim is twice paid off before losing his money.
Play to the wall — Simulated stock exchange.
Putting the bee — Making a crook pay for protection.

Rap — Complaint against a crook.
Retie — Trimming a victim for a second time.

Sale, or beat — Trimming a sucker.
Salted-mine — Mine with ore fixed to resemble high grade.
Score — Amount of the swindle.
Show-up — Exhibition of arrested men before the detectives.
Slicker — Con-man.

Spieler — Second inside man, or mysterious stranger.
Spring — Get out on bond.
Squealer — One who talks to the Law.
Steer, steerer or salesman — Pick-up man.
Stir — Penitentiary.
Stool-pigeon — Police spy.
Store or joint — Fake stock exchange or race parlor.
Store-booster — Shoplifter
Store-men — Con-men.
Straw-bond — Bail bond with worthless signers.
Sucker, boob, chump, egg, customer — The victim.

Tailer — The man who follows the victim.
Take for a ride — Convey a man to an out-of-the-way spot and kill him.
Tied — When victim sends for money.
Tied-up — When victim enters stock exchange.
Tip-off — Underworld surveillance on police.

Work the streets — Street-walking.

# *Index*